concrete toronto

a guidebook to concrete architecture from the fifties to the seventies

editors **michael mcclelland**
graeme stewart
designer **steven ho yin chong**

Canada Council for the Arts   Conseil des Arts du Canada

ONTARIO ARTS COUNCIL
CONSEIL DES ARTS DE L'ONTARIO

Canadä

This publication was funded in part by the the Assistance for the Promotion of Architecture program at the Canada Council for the Arts. The publisher would also like to thank, for their support, the Block Grant programs of the Canada Council for the Arts and the Ontario Arts Council. We also acknowledge the Government of Ontario through the Ontario Book Publishing Tax Credit program and the Government of Canada through the Book Publishing Industry Development Program.

Library and Archives Canada Cataloguing in Publication

Concrete Toronto : a guide to concrete architecture from the fifties to the seventies / edited by Michael McClelland and Graeme Stewart.

ISBN 978-1-55245-193-9

1.Architecture--Ontario--Toronto--20th century. 2.Concrete construction--Ontario--Toronto--History--20th century. 3.Toronto (Ont.)--Buildings, structures, etc.--History--20th century. I.McClelland, Michael, 1951- II.Stewart, Graeme, 1981-

NA4125.C66 2007   720.9713'54109045   C2007-905650-4

With generous support from:

docomomo canada ontario

Contents

Infrastructure

The Modern Suburbs

Beyond Toronto

Building with Concrete

Afterword

'I have to say that from the beginning I was fortunate in coming into my practice during the pulsating '60s of this country's enormous growth, which offered all sorts of opportunities ... One could make experiments. One could find clients wanting to try new things ... Sometimes they succeeded and sometimes they didn't. But it was a very rich, vibrant time we've had. And architects everywhere have benefited from that ...'

Irving Grossman

'*Canadian architecture, remarkably producing quality building after quality building at a tremendous rate …*'

Progressive Architecture

'Thanks are due to the City of Toronto, for having the courage and foresight to invite the whole architectural world to contribute towards erecting the first civic centre of this century worthy of the name ...'

Siegfried Giedion

Why *Concrete Toronto?*

Graeme Stewart and Michael McClelland
Editors

This publication celebrates the concrete architecture that was built in Toronto in the 1950s, '60s and '70s. This important period was a time of immense prosperity, when considerable public and private investment had a major influence in shaping Canadian cities. But more significantly, we now suffer a cultural amnesia about this period; we remain critical yet uninformed about its architecture and leave its very large impact on our environment without thoughtful assessment. An appreciation for the architecture of the recent past is a contemporary cultural blind spot. If the making of architecture and the making of cities are inexorably linked, it is clear that the understanding of one requires an understanding of the other. A better appreciation of our recent architectural past gives us greater continuity with the intent, knowledge and ambition of previous generations and a stronger sense of our direction as our city continues to grow.

At the centre of our limited understanding of the architecture of this era is the confusing term *Brutalism*, now broadly used to cover the style of almost all concrete buildings erected during the period. The word comes principally from the work of English architects Peter and Alison Smithson, who, with their friend Reyner Banham, used the phrase the *New Brutalism* to propose a practical, honest and no-nonsense antidote to what they regarded as the frivolous modernism of the 1951 Festival of Britain. Banham's early-1950s book was entitled *The New Brutalism: Ethic or Aesthetic?*, and the title tellingly underlines the implicit contradictions in the Smithsons' work – can an architectural idea be equally about ethics and aesthetics?

But Brutalism also applies to Le Corbusier's use of raw concrete – known in French as *béton brut* – for the exposed finish of his buildings such as the Unité d'Habitation, completed in the early 1950s. Today we're left uncertain to what degree Toronto architects were influenced by the Corbusian French *béton brut*, which has some of the same connotations as *champagne brut* or *diamant brut* – a diamond in the rough – and how much they were influenced directly by the Smithsons' English utopian experiments in social housing ... or if neither was actually a strong reference. A closer look suggests many other non-Brutalist cultural connections fed into the design of Toronto's concrete buildings. They are as diverse as Rudolf Schindler, the extraordinary Californian architect for whom Irving Grossman had worked, or the engineering innovations of Maillart or Nervi, which influenced Morden Yolles, or simply the sheer impact of the immigrant populations who brought the right skills and trades at the right time.

Richard Serra's rare 1970s concrete sculpture in King City shows that concrete was a material for artistic experimentation. At the time, concrete must have seemed incredibly liberating for architects, allowing them to move beyond many of the limitations of earlier construction materials. Concrete could be compressive and tensile and could be made into almost any form imaginable. Where architecture had previously been built on a codified set of values for materials and techniques, like status goods, concrete was inexpensive, locally produced and readily available, and it broke from established practice. Concrete was the perfect material for the postwar period.

But as we celebrate this architecture, we recognize that it will pose interesting questions about taste, as many of the buildings included in this publication still remain controversial both for architects and the general public.

Why is it that we like some buildings and dislike others? And are our likes and dislikes more valid than those of others? These are questions worth asking, but there are no simple answers. We can remind ourselves that values, like tastes in fashion, will change. We can remember that until the 1970s, Toronto's Old City Hall was regarded with disdain, as obsolete, fussy, oppressive and cumbersome – all too Victorian, in a bad way. Or we can recognize that our values in architecture, even beyond issues of taste, still flow from evolving fields of cultural production and consumption that establish the context for valuation.

We can point out that buildings old and new all need to be assessed on what they contribute to the community as a whole, and that positions and arguments will often vary. As buildings age, they may attain a canonic value – something like that which we see in Old City Hall. We don't mean to imply that all these concrete buildings have now reached this canonic or heritage value, but we propose that many may do so.

Beyond the question of taste, the more important direction for questioning is what we can learn from the recent past. Whether through knowing our history better we can build on its strengths and enrich our contemporary environment. Whether through seeing these buildings through fresh eyes we can see new possibilities. These concrete buildings, a significant part of the built fabric of the city, are ready for a careful second look.

Methodology: The Individual Voice

Graeme Stewart and Michael McClelland
Editors

Our architectural office is located on the eighth floor of a building at the corner of St. Mary and Yonge streets. The architects Mathers and Haldenby had built and occupied the building in the 1950s. We are surrounded by the commercial buzz of the low-scale Victorian structures on Yonge, by the quiet, treed residential character of St. Nicholas and by a number of high slab apartment towers to the north and the west. Two of our largest local landmarks are the Manulife Centre, one block to the north, and the Robarts Library, far off to the west, visible between the older buildings of the University of Toronto. These are landmarks, undeniable in their urban presence, yet invisible in our contemporary architectural discourse. We wanted to change that. We wanted to make the invisible visible. We wanted to talk about the architecture of our recent past, to learn about the people who designed the structures and to explore their ideas.

The underlying premise of the book is that a greater understanding of our immediate environment and how it has evolved will provide us with better tools for discussing current issues of urbanism and architecture. Understanding the past will give us a vocabulary to talk about the future.

The material in the book is focused on the distinctiveness of the individual voice. We asked for brief written descriptions on the topic of 'concrete buildings from the 1960s period' from a wide range of people, hoping their varied perspectives would provide unfiltered documentation. But none of the documentation is neutral. Equally valuable are the new and period images. Like the written articles, all of the images are a positioning of an opinion.

Wishing to involve a diverse group on a single topic has created unique responses to similar subjects, as well as the introduction of unexpected material, some from beyond the city's borders, and much from Toronto's remarkable modern suburbs. The result is not the definitive list of modern concrete structures in Toronto but rather *a* list, affected by our biases and those of our contributors. For the purposes of presentation, the collected material has been loosely categorized, yet many of these projects challenge conventional organization as they do the conventional understanding of our city.

As with a previous publication called *East/West: A Guide to Where People Live in Downtown Toronto*, we are purposely presenting diverse opinions as a challenge to current wisdom, as a suggestion that experiences are different and that our urbanism is complex. There is no implication that a détente will be easily reached between the ideas of the '60s and the present day or that the issues raised by the discussion need be resolved, summarized or even itemized. This book is moulded around the idea of the city as a continually evolving enterprise.

Fig. 4 View of Robarts Library from the office of E.R.A. Architects at 10 St. Mary Street

Concrete Projects

Guidebook Entries

Additional Projects

Navigation Bar

The guidebook provides information for a selected list of projects. It also functions as an index to help you make your way through the book. Tabs in the navigation bar direct you to articles, interviews, technical information and photographs that feature specific buildings.

concrete toronto   guidebook

32

FINCH AVENUE WEST

56   WESTON ROAD   59   62

SHEPPARD AVENUE WEST

43   34

04

JANE STREET   KEELE STREET   YONGE STREET

07   03   EGLINTON

33

ST. CLAIR AVENUE

40   61

39

GUIDEBOOK ENTRIES

03. Yonge Eglinton Centre
04. Yorkdale Shopping Centre
07. Eglinton West Station
08. Don Valley Parkway
32. Ross Building
33. Holy Blossom Temple

34. Beth David Synagogue
39. Palace Pier
40. House on Ardwold Gate
43. Jane Exbury Towers
48. Crescent Town
49. Scarborough College

TORONTO CITY-WIDE MAP 1:125 000

LEGEND

Guidebook Entry

Additional Projects

Subway
Subway Stop
Major Streets
Streets

2000m

Street labels visible on map: BLOOR STREET · HARBORD STREET · COLLEGE STREET · CARLTON STREET · WELLESLEY STREET EAST · QUEEN STREET WEST · QUEEN STREET EAST · KING STREET WEST · KING STREET EAST · BATHURST STREET · SPADINA AVENUE · ST. GEORGE STREET · UNIVERSITY AVENUE · BAY STREET · YONGE STREET · JARVIS STREET · PARLIAMENT STREET

GUIDEBOOK ENTRIES

01. New City Hall
02. CN Tower
05. Gardiner Expressway
06. Rosedale Valley Bridge
13. 45 Charles Street East
14. Sears Canada
15. National Life
16. The Manulife Centre
17. The Sheraton Centre
18. Toronto Hilton Hotel

19. Four Seasons Hotel
20. Sutton Place Hotel
21. Rochdale College
22. Tartu College
23. OISE
24. The Clarke Institute
25. Sidney Smith Hall
26. New College
27. Robarts Library
28. Medical Sciences

29. Central Tech Art Centre
30. McLaughlin Planetarium
35. Polish Combatants
37. The Colonnade
38. Harbour Square
41. 44 Walmer Road
42. 20 Prince Arthur
44. Allen Brown Building
47. St. Jamestown

ADDITIONAL PROJECTS

53. Regent Park South (p. 59)
54. City Park Apartments (p. 132)
60. Dupont Station (p. 288)

DOWNTOWN MAP 1:35 000

500 M

DON MILLS ROAD

11

WYNFORD DRIVE

12

36

09

10

EGLINTON AVENUE EAST

31

NORTHLINE ROAD

46

OVERLEA BOULEVARD

THORNCLIFFE PARK DRIVE

45

OCONNOR DRIVE

08

ST CLAIR AVE EAST

OCONNOR DRIVE

GUIDEBOOK ENTRIES

08. Don Valley Parkway
09. Bata Headquarters
10. Imperial Oil
11. Ortho Pharmaceutical Plant
12. Oxford University Press
31. Ontario Science Centre
36. Noor Cultural Centre
45. Thorncliffe Park
46. Flemingdon Park
48. Crescent Town

DON MILLS / FLEMINGDON PARK MAP 1:35
000
500 M

48

1. New City Hall

ARCHITECT **VILJO REVELL**
WITH JOHN B. PARKIN ASSOCIATES
CLIENT **CITY OF TORONTO**
LOCATION **100 QUEEN STREET WEST**
DATE OF CONCEPTION **1957**
DATE OF COMPLETION **1965**
STATUS **STANDING**

The City's symbol, New City Hall brought Toronto into the modern age as well as onto the international stage. The product of what was at the time the world's largest international architecture competition, with over 500 entries, City Hall was called by many the architectural event of the decade. Providing Toronto with a centre, its first large public space and a benchmark for the extensive modern design that followed throughout the city, City Hall is perhaps Toronto's most important building, and continues to be its most loved.

2. CN Tower

ARCHITECT **JOHN ANDREWS WITH WZMH**
CLIENT **CN RAILWAY**
LOCATION **FRONT STREET AND JOHN STREET**
DATE OF CONCEPTION **1968**
DATE OF COMPLETION **1976**
STATUS **STANDING**

The CN Tower enjoyed 31 years as 'the world's tallest self-supporting tower on land,' a description that nicely distinguished it from other tall things, like the Petronius oil platform in the Gulf of Mexico, which is taller but mostly underwater. In September 2007, it was overtaken by the Burj Dubai in the United Arab Emirates.The tower was intended to have been the centrepiece in a massive Metro Centre development of the CN/CP railway lands planned for during the 1960s. It is all that's left of that big dream, but its slipform concrete still stands proud as an example of Canadian engineering ingenuity.

3. Yonge Eglinton Centre

ARCHITECT	**BREGMAN + HAMANN**
CLIENT	**NORTH TORONTO DEVELOPMENT**
LOCATION	**2300 YONGE STREET**
DATE OF CONCEPTION	**1965**
DATE OF COMPLETION	**1974**
STATUS	**STANDING**

Catalytic to the intensification of the suburbs, this multi-towered mixed-use project rises up above what was originally the end of Toronto's first subway line. Today the centre of midtown, this megastructure's underground walkways, public plaza, apartments and office towers are given texture through various application of cast-in-place and precast concrete. Sitting among a sea of neighbouring high-rises, it constitutes the centre of an area of Toronto that now rivals downtown.

4. Yorkdale Shopping Centre

ARCHITECT	**JOHN GRAHAM AND COMPANY, JOHN B. PARKIN ASSOCIATES**
CLIENT	**SIMPSON'S & EATON'S COMPANIES**
LOCATION	**1 YORKDALE ROAD**
DATE OF CONCEPTION	**1958**
DATE OF COMPLETION	**1964**
STATUS	**STANDING**

Canada's first true shopping mall, Yorkdale Shopping Centre opened to great fanfare, bringing downtown retail sophistication to the expanding suburbs. Built at the nexus of the 401 and Spadina Expressway, and now a regional hub for the subway and GO Transit, Yorkdale continues to be the social and commercial centre of North Toronto. Though continually evolving, the pure concrete forms of the original Simpson's building, designed by John Andrews during his tenure at Parkin, sits monumental, timeless and solid amid the infinite landscape of its suburban surroundings.

5. Gardiner Expressway

ARCHITECT	METRO WORKS
CLIENT	METROPOLITAN TORONTO
LOCATION	CENTRAL WATERFRONT
DATE OF CONCEPTION	1943
DATE OF COMPLETION	1964
STATUS	STANDING

A project infamous for both the highway and the Metro chair for whom it is named, the Gardiner Expressway is perhaps Toronto's most contentious piece of infrastructure. Built on vacant industrial lands as a dynamic elevated expressway, the Gardiner was Toronto's first introduction to rapid motor transit beginning in 1955. While its place in Toronto's post-industrial landscape is currently undecided, this vital piece of infrastructure provides hundreds of thousands of daily commuters with unparalleled views of the city's ever-changing skyline, waterfront and the Toronto Islands.

6. Rosedale Valley Bridge

ARCHITECT	JOHN B. PARKIN ASSOCIATES
	WITH DELCAN CATER & CO.
CLIENT	TORONTO TRANSIT COMMISSION
LOCATION	ROSEDALE RAVINE AND BLOOR
DATE OF CONCEPTION	1954
DATE OF COMPLETION	1966
STATUS	STANDING

The little brother of the Bloor Viaduct, the Rosedale Valley Bridge brings the Bloor-Danforth subway gracefully across the Rosedale Ravine's deep gorge. Soaring over treetops, this open spandrel concrete arch bridge is enclosed to prevent train noise from disturbing the neighbourhood around it. Its simple modern character references pioneering concrete bridges constructed earlier in the century, such as those of Robert Maillart. Unnoticeable to subway passengers and difficult to see from above, this magnificent structure is best experienced from the ravine below.

7. Eglinton West Station

ARCHITECT   ARTHUR ERICKSON
CLIENT   TORONTO TRANSIT COMMISSION
LOCATION   EGLINTON AND ALLEN EXPRESSWAY
DATE OF CONCEPTION   1972
DATE OF COMPLETION   1978
STATUS   STANDING

8. Don Valley Parkway

ARCHITECT   METRO WORKS
CLIENT   METROPOLITAN TORONTO
LOCATION   DON VALLEY
DATE OF CONCEPTION   1960
DATE OF COMPLETION   1966
STATUS   STANDING

The most 'concrete' of Toronto's modern transit stations, Eglinton West features a 70-metre concrete waffle slab roof that appears to float above the Allen Expressway's artificial cliff face. The station cascades toward the subway platform below, while its raised bus terminal offers panoramic views of the highway and modern communities to the north. Murals by artist Gerald Zeldinwith inhabit the double-height spaces created by the station's gradual terracing.

Curving gracefully within the bed of the Don Valley, the DVP brought new mobility and speed to the growing metropolis in the early 1960s, as well as the rare experience of complete immersion in Toronto's vast ravine system. Enabling the growth of Toronto's modern communities along its length, the expressway embodied a 'jet set' pleasure ride, providing unparalleled views of Toronto's natural and modern landscapes.

9. Bata Headquarters

ARCHITECT   JOHN B. PARKIN ASSOCIATES
CLIENT   BATA SHOES
LOCATION   59 WYNFORD DRIVE
DATE OF CONCEPTION   1963
DATE OF COMPLETION   1965
STATUS   GONE

10. Imperial Oil

ARCHITECT   JOHN B. PARKIN ASSOCIATES
CLIENT   IMPERIAL OIL LTD
LOCATION   EGLINTON AVENUE
        AND DON MILLS ROAD
DATE OF CONCEPTION   1960
DATE OF COMPLETION   1962
STATUS   GONE

The temple-like Bata Headquarters was sited on a rise overlooking Eglinton and the Don Valley. Three rows of colonnades support the cantilevered box above with concrete triangulated panels branching outward from individual column 'trunks' centralized within repeated square structural panels. John Parkin celebrated modular precast concrete construction in this building by setting its organic frame against smooth sheets of glass.

Winner of the Massey Silver Medal and an honourable distinction at the São Paulo International Biennale of Architecture and Design, Imperial Oil sat on its perch at the corner of Don Mills and Eglinton as a shining emblem of the new Canada. Supported by a rectilinear steel skeleton, a gleaming concrete skin of 360 white precast panels float within the generous site's mature trees. A rigid modern plan with logia and a three-storey atrium brought a classical rigour to the winding streets of Don Mills.

11. Ortho Pharmaceutical Plant

ARCHITECT	JOHN B. PARKIN ASSOCIATES
CLIENT	ORTHO PHARMACEUTICAL
LOCATION	19 GREEN BELT DRIVE
DATE OF CONCEPTION	1954
DATE OF COMPLETION	1956
STATUS	STANDING

The bright white concrete exoskeleton of this structure was John Parkin's answer to Don Mills master planner Macklin Hancock's ideals for his modern town: clean, sleek and, most importantly, modern. Bringing both light industry and high design to a pasture in the city's northeast, Ortho Pharmaceutical introduced modernism to the suburbs and helped complete Don Mills' mandate of live, play and work. Highly published, Ortho became an icon and was catalytic to modern design in Canada.

12. Oxford University Press

ARCHITECT	FAIRFIELD AND DUBOIS
CLIENT	OXFORD UNIVERSITY PRESS
LOCATION	1-70 WYNFORD DRIVE
DATE OF CONCEPTION	1961
DATE OF COMPLETION	1963
STATUS	STANDING

Relocating to Don Mills in the early 1960s, Oxford University Press sought an innovative design to announce its presence within Toronto's modern industrial corridor. A suburban departure from DuBois's catalogue of urban projects, Oxford University Press was designed as a stand-alone object that takes advantage of its generous site. Emphasis is placed on the horizontal through its layered low form and linear concrete block pattern. Displaying influences ranging from Le Corbusier to Frank Lloyd Wright, Oxford University Press redefined the light industrial building as a work of art.

240 | ARTICLE

59 | INTERVIEW

102 | INTERVIEW

ORTHO

OXFORD

13. 45 Charles Street East

ARCHITECT	**FAIRFIELD AND DUBOIS**
LOCATION	**45 CHARLES STREET EAST**
DATE OF CONCEPTION	**1964**
DATE OF COMPLETION	**1966**
STATUS	**STANDING**

14. Sears Canada

ARCHITECT	**MAXWELL MILLER**
CLIENT	**SEARS CANADA**
LOCATION	**222 JARVIS STREET**
DATE OF CONCEPTION	**1968**
DATE OF COMPLETION	**1971**
STATUS	**STANDING**

The geometric individuality of this mid-block office building separates it from the neighbouring architecture on Charles Street East. The structure's 45-degree angles allow for a unique eight-corner structure, offering generous outdoor terraces with significant plantings. Originally housing the practice of building designer Macy DuBois, this distinctive modern form, composed of patterned precast concrete panels, is a refreshing alternative to the standard glass box so typical of office design.

Clad in brick as a homage to its material surroundings, yet unmistakably Brutalist in form, the Sears Canada building is Toronto's iteration of the early postwar fascination with cantilevered block volumes, made famous with Le Corbusier's La Tourette, and Boston City Hall. As an inverted ziggurat, it is a striking monument within the architectural eclecticism of Jarvis Street.

15. National Life

ARCHITECT	JOHN B. PARKIN ASSOCIATES
CLIENT	NATIONAL LIFE
LOCATION	522 UNIVERSITY AVENUE
DATE OF CONCEPTION	1971
DATE OF COMPLETION	1974
STATUS	STANDING

16. The Manulife Centre

ARCHITECT	CLIFFORD AND LAWRIE
CLIENT	MANULIFE FINANCIAL
LOCATION	55 BLOOR STREET WEST
DATE OF CONCEPTION	1967
DATE OF COMPLETION	1974
STATUS	STANDING

National Life was designed as a modern addition to the monumental streetscape of University Avenue. Using its precast panels as a nod to context, its warm light limestone aggregate echoes its neighbouring masonry structures. Sculptural piers lift the building's heavy bulk, under which hangs the cantilevered second storey. Its generous free-plan lobby provides access from the ordered grandeur of University Avenue to the quiet streets of Baldwin Village to the west.

Located above the Bay subway station, the Manulife Centre brought downtown to Bloor Street. With an office block, 51-storey residential tower, podium of shops, restaurants and cinema, as well as subterranean connection to its neighbours, the Manulife Centre has remained the area landmark and infrastructural epicentre for over three decades. With a podium-level roof garden and 51st-storey swimming pool, it offers 'modern living' as much now as it did in 1974. Constantly evolving retail has neatly knitted this concrete mega-structure into the community, and its rooftop patio offers unbeatable views of the city.

17. The Sheraton Centre

18. Toronto Hilton Hotel

ARCHITECT JOHN B. PARKIN ASSOCIATES
CLIENT SHERATON HOTELS LTD.
LOCATION 123 QUEEN STREET WEST
DATE OF CONCEPTION 1965
DATE OF COMPLETION 1972
STATUS STANDING

ARCHITECT NORR LIMITED AND
RENO C. NEGRIN AND ASSOCIATES
CLIENT WESTERN INTERNATIONAL HOTELS
LOCATION 145 RICHMOND STREET WEST
DATE OF CONCEPTION 1972
DATE OF COMPLETION 1975
STATUS STANDING

Built in concrete to achieve a contextual relationship with the New City Hall, the Sheraton Centre was part of an effort by the City to surround its new urban square with a modern project worthy of Revell's celebrated icon. The project's tower and podium were carefully placed to prevent shadows on the square, and bound a publicly accessible sky garden and waterfall. Not merely a hotel, the project was planned as a piece of urban infrastructure, containing shops, restaurants and offices, as well as connections to the underground PATH system, subway, and the city's now-defunct plus-15 pedestrian sky-bridge system.

The hotel component of Toronto Place, a multi-tower complex built between the Osgoode and St. Andrews subway stations, the Hilton distinguishes itself as a clean, opaque volume in relation to its mirrored-glass neighbours. Its smooth and tightly placed precast panels are a further iteration of the concrete surface of its big brother, the Sheraton Centre to the north. Glass elevators break through its monolithic east and west elevations. A raised plaza, featuring an indoor/outdoor, pool provides access to the hotel's impressive atrium lobby, as well as to shopping in the underground concourse below.

19. Four Seasons Hotel

ARCHITECT	WZMH PARTNERSHIP
CLIENT	HYATT REGENCY
LOCATION	21 AVENUE ROAD
DATE OF CONCEPTION	1969
DATE OF COMPLETION	1971
STATUS	STANDING

20. Sutton Place Hotel

ARCHITECT	WZMH PARTNERSHIP
CLIENT	AFFILIATED REALTY
LOCATION	955 BAY STREET
DATE OF CONCEPTION	1964
DATE OF COMPLETION	1967
STATUS	STANDING

A mountain at Cumberland and Avenue, the Four Seasons was catalytic to the transformation of Yorkville. The flagship of the Toronto-based luxury hotel chain, the project was one of the larger, later infrastructural pieces of WZMH Partnership, whose extensive portfolio in Yorkville spans several decades. Along with the neighbouring Renaissance Plaza, the project brought density to Avenue Road, while its low podium integrates with a fabric of adjacent mid-rise and low buildings. Excellent quality concrete finishes and the service of its legendary owner has made the Four Seasons an area landmark for decades.

The tallest building north of Queen Street when erected, the Sutton Place Hotel brought glamour and big investment beyond the financial district. The 32-storey building is clad in rough ribbed 'corduroy' panels, which, also found on the Four Seasons Hotel, became synonymous with luxury. Though its Victorian interior betrays its Brutalist face, Sutton Place quickly became a symbol of affluence and today remains a textured landmark among Bay Street's less distinguished glass and postmodern towers.

21. Rochdale College

ARCHITECT	TAMPOLD WELLS ARCHITECTS
CLIENT	ROCHDALE COLLEGE
LOCATION	341 BLOOR STREET WEST
DATE OF CONCEPTION	1964
DATE OF COMPLETION	1968
STATUS	STANDING

An icon of late-1960s counterculture, this sleepy seniors' residence began its life as Canada's first 'free' university and quickly became a creative hotbed for all that embodied that turbulent decade, before being closed in 1971 by federal decree. Composed of cast-in-place and precast elements with textured board forming, this modern high-rise offered a new mode of campus living and brought Bloor Street into the space age. Its impact still resonating in the city through a progeny of dozens of active cultural institutions, Rochdale the building and Rochdale the short-lived social experiment have influenced Toronto's cultural landscape for four decades and counting.

22. Tartu College

ARCHITECT	TAMPOLD WELLS ARCHITECTS
CLIENT	TARTU COLLEGE
LOCATION	310 BLOOR STREET WEST
DATE OF CONCEPTION	1967
DATE OF COMPLETION	1969
STATUS	STANDING

This university student residence sits on the fringe of the University of Toronto, its monumental form a marker for the campus's northwestern edge. Details such as textured cedar board forming and subtle setbacks at each street front elevation give Tartu's massing a refined and light presence. With a second allegiance to Tartu University in Estonia, its exterior graphic details pay homage to both to this European school as well as the limitless forms that concrete can create.

23. OISE

ARCHITECT	K. R. COOPER
CLIENT	PROVINCE OF ONTARIO
LOCATION	252 BLOOR STREET WEST
DATE OF CONCEPTION	1966
DATE OF COMPLETION	1969
STATUS	STANDING

The Ontario Institute for Studies in Education stands as an archetypal representation of educational architectural in modern Toronto. While its proportions are massive and its scale monumental, great care is dedicated to the refinement of this structure, both inside and out. Incised windows and a lofty colonnade offset the facade's heavy concrete skin. Inside, warm materials and technical precision quiet the subway running underground, as well as the building's former critics.

24. The Clarke Institute

ARCHITECT	JOHN B. PARKIN ASSOCIATES
CLIENT	PROVINCE OF ONTARIO
LOCATION	250 COLLEGE STREET
DATE OF CONCEPTION	1961
DATE OF COMPLETION	1964
STATUS	STANDING

Associated with the westward expansion of the University of Toronto, the Clarke Institute was the area's first modern tower, predating the McLennan Physical Laboratories by a matter of months. Yet while the latter is clad in limestone, the Clarke's bright white moulded concrete precast panels brought out the sculptural possibilities and simplicity of the modern material. Sited on a generous property that echoes the grounds of its historic Queen Street sister facility, the Clarke represents a modern investment in general social welfare.

292
138 | ARTICLE

OISE
──────────────────────────── 33
CLARKE INSTITUTE

59 | INTERVIEW

25. Sidney Smith Hall

ARCHITECT	PARKIN ASSOCIATES
CLIENT	UNIVERSITY OF TORONTO
LOCATION	100 ST. GEORGE STREET
DATE OF CONCEPTION	1960
DATE OF COMPLETION	1962
STATUS	STANDING

26. New College

ARCHITECT	FAIRFIELD AND DUBOIS
CLIENT	UNIVERSITY OF TORONTO
LOCATION	300 HURON STREET
DATE OF CONCEPTION	1964
DATE OF COMPLETION	1968
STATUS	STANDING

The first building in the University of Toronto's westward expansion, Sidney Smith's tower, podia and plaza marked a bold new direction for the historic campus. The home of the Faculty of Arts and Sciences, Sidney Smith has been the centre of campus life for thousands of students annually for over 40 years. The plaza facing St. George has evolved into one of Toronto's most used public spaces. An early and refined example of postwar modernism in Canada, the building has evolved to meet changing demands. Precast concrete panels decorate the podium's east and west facades.

Built in response to growing student demand, New College was the first 'new' addition to the University of Toronto's college system. Built in phases, New College's two marvellously undulating concrete slab halls bound a generous interior landscaped courtyard. Its boxy west facade was planned as a buffer between students and the aborted Spadina Expressway.

27. Robarts Library

ARCHITECT	WARNER, BURNS, TOAN + LUNDE, MATHERS AND HALDENBY
CLIENT	UNIVERSITY OF TORONTO
LOCATION	130 ST. GEORGE STREET
DATE OF CONCEPTION	1968
DATE OF COMPLETION	1974
STATUS	STANDING

With raised podia, suspended fourth floor and soaring triangular mass cantilevered above St. George, Robarts is one of the more remarkable and controversial concrete buildings in Toronto. Sited in a field of open space and mature trees, the massive bulk of the St. George Campus's largest building houses the majority of the University of Toronto's 15–million (and counting) collection, making Robarts Canada's most prolific research institution. The remarkable Thomas Fisher Rare Book Library is housed at its southern end.

28. Medical Sciences

ARCHITECT	PETER GOERING
CLIENT	UNIVERSITY OF TORONTO
LOCATION	1 KING'S COLLEGE CIRCLE
DATE OF CONCEPTION	1966
DATE OF COMPLETION	1969
STATUS	STANDING

Home to U of T's Medical School, the sprawling concrete complex of 'Med Sci' sits at the southeast corner of King College Circle as Toronto's largest modern sculpture. Originally proposed to be clad in blank stone, concrete was instead chosen for its sculptural and modern qualities. The building's arts budget was dedicated to the creation of thousands of precast panels designed by artists Ted Bieler and Robert Downing.

29. Central Tech Art Centre

ARCHITECT	FAIRFIELD AND DUBOIS
CLIENT	TORONTO DISTRICT SCHOOL BOARD
LOCATION	725 BATHURST STREET
DATE OF CONCEPTION	1957
DATE OF COMPLETION	1962
STATUS	STANDING

The first exposed concrete building erected in Toronto after the war, the Central Tech Arts Centre represents a large leap forward for design in the city. Complementing the neighbouring building's rusticated stone face, while also plastic and fluid in its expression, the use of concrete allowed for forms otherwise cost-prohibitive. A series of terraced artist studios allow generous exposure to northern light.

30. McLaughlin Planetarium

ARCHITECT	ALLWARD AND GOUINLOCK
CLIENT	ROYAL ONTARIO MUSEUM
LOCATION	100 QUEEN'S PARK CRESCENT
DATE OF CONCEPTION	1965
DATE OF COMPLETION	1968
STATUS	STANDING BUT NOT IN USE

Following in the tradition of the Pantheon and Étienne-Louis Boullée, this reinforced-concrete structure was constructed by the Royal Ontario Museum as a means through which to understand and embody the cosmos at the height of the space race. A dual-layered dome allows the interior of this building to receive a projection of the universe from a central Zeiss planetarium projector. Though it opened to great fanfare in 1968, it closed its doors in 1995. Its future use is currently undecided.

97 | INTERVIEW

31. Ontario Science Centre

ARCHITECT	MORIYAMA AND TESHIMA
CLIENT	PROVINCE OF ONTARIO
LOCATION	770 DON MILLS ROAD
DATE OF CONCEPTION	1964
DATE OF COMPLETION	1969
STATUS	STANDING

32. Ross Building

ARCHITECT	GORDON S. ADAMSON
CLIENT	PROVINCE OF ONTARIO
LOCATION	4700 KEELE STREET
DATE OF CONCEPTION	1962
DATE OF COMPLETION	1968
STATUS	STANDING

Opening in 1969 to international acclaim, the Ontario Science Centre transformed the notion of the 'museum' and represented a significant cultural investment in anticipation of Canada's centennial. The centre is sited within the Don Valley at Flemingdon Park, and great measures were taken to limit the ecological impact and heighten the relationship between the textured concrete structure and its natural setting. A 'hands-on' approach defines the programs of this building, while the centre's design consists of flexible blocks connected by links that capitalize on views of nature and beyond.

Emerging from a farmer's field north of the city, the Ross Building's 10 storeys and nearly 200-metre length announced York University's arrival to North Toronto. A mega-structure consisting of offices, lecture halls and student amenities, the Ross Building formed the centre of an extensive modern master plan. The plan itself was designed through a partnership between John B. Parkin Associates, Shore and Moffat and Partners, as well as Hideo Sasaki, head of Landscape Architecture at Harvard. Its generous open space, ring road and pedestrian-oriented centre has allowed the campus to flexibly grow these past 40 years.

33. Holy Blossom Temple

ARCHITECT	CHAPMAN AND OXLEY
CLIENT	CONGREGATION
LOCATION	1950 BATHURST STREET
DATE OF CONCEPTION	1932
DATE OF COMPLETION	1938
STATUS	STANDING

Exhibiting a rare pre-war use of exposed concrete for non-industrial purposes, Holy Blossom was described by Eric Arthur as the only pre-war example of exposed concrete architecture 'that we can point to with any pride.' Built in the 1930s as the Jewish community established itself in new suburbs north of the city, Holy Blossom continues to be one of Toronto's unique and enduring examples of religious architecture.

34. Beth David Synagogue

ARCHITECT	IRVING GROSSMAN
CLIENT	CONGREGATION
LOCATION	55 YEOMANS ROAD
DATE OF CONCEPTION	1957
DATE OF COMPLETION	1959
STATUS	STANDING

This 'jewel box' was created in collaboration with Graham Coughtry, a local artist whose use of prefabricated concrete forms a symbolic facade. Site-specific emblems repeatedly produced from formwork designed by the artist create the synagogue's structure and ornament. Jewish traditions, expressed through sculpture and aligned with innovative construction practices, make the Beth David B'nai Israel Beth Am Synagogue a temple of the modern age.

35. Polish Combatants

ARCHITECT	**WIESALW WODKIEWICZ**
CLIENT	**POLISH COMBATANTS ASSOCIATION**
LOCATION	**206 BEVERLEY STREET**
DATE OF CONCEPTION	**1967**
DATE OF COMPLETION	**1973**
STATUS	**STANDING**

Sited on Beverley Street, the Polish Combatants Association Branch No. 20 offers expressive institutional Brutalism on a quite residential scale. Floating on piers over a sunken, open-air parking lot, the compact bulk of the building houses offices, restaurant and banquet hall, and remains a lively staple for the Polish community. A cast-in-place frame and rugged precast 'corduroy' concrete panels have made the building a neighbourhood landmark within its Victorian surroundings.

36. Noor Cultural Centre

ARCHITECT	**MORIYAMA AND TESHIMA**
CLIENT	**JCCC FOUNDING FAMILIES**
LOCATION	**123 WYNFORD DRIVE**
DATE OF CONCEPTION	**1957**
DATE OF COMPLETION	**1963**
STATUS	**STANDING**

Originally built as the Japanese Canadian Cultural Centre, the project was designed to honour the place of Japanese ancestry within Canada. Located in Flemingdon Park, the project marked an expansion of the city's cultural landscape to the growing suburbs. Precast concrete elements pay homage to Japanese heritage. Recently renovated by Moriyama & Teshima as the Noor Islamic Cultural Centre, the building continues to be operated as a sacred and vital community hub.

37. The Colonnade

ARCHITECT	GERALD ROBINSON AND TAMPOLD WELLS ARCHITECTS
LOCATION	131 BLOOR STREET WEST
DATE OF CONCEPTION	1961
DATE OF COMPLETION	1964
STATUS	STANDING

The first modern mixed-use building in the city, this concrete mid-rise defines a character of urban living unlike any others in the surrounding Yorkville neighbourhood. Twelve floors of residences sit above offices, two levels of shops and a public forecourt. A lattice skin, formed by a repetitive concrete structure, provides an inherent flexibility essential to the modern ideal. The free-standing concrete courtyard contains a swooping staircase said to be the largest unsupported staircase of its kind when built.

38. Harbour Square

ARCHITECT	BREGMAN + HAMANN
CLIENT	CAMPEAU CORPORATION
LOCATION	33 HARBOUR SQUARE
DATE OF CONCEPTION	1972
DATE OF COMPLETION	1979
STATUS	STANDING

The first project of a revitalized waterfront, Harbour Square, along with the Westin Harbour Castle, brought residences, retail, tourist attractions and most importantly ample greenspace to a decommissioned industrial harbour. Planned originally to include similar buildings on an adjacent quay, as well as in conjunction with the massive Metro Centre development on the rail lands, these buildings represent the realized portion of an era of ambitious waterfront planning. With a generous garden roof, terrace units that face mature trees at the lake edge, and Brutalist ferry docks providing an escape to Toronto Island, concrete has never looked so green.

39. Palace Pier

ARCHITECT	E. I. RICHMOND
LOCATION	2045 LAKE SHORE BLVD WEST
DATE OF CONCEPTION	1975
DATE OF COMPLETION	1978
STATUS	STANDING

This luxury concrete residence, located by the Humber River, has been an Etobicoke landmark for over three decades. With views of the lake and distant central city skyline, the 46-storey cruciform canonical tower-in-the-park functions as a modern private estate by the western waterfront. Joined by a metal clad twin in the late 1980s, and more recently by an eclectic swarm of mid-rise turn-of-the-century glass condos, Palace Pier's generous site planning and concrete form remains the modern ideal.

40. House on Ardwold Gate

ARCHITECT	TAIVO KAPSI
LOCATION	ARDWOLD GATE
DATE OF CONCEPTION	1966
DATE OF COMPLETION	1968
STATUS	STANDING

Featuring rough cast-in-place concrete on both its interior and exterior, this modern home was something of a shock to its North Toronto neighbours. Generous terraces and open plan takes full advantage of its idyllic ravine site, and texture from saw-cut timber forms heightens this relationship between structure and nature. Reminiscent of the work of Rudolf Schindler, tucked away within the tree canopy of Roycroft Park, this house is one of Toronto's hidden architectural gems.

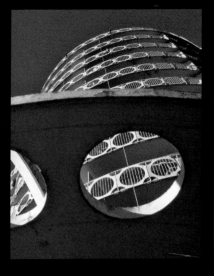

41. 44 Walmer Road

ARCHITECT	UNO PRII
LOCATION	44 WALMER ROAD
DATE OF CONCEPTION	1967
DATE OF COMPLETION	1969
STATUS	STANDING

42. 20 Prince Arthur

ARCHITECT	UNO PRII
LOCATION	20 PRINCE ARTHUR STREET
DATE OF CONCEPTION	1963
DATE OF COMPLETION	1965
STATUS	STANDING

Known to have realized hundreds of buildings and designed many more, the prolific Estonian-Canadian architect Uno Prii brought radical design to Toronto's booming development market of the '60s and '70s. The building at 44 Walmer brought a light, modern motif to the dense Victorian architecture of Toronto's West Annex neighbourhood. Modest in scale compared with other Prii projects, this cruciform point tower has become a neighbourhood icon through its curvilinear balconies, sculptural fountain and porte cochère.

This modern tower has become the canonic Prii statement, its sweeping form a symbol of mod 1960s sophistication in a style unique to Toronto. Surrounded by Victorian streetscapes, its space-age look has come to help define the eclectic character of the historic Annex neighbourhood over the last four decades. Along with several other notable project by the architect, 20 Prince Arthur was added to the City's list of heritage properties in 2003.

43. Jane Exbury Towers

ARCHITECT	UNO PRII
LOCATION	2335 JANE STREET
DATE OF CONCEPTION	1968
DATE OF COMPLETION	1970
STATUS	STANDING

Landmarks visible for miles, and an entry marker to the city when driving from the north on Highway 400, the Jane Exbury Towers are a modern statement in Toronto's northern fringe. A further iteration of Uno Prii's characteristic sweeping forms, the true uniqueness of these sculptural, buttressed tower blocks is their arrangement as a series. Five identical towers, repeated in typical modern fashion, bring a remarkable coherence and originality to this ravine site.

44. Allen Brown Building

ARCHITECT	UNO PRII
CLIENT	HOSPITAL FOR SICK CHILDREN
LOCATION	77 ELM STREET
DATE OF CONCEPTION	1979
DATE OF COMPLETION	1981
STATUS	STANDING

A stylistic departure for Uno Prii, 77 Elm Street pushes the architect's sculptural vocabulary from the swooping to the rough and angular. Sitting above a multi-storey parking garage, the playful use of exposed and precast concrete creates several allusions to the human body through abstracted ornamental heads at grade, and expressive figures emerging from protruding shear walls. Following the mandate of the typical residence, yet pushing the sculptural potentials of concrete, 77 Elm Street is a building like no other within the city's vast catalogue of concrete high-rises.

45. Thorncliffe Park

ARCHITECT	ALEXANDER BENEDEK
CLIENT	THORNCLIFFE PARK LTD
LOCATION	85 THORNCLIFFE PARK DRIVE
DATE OF CONCEPTION	1955
DATE OF COMPLETION	1971
STATUS	STANDING

In the 1960s, Thorncliffe Park was constructed on the site of a horse-racing track that lay cut off from the city by two branches of the Don River. The objective was to create a self-supporting urban hub, a new town overlooking the Don Valley, characterized by distinctive apartment towers. The success of this program was evident as Thorncliffe Park was officially renamed East York Centre in 1993. The concrete residential Leaside Towers of 1970, at 130 metres, have been the tallest buildings north of Bloor Street for 37 years.

46. Flemingdon Park

ARCHITECT	IRVING GOSSMAN
CLIENT	WEBB AND KNAPP
LOCATION	10 GATEWAY BOULEVARD
DATE OF CONCEPTION	1959
DATE OF COMPLETION	1965
STATUS	STANDING

Influenced by Sweden's Vallingby and London's Roehampton, Flemingdon Park was conceived in 1959 as a modern town of 14,000 people, containing apartment towers, commercial districts, transit and a full complement of community facilities. Not all of this was realized, yet the concrete towers of Flemington Park initiated a distinctly new way of developing suburban Toronto. The neighbourhood contains examples of remarkable housing by Irving Grossman and cultural facilities by Raymond Moriyama.

47. St. Jamestown

ARCHITECT	VARIOUS
CLIENT	MERIDIAN
LOCATION	495 SHERBOURNE STREET
DATE OF CONCEPTION	1956
DATE OF COMPLETION	1973
STATUS	STANDING

The first towers completed in the early 1960s, St. Jamestown includes variations of the high-rise apartment tower form – a diversity not typical of such mass residential estates. Seen from afar, it has the skyline of a city within a city. Up close, its culturally diverse population shows that it is in fact a global village. Contrary to tendencies of modern standardization, St. Jamestown represents an array of social and architectural expression. Continuing to evolve with new infill projects, the area contains some of the largest publicly accessible open spaces downtown.

48. Crescent Town

ARCHITECT	MARLIN DIETRICH
CLIENT	BELMONT CONSTRUCTION
LOCATION	2 THE MARKET PLACE
DATE OF CONCEPTION	1969
DATE OF COMPLETION	197
STATUS	STANDING

Construction began in September 18, 1969, for Crescent Town, an entire community contained within one immense building, built on a farm originally owned by the Massey family. With parking below and a walkway to Victoria Park subway station, a collection of towers, townhouses and courtyards on top promised new residents a space of their own. Including shops, restaurants, a library and even an elementary school, the complex truly is a town within one concrete mega-structure built adjacent to the quiet forests of Taylor Creek.

49. Scarborough College

ARCHITECT	**JOHN ANDREWS WITH PAGE AND STEELE**
CLIENT	**UNIVERSITY OF TORONTO**
LOCATION	**1265 MILITARY ROAD**
DATE OF CONCEPTION	**1963**
DATE OF COMPLETION	**1965**
STATUS	**STANDING**

Among the few Canadian projects routinely listed in global surveys of modern architecture, Scarborough College is Toronto's educational landmark in concrete design. Cascading along its site's generous topography, the project, originally planned to be expanded in several phases, redefined campus planning and built form. Immediately a star showcased in popular media, this innovative project epitomizes the period of experimentation, innovation and large scale cultural investment that characterized the 1960s in Canada.

50. Trent University

ARCHITECT	**RON THOM**
CLIENT	**PROVINCE OF ONTARIO**
LOCATION	**1600 WEST BANK DRIVE PETERBOROUGH**
DATE OF CONCEPTION	**1966**
DATE OF COMPLETION	**1968**
STATUS	**STANDING**

Situated within the banks of the Otonabee River, rubble aggregate concrete composes the planes and platforms of this 1,500-acre riverside campus. Subtle references to traditional university design create a human-scaled campus that explores the plastic possibilities of concrete, as exemplified in the heroic Reginald Faryon Bridge. The use of concrete as structure and surface material, with a direct relationship to the surrounding natural landscape, has persuaded many to distinguish Trent as Canada's premier modern campus.

51. McMaster Health Sciences

ARCHITECT	CRAIG, ZEIDLER AND STRONG
CLIENT	MCMASTER UNIVERSITY
LOCATION	1280 MAIN STREET WEST
	HAMILTON
DATE OF CONCEPTION	1967
DATE OF COMPLETION	1973
STATUS	STANDING

Echoing space-race functionalism, McMaster's Health Sciences Centre in Hamilton was an internationally celebrated experiment in flexible design and new campus planning. Its opaque precast concrete facade is broken by a series of steel and glass mechanical piers, and the bulk of this megaplex is bisected by a series of public spaces. Its active 'Student Street,' containing open-air atria, bridges and walkways, showcases all the ideals of the mega-structural urbanism from which this building was born.

52. University of Guelph

ARCHITECT	HANCOCK, LITTLE,
	CALVERT AND ASSOCIATES
CLIENT	PROVINCE OF ONTARIO
LOCATION	50 STONE ROAD, GUELPH
DATE OF CONCEPTION	1964
DATE OF COMPLETION	1974
STATUS	STANDING

A result of the massive investment in education in the 1960s, the University of Guelph represents a remarkable international collaboration in monumental campus planning. Consultants for the project, including John Andrews, Macklin Hancock, Morden Yolles and then head of the Harvard School of Design, José Luis Sert. Together they achieved a pedestrian-oriented refined Brutalism that remains coherent, monumental and marvellously integrated into landscaped open spaces of the historic campus.

On *Concrete Toronto*

George Baird

Dean, Faculty of Architecture, Landscape and Design, University of Toronto

Partner, Baird Sampson Neuert Architects Inc.

I have tended to think of myself as a dubious contributor to this volume, on account of my very mixed feelings about concrete as a finishing building material – particularly in a climate such as that of Toronto. It is my view that cast-in-place concrete is a problematic material in our climate, given that our sunlight is rarely intense, and that there are substantial parts of the year when we have no sunlight at all. Even a great building such as Le Corbusier's Carpenter Center at Harvard – a venue with a climate much like Toronto's – is difficult to love unreservedly, with its shadowy undercroft and its rain- and snow-stained concrete looking dank for much of the year.

Then there is the matter of the fateful remark I made many years ago, to the effect that Toronto has 'some of the best second-rate architecture in the world.' This comment of mine – originally made in a circle of friends – was later quoted publicly by Bruce Kuwabara, triggering a small storm of local indignation. The remark was made, I confess, somewhat ironically, but it was also intended to compliment a genre of local precast-concrete-clad buildings – such as Mount Sinai Hospital – that I thought demonstrated a real sophistication, even if the buildings themselves were not masterpieces. In my view, precast concrete cladding fares better in our sometimes cold and often wet climate than does cast-in-place concrete.

None of this line of thinking, it seemed to me, added up to enough to justify a contribution to the present volume.

But then, all of a sudden, I thought again of John Andrews' original building for Scarborough College, that amazing icon of the '60s that is one of the few internationally consequential modern Canadian buildings. And once the Scarborough building – an extravaganza of cast-in-place concrete – had come to my mind, I had to ask myself if I was as sure of my position as I had once thought. What is it about the Scarborough building that enables it to elude most of the problematic visual effects of other cast-in-place buildings in our city?

I can cite at least three features that help it do so. First is that its exterior is viewed largely within a natural landscape – virtually all of its south face, and much of its north one, describes what it is the south and north face are facing. Somehow this natural setting enables the building to elude the dankness I associate with so many of its peers. Then, too, unlike the Carpenter Center or the Robarts Library, Scarborough has very few exterior undercroft areas. Finally, there is the fact that the building's most astonishing plastic effects are on its interior, where the level of control of the appearance of its finishes is much greater than it can be on the building's exterior. I have no doubt that the interior spatial systems at Scarborough remain as visually charged today as they were at the time of the building's completion.

Does this mean, after all, that the editors of this volume are right and that I am wrong? And that it truly is possible to treat concrete as an appropriately Torontonian finishing building material? Certainly this is a question that requires due consideration.

Fig. 1. South view from the terraced balconies of the Science wing, Scarborough College

Concrete Materiality: Text and Texture

David Lieberman

Faculty of Architecture, Landscape and Design, University of Toronto; School of Architecture, University of Waterloo; Faculty of Environmental Studies, York University

The idealist utopian experiments of the early modern period were quickly forgotten in the economic woes and political strife of the 1930s, and with the world at war, concrete was the material of fortress and buttress, thickened to unprecedented mass and weight to both accommodate and resist the force of bombardment and armament. The coasts of Normandy are still littered with constructed cliff faces, the remnants of concrete gun emplacements partially absorbed by the shifting landscape, but grim reminders of an historical past not to be forgotten. With the end of the war and the returning troops, Canada sought to build anew, and to build cities at a ferocious pace with zealous optimism. The rural agricultural past was quickly replaced by urban dreams and ambitions.

Concrete was the material and the substance of that building. Roadways and bridges, water mains and sewers were required – infrastructure to support a new population. Architects needed a material with which to construct and to mould their imaginings. Concrete in its liquid state had infinite possibilities and could be shaped to accommodate the widest range of structures. Concrete had thermal mass and both solidity and stability. Concrete, when reinforced with steel in a variety of ways, could form delicate shells or beams with the capacity to span extraordinary distances. Moulds or forms could be reused either on-site or in the controlled conditions of the factory; construction was both craft and industrial production.

Schools and hospitals, office and apartment towers – concrete made possible the beginnings of a new nation, and certainly the 1950s, '60s and '70s in Toronto were filled with new building. The fly form allowed for repetition; towers often rose as quickly as a floor per week.

Concrete again made possible invention and innovation. Form was limited only by the sculptural ambition of the designers; architects and engineers had a material to shape and to mould. Concrete was also unique in its material presence; embedded in its surface was the trace of its making: the composition of the mix; the size, shape and colour of its aggregate; and, perhaps most importantly, the text and texture of the temporary formwork of its casting, be it the roughness of raw lumber, the smooth touch of steel or the waxed surface of a form giving the finely honed or polished surface of some new and rich stone. Concrete was no longer simply a cold, unfeeling material of support, but was resonant with tectonic eloquence and the subtleties of variable surface. Here was a material that could accommodate the delicate tendrils of climbing ivy or, in its polished state, reflect the bright light of the sun.

Not all experiments were successful; the grey of February draped many buildings with a depressing shadow of a too long winter, and the more absorptive of surfaces often were stained in the dampness of a rainfall. Building science and the necessities of enclosure had not sufficiently understood the issues of thermal transfer and the havoc that would be wreaked by the rigours of the freeze-thaw cycle of the Canadian climate. Certainly, no one predicted the necessity of rebuilding parking garages subject to deterioration of both concrete and reinforcing steel. Even in failure, and in recognition of material limitations, concrete afforded architects the opportunity to draw and model at full scale in response to the rapidly changing needs of the emerging metropolis. For the most part, these heroic structures were a great success, and the opportunities of a material mutability produced architecture of invention and quality.

Moreover, building and infrastructure had a sense of foundational permanence: these concrete structures shaped and evolved our cities. Concrete is not always revealed, but it remains fundamental to building. In the 21st century, with current technical developments of higher strengths, articulated surfaces and even translucency, concrete will again have architects dipping their hands into wet cement, dreaming and shaping concrete poetry as the fabric of the cities in which we dwell.

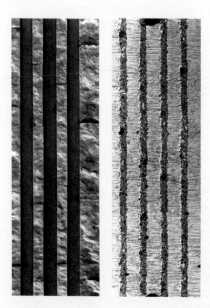

Figs. 2, 3. Examples of concrete textures achieved through different processes of formation: precast (left) and cast in place (right)

Canadian Concrete

David Rich

Partner, WZMH Partnership

Concrete has been a major feature of Toronto buildings since World War II – unlike its U.S. counterparts. Among the reasons for this has been the relative economy of concrete over steel in Canada, as compared to the U.S., together with the significant influence in Canada of European architects who have been more open to the use of concrete. Moreover, the giant U.S. steel industry has not been as influential in Canada as in the U.S. when it has come time to make decisions. Some of Toronto's major tall buildings have been constructed of concrete on a continent where steel had generally been the accepted norm. It is interesting to note that of Toronto's tallest commercial towers after 1960, those designed in U.S. with U.S. structural engineers have been built of steel, while those designed in Canada with Canadian architects and structural engineers have been built of concrete (for example, the CN Tower, Royal Bank Plaza and Scotia Plaza). Also, the large Canadian contractors, particularly through the '60s, '70s and '80s, developed a reputation for innovative concrete construction methods in large buildings, ahead of their U.S. counterparts.

This has led, in turn, to subtle differences in design approach, taking into account the greater plasticity of concrete as distinct from the more formal and taut character of steel. And, of course, the great bulk of large residential buildings being erected currently are built of concrete – in 'surface' structure format as distinct from steel frames.

Building skins have taken a different path. The use of heavy precast elements (and stone) stapled onto the outside structural frames has been waning, in favour of lighter skins and more developed exterior-wall technology. However, Toronto has several fine examples of earlier precast exterior skins, notably the Colonnade on Bloor Street, the Tower Hill apartments at St. Clair and Spadina, and Bata Headquarters.

The use of concrete in Toronto since 1950 enabled architects such as Peter Dickinson to easily conceive of projects such as Benvenuto Place to enlarge on the 1930s Modern Movement of Europe, with an expression of flat, cantilevered slabs and projecting balconies. In addition, the plastic quality of concrete has allowed designers to readily conceive of buildings with significant curved qualities. City Hall is a supreme example of this, and this in time has influenced the design of much subsequent work – for example, Scarborough College, which, when it opened in the mid-'60s, was the subject of great interest. These two buildings were seminal for future work in the city. Even some office towers have changed more recently by taking advantage of the cantilevering ability of concrete, to move major structural elements to the inside of office floor plates where this is deemed desirable, thereby leaving exterior walls free to be expressed without column intrusion.

Fig. 4. At the south end of the site, Robarts emerges behind a concrete gazebo that was used to test architectural finishes as well as marking a time capsule containing artifacts from the early 1970s

Looking and Seeing: Concrete Toronto and the Education of the Architect

George Thomas Kapelos

Chair, Associate Professor, Department of Architectural Science, Ryerson University

I am an architect who takes every opportunity to travel and look at architecture. I enjoy exploring new cities; I look and I see; I observe and I remember. Every city has its own character that leaves an imprint on the mind's eye. Sometimes the remembrance is in materiality: grey stone for Montreal or honey-coloured limestone for Jerusalem. Sometimes it's in the city's form: New York's high-rise canyons or the Parisian mat of boulevard and building. Sometimes the character is defined by the section: Chicago's layers of river, railway, street and building, or Hong Kong's escalators, running up hillside neighbourhoods. Or perhaps the definer is more abstract and ephemeral. In Vancouver, there's the idea of the 'other,' where mountains and sea remind the city dweller of places out of range of daily urban life. In L.A., it's the 'infinite,' the imagined point on the horizon, framed by windshield and experienced only by endless driving. But what might be Toronto's essential character? Is it the ravines? The waterfront? How does architecture shape this character?

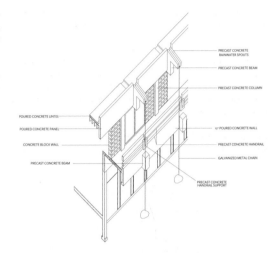

Concrete Toronto brings to light new evidence to help answer this question. When Michael McClelland

and Graeme Stewart proposed the idea for this book, their enthusiasm and passion about Toronto's modern concrete architectural heritage led me to speculate whether this could be a new way to understand our city. *Concrete Toronto* is also timely. As the instructor in ARC512 – Theory III in the four-year Bachelor of Architectural Science degree program at Ryerson University, I am always on the lookout for new ways to engage students in understanding the relationship between technique and theory.

The fit of *Concrete Toronto* to my course was therefore obvious. In the fall of 2006, I asked students to examine a Toronto-area building from the period 1950–80 whose design and construction emphasized the architectonic use of concrete. The *Concrete Toronto* assignment draws

its inspiration from Edward R. Ford's, *The Details of Modern Architecture*, a particularly important work for the architecture student. A key component of Ford's methodology was the examination of construction details and working drawings that would be subsequently redrawn in simple-to-understand line drawings. I am

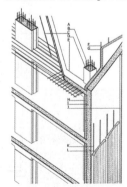

pleased that many of the outcomes of this work have been included here.

In looking at these buildings, *Concrete Toronto* leads us to see our city in a new way. Certainly Toronto's place in the history of Canadian architecture is only now being fully explored. The period of rapid expansion, postwar growth, new capital, optimism and experimentation may well be one of the key definers of this

city. The built artifacts of this period – many of which were executed in concrete – help explain who we are, both to ourselves and to our visitors. Examining Toronto through the exuberant and vibrant constructions of *Concrete Toronto* confirms that our modern concrete legacy is a critical element that distinguishes our city.

The drawings throughout this book have been selected by the editors of

Concrete Toronto from thoes submitted by students to the instructor, and are accompanied by similar drawings undertaken by students from the University of Toronto working with professor Pina Petricone. They by no means represent all the projects yet exemplify a range of work. I am grateful to all my students for their co-operation and enthusiasm in effecting this project.

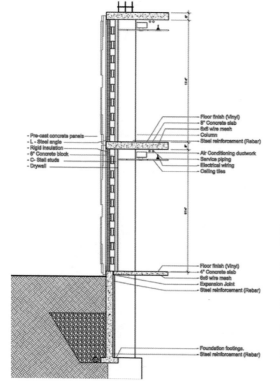

Fig. 5	Fig. 8 Fig. 9
Fig. 6 Fig. 7	

Fig. 5. Japanese Canadian Cultural Centre

Fig. 6. Council Chamber, New City Hall

Fig. 7. Office Block, New City Hall

Fig. 8. Medical Sciences Building

Fig. 9. John P. Robarts Library

55

Vincent Tovell: Documenting A Cultural Explosion

Interview with Vincent Tovell

Producer, CBC Television

VINCENT TOVELL was a pioneering CBC television producer whose broad focus included modern architecture. He was interviewed by E.R.A. Architects in his modern apartment in the Annex in November 2006.

E.R.A. The '60s marked a big change in Canadian culture – it is always mythologized as Canada coming into its own. What do you see as the big changes?

Vincent Tovell   The '60s, of course, are very easy to talk about. There was a kind of dynamism that had not existed. It wasn't possible during the Depression, and it couldn't be done during the war. War was static. It was great for industrialization. It was great for building all sorts of things that hadn't got built before, like tanks. That was the industrial profit of the war; we profited well out of the second war. No doubt about that. Look at the ships, look at the cordites that got built in Collingwood, and all that. But it didn't affect domestic architecture until we got to the postwar stages. The advances in arts and culture that were starting in the '20s pretty well stopped for two decades, then shot off with a bang after the war. The '60s were really a wonderful period. New ideas were for everyone, not just an elite.

There was a whole new generation of people after the war who travelled, who were open to new ideas. There came a kind of new middle class with the possibility of university education, who had worked in the forces. Men and women. And there were new kinds of families. A great flourishing of Scandinavian furnishing for small apartments, which is where all the young couples had to live. They didn't inherit great houses to live in; they had to make do. And the great market for the Scandinavian furniture flourished

everywhere across the country, and I think it's beneficial. I have some. Everybody did.

E.R.A. **How did this new cultural attitude express itself in terms of design?**

Vincent Tovell   Through very sophisticated architecture. There was the wave of confidence, there's no doubt about that, prosperity after the war. And I do think it's terribly important that the architects were one of the beneficiary groups in this. There were talented architects ready to push the old guard out. And they were – you can think of them now in retrospect – the giants of the period. Parkin was a big leader in this, undoubtedly. John had an enormous influence on many people, not just as the modernist, which is how he got labelled most quickly – like Gropius and all the others from Harvard. But he really was eager to break the patterns and change. And he was a force in the world of the emerging Canada Council – getting them to think in new terms. He wasn't the only one, but he certainly was a leader. The idea of the Bata was one of the great ones for him. He won the National Gallery Competition, if I remember correctly – one of the ones they didn't build.

And it's a pity there isn't more published about John Parkin. He had a tremendous influence in this country.

Fig. 11. Bata Headquarters

Fig. 12. Imperial Oil

Four projects by John B. Parkin Associates (Now NORR Limited Architects & Engineers)

Eric Arthur is another one, in his own way. Based at the University of Toronto, with his interest in not just the historical material, which he shared with Tony Adamson to some extent. He got the students activated to get the new City Hall of Toronto competition going. He really guided that competition. It was a shock for Toronto. They even called Frank Lloyd Wright – I don't know which of the newspapers did – to get him to say something outrageous. Of course he hadn't seen anything, but he proceeded to say it anyway. But it was a worldwide story for architecture.

E.R.A. **There was a flood of modern architecture that came forward in the '60s. Quite a radical change. What was the public reaction? Did people like these buildings?**

Vincent Tovell   They definitely did. I have no hesitation in saying this. People were curious. This was something people here had never seen before. There was sheer curiosity. City Hall, for instance, was a storm, and it was wonderful, because it looked strange. 'What was this going to be like?' In retrospect, you'd have to say it was very, very well received early. It was so exciting. And clearing away all of that downtown mess. Regrettably, the old Shea's Theatre with its old vaudeville shows – I missed that. Not to mention the casino across the way. All those closed. And then the big storm about the Henry Moore sculpture in the plaza. Well, you see, it broke through! It wasn't just art gallery stuff. It *belonged* in a public place.

Fig. 13. Ortho Pharmaceutical

Fig. 14. The Clarke Institute

E.R.A.   **Is it true that the old architectural guard in Toronto never forgave Eric for the City Hall competition?**

Vincent Tovell   Maybe the public was receptive of new pieces, but I think the old guard was less receptive of new or younger architects. It may be that younger architects had a hard time breaking into the successful contracts, but that didn't last long – it became a wide-open game. Something got lost, however, because the old guard had skills. They also had styles they were masters of. You couldn't build a building like the Medical Arts Building today. I don't suppose any of the young architects would have any idea how to go about thinking that way. It was all about innovating – but when you're always innovating, do you know how to detail that?

E.R.A.   **And how did people react to characters like Peter Dickinson and Mies van der Rohe? What was the idea of architecture as a personality?**

Vincent Tovell   Peter Dickinson was a great success, wasn't he? Benvenuto, which is still his place, that was successful at every level, wasn't it? People liked it. And it worked in business/commercial terms. And there was the O'Keefe Centre and the tower's at Regent Park (MAP P. 20). I don't remember hearing of him as particularly controversial. He was certainly 'of the times.' And he seemed to understand what could be done and got them built, and of course he was so young when he died, wasn't he?

Fig. 15. Ontario Science Centre, Moriyama and Teshima

Fig. 16. Revell presenting his winning scheme

E.R.A.   **Thirty-six ...**

Vincent Tovell   And that was a shock. Because he was a leader, obviously. I'm not sure that Mies represented any great disturbing aesthetic. It looked so practical for a start. And then an awful lot of the business people, the money people – the big money – liked that building because they looked as important as they would in Chicago or New York or somewhere they really would fit. I had friends who were young lawyers working in that part of the new Canada, the big corporate structure that was evolving, and they were very proud to be around there: We're big-time now.

When you think of the sheer scale of the projects through the progress of the '60s, you can see the really interesting trends emerging and you can make your own lists of the architects. Think again of John Parkin, of course, and Ray Moriyama ... and the list goes on.

E.R.A.   **Was there the notion of architect as celebrity as there is today?**

Vincent Tovell   Not like today. But John Andrews was a real showman. He said to me, 'Architecture is a performing art. If you can find yourself in the *New York Times* or the centre spread of *Time* magazine, then you've made it.' And he accomplished all of the above, the latter with Scarborough College.

Figs. 17, 18. Scarborough College, John Andrews

E.R.A. Many of these projects were a radical departure from what people were used to. Was the country generally receptive of international ideas?

Vincent Tovell Absolutely. This is most evident in Expo. People still prattle on about Expo as the most exciting time they ever spent – because there was money available one way or another to go to Montreal and actually wander around. Some of the Canadian buildings were in themselves landmarks. Real landmarks! Arthur Erickson did one. The federal building was done by Colin Vaughan. And Grossman's News and Administration building.

The centennial itself was huge. Of course with Expo, but also there were celebrations right across the country. The government decided to put money into it, which all the towns had access to, some provincial, some federal. And all kinds of activities that had never happened before. The celebrations were all about moving forward.

E.R.A. Expo, the centennial – there seems to be huge investments in all directions. Would you say this time reflects a period of country-building?

Vincent Tovell Country-building, absolutely right: national libraries, the Canada Council, investment in universities, and on and on. This was all in response to the population exploding, and a new sense of what the government could do. The country was growing at such a rate, and with the mixing of people from all over the world, there was a new kind of public, and a real need for investment.

The '60s were the beginning of all the new performing centres. Then in 1967 you had the Ontario Science Centre project. There was no precedent for that, a new centre for learning, with all the public schools rearranging their curriculums to have school trips there.

The whole educational apparatus became much, much bigger, as did the hospitals, as did everything. This era was the laying out of the key infrastructure, which is still today the sacred backbone of most Canadian cities. And the leadership of the governments, especially here in Ontario, encouraged all these things. They kept nurturing it, and this was very necessary.

E.R.A.   **Through all of this, do there think there was a developing sense of a Canadian style in the '60s?**

Vincent Tovell   Well, that's part of a subtle issue. I think architecturally you can argue yes. Ron Thom, Arthur Erickson certainly, represented something that was particularly western, particularly BC, as we know it. The use of materials, the sense of outdoor/indoor. Whereas you could say the Parkin-Gropius line really was much more related, perhaps, to central Canada, with its climate issues. Opening of glass was very important – gets lots of light – long winters. Certainly there was that. But I don't know that you could say there's a unified style right across the country. But everybody was encouraging diversity. I don't think anybody wanted to impose anything particular. Also, it was not easy to get around in this country; it was expensive to travel. The growth of airlines helped. The growth of television helped enormously.

E.R.A.   **You worked as a broadcaster at the CBC, communicating to the nation. You had Revell and John Andrews as features on your show** *Explorations*. **Some today might be surprised that Scarborough College's concrete was a star.**

Vincent Tovell   As I said, people were interested in new ideas. We were all learning, including us at the studio. Television was a new way of connecting our vast country, and the CBC took full advantage. Our program was introducing our audience across Canada to any and all interesting bits of arts and culture from around the world – from Japanese temples in Kyoto to Le Corbusier's concrete La Tourette in France. And of course modern architecture here in Toronto. Most people had previously never seen images of these things, and there was a tremendous excitement about learning. It was all new to us, regardless of what time period it was from. World travel was still expensive, though it was becoming cheaper, but now it was possible to see the world through television. Also, colour photography was just beginning to expand after the war, and it changed our whole way of looking at everything. It's interesting how much our visual horizon has changed.

E.R.A.   **Before we go, any thoughts about concrete?**

Vincent Tovell   The use of concrete was partly a practical solution, wasn't it? The massive growth and the sheer number of buildings that needed to be built – and built quickly, I suppose – demanded concrete, and architects used this to design a new kind of expression. You couldn't build the old way. Couldn't get the stonemasons, in fact, is what it boiled down to. You couldn't afford to pay them. The kind of stone work from Richardson and Lennox, that was another generation, and this was a new type of architecture. It seems like after the City Hall the fashion of the day was the new ideas, the new generation. It became the point at which to go with the old guard would have been a bad move.

They were remarkable times, really worth remembering. And looking back, it was quite something being in the middle of it.

Fig. 1. Downtown Toronto, late 1960s, from the Park Plaza Hotel

concrete toronto   downtown

Reinforced Concrete in Toronto: An Early History

Robert G. Hill

Architect, Historian, KPMB Architects

Despite American precedents recorded as early as 1895, the pioneering use of reinforced concrete in general construction did not occur in Canada until after the turn of the century. Considered ideal for use in commercial and industrial buildings, the material offered significant advantages for architects and engineers, including its inherent strength, its fire-resistant quality and the large, unobstructed spans made possible with few, if any, supporting columns to obstruct activity within the building.

Following the patented invention of the Kahn system of reinforced concrete framing in the United States in 1903, it wasn't long before a competing system, developed by Ferro-Concrete Construction Ltd., was introduced the same year. Within five years, virtually all major Canadian cities had begun to debate and formulate bylaws and codes to regulate the use and standards of this construction method.[1]

Among the earliest buildings in Toronto to be constructed in concrete was a six-storey loft building at 60 Front Street West, just west of Bay.[2] This landmark work would later draw the attention of Eric Arthur when he published an illustration of the rear of the building in *Toronto: No Mean City* (University of Toronto Press, 1964). The illustration is erroneously dated by Arthur as 'c. 1900' and unattributed; it is only recently that new research conducted by this writer has uncovered information about the architects who designed the building, enabling an accurate dating of the work to 1905–06. This confirms it as one of the first buildings erected after the Great Fire of April 1904, when the entire north side of Front Street West, both east and west of Bay, had been completely engulfed in flames

and destroyed. Cited as a vacant building in city directories in 1906, the new building was fully occupied by 12 business tenants from 1907 onward; by 1920, the building had been renamed Wilson Warehouses Building. The designers of this innovative structure are Symons and Rae, who applied for a building permit on June 24, 1905, for a '6 storey concrete warehouse and office building for Mr. S. Frank Wilson ... located at 60–62 Front Street West'. Sadly, this early and important work, one of the first of its kind in Canada, was demolished in 1958 to make way for additions to the Royal York Hotel.[3]

While major advances in reinforced-concrete construction were occurring in Calgary, Vancouver, Winnipeg and Montreal during the first decade of the 20th century, the introduction of this innovative construction method in Toronto suffered a significant setback with the appointment of Robert McCallum as City Architect in late 1905. McCallum (1851–1916), an engineer by training, was known for his conservative views on the introduction of this new building technology, and he frequently refused to grant permits for concrete buildings, declaring this construction method flimsy, dangerous and unproven. His demands, outlined in an illuminating article published in Toronto in *The Contract Record* in June 1908, included requiring architects to overdesign the building strength of the concrete by a factor of 25 percent and requiring owners of new reinforced-concrete buildings under construction to employ, at their own expense, a special inspector to supervise the mixing and placing of concrete and steel.[4] By June 1911, McCallum was increasingly intransigent on the issue of relaxing standards to allow for wider use of the method,[5] but by late 1913 he had resigned his position after

Fig. 2. 60 Front Street West

extensive criticism from City Council committees who accused him of mismanagement.[6]

Only after his departure did the full-fledged, large-scale innovation of this new construction technique flourish, with outstanding examples including the Methodist Book Publishing Warehouse (1913; now Citytv), Queen Street West at John, designed by Burke, Horwood & White, and the sprawling Robert Simpson Co. Warehouse (1916; now the Merchandise Lofts complex), Dalhousie Street at Gould, designed by Max L. Dunning.

Notes

1. For details of the development and use of cement and reinforced concrete in Canada, see Thomas Ritchie, *Canada Builds 1867–1967* (Toronto: University of Toronto Press, 1967), 228-251.

2. For an illustration of the front facade of 60 Front Street West, see the photograph in the Salmon Collection dated Oct. 1955, Acc. S 1-3163B, Baldwin Room, Metro Toronto Reference Library.

3. City of Toronto Archives, Building Permit No. 1326, 24 June 1905, issued to Symons and Rae, Architects, Toronto.

4. See the criticism of Robert McCallum's views in *The Contract Record* XXV (14 June 1908), 37–38.

5. McCallum's conservative opinions on the use of concrete appear in a lengthy article entitled 'McCallum Sticks to His Guns' in *The Evening Telegram* (6 June 1911), 17.

6. A judicial enquiry into the activity of the City Architect was called by City Council in 1913, according to City of Toronto Council Minutes, 24 November 1913.

New City Hall

Christopher Hume

Urban critic, *The Toronto Star*

Though much unloved, concrete has changed the cities of the world, even made them possible. Sadly, architects have not always taken full advantage of its expressive properties, but Viljo Revell was different. The Finnish practitioner, chosen in 1958 through an international competition to design Toronto City Hall, fully understood the sculptural potential of this ancient medium. More than four decades after his masterpiece was completed, it still stands among the supreme examples of architectural concrete in the world.

True, people complain that Toronto City Hall lacks colour, but that's more than adequately compensated for by the spectacular forms of the complex. The two curved towers, 27 and 20 storeys, embrace the 'flying saucer' that contains the council chamber. Revell's concept, however abstract it may seem, expresses the civic ideal and the democratic spirit that lie at the heart of the modern city.

It was concrete that enabled Revell to achieve the organic, curvilinear qualities so essential to his vision. Though inspired by classical notions of civic architecture, his interest was not formal. Unlike, say, Ludwig Mies van der Rohe, who sought to mesh the rationality of classical models with 20th-century technology, Revell took a more humanist stance. The rigid geometry of the Miesians held little appeal for Revell; he opted for a kinder, gentler architecture ideally suited to the plasticity of concrete.

Thus, City Hall is defined by its flow, soft edges, curves and circularity; it is a complex where every element connects seamlessly with the next. The ribbed tower walls, for example, are informed by Revell's concerns for shape and texture. They feel more gestural than structural, more handmade than constructed. There is a fluidity here rarely found in architecture, especially in a building such as City Hall, which must bear the weight of municipal symbolism. In this case, it's concrete that made such expressiveness possible.

Best of all, Revell does not seem to have approached concrete as a substitute for some other material. One doesn't look at City Hall and wish it were clad in marble or limestone – that wouldn't be appropriate. His building makes a virtue of the specific characteristics of concrete, its ability to take any shape, its almost liquid quality. Unlike some Brutalist building, with its fixation on surface and texture, Revell's structure concentrates on forms and shapes.

Interesting, too, that even the now-legendary City Hall competition also helped set the stage for the acceptance of concrete as a material for use in a civic icon. Among the architects the contest drew to Toronto was John Andrews, whose submission was one of seven chosen from 510 entries sent from 42 countries. Though he eventually lost to Revell, Andrews went on to design several local landmarks, including the CN Tower and Scarborough College, both remarkable examples of sculptural concrete.

It is a testament to Revell's genius and the power of concrete that City Hall ranks among the most beloved buildings in Toronto.

Fig. 3. Viljo Revell's winning competition model superimposed onto site

Fig. 4. The 'Ward,' site of New City Hall before clearance

Fig. 5. Site cleared, in use as parking prior to construction of New City Hall

Fig. 6. Photo montage of Revell's winning design

Fig. 7. New City Hall, giving Toronto an icon and vaulting it into the modern era

Design in Concrete and Architectonic Form in Viljo Revell's Toronto City Hall

Ronald Mar

Associate, Stantec Architecture Ltd. His father, Jack B. Mar, was Project Architect with John B. Parkin Associates, Architects and Engineers, who were the Associate Architects with Viljo Revell for New City Hall.

As pure, mannered sculptural form, Viljo Revell's City Hall, with its iconic boomerang-shaped towers poised above the largest public square in the metropolis, has, since its inception, occupied a place in the collective imagination of the City of Toronto. With a futuristic architectural concept translated largely intact from the original 1958 competition-winning scheme to the built project that officially opened in September 1965, the project embodied the post–World War II spirit of optimism, looking forward to the new modern era in the second half of the century.

While the architectural form and design image of City Hall is the subject of other articles in this publication, Revell's project was also firmly rooted in the spirit of technological and structural innovation, especially in terms of design in concrete. The formal expression of concrete was most apparent in the fluid structural shapes of the civic square and podium elements, but also in the overall building language of the two office towers' concrete-shelled arcs and the spaceship form of the Council Chamber.

The structure is essentially a composition of three components – the towers, the Council Chamber core and the podium/base with civic plaza – with each component placing a great emphasis on concrete as a visible structural system that:
• creates an enclosing shell, keeping the elements at bay (commodity)
• resolves the forces of gravity and wind (firmness)

• forms a series of exterior and interior spaces for public and private interaction in activities that range from the mundane payment of one's city realty tax bill to the esoteric pleasure of ice-skating outdoors (delight)

Structural Design: Towers

Each of the two office towers (20 and 27 floors) was conceived as a sliver-like convex curved vertical shell with a hard blank outer skin that opened up to reveal a glazed transparent inner skin.

The plan form of each tower is similar but different in size (with long arc dimensions of approximately 255 feet and 325 feet), being more boomerang in form than pure arc as they bulged out at the midpoint to house vertical circulation cores. The constructed structural design of these vertical shells was based on a massive 18-inch-thick reinforced concrete bearing wall along the outer convex line, commonly referred to as the 'back wall,' and a single interior line of column elements. The back-wall element is pinned from ground to roof at the midpoint of the arc by the elevator-services core and at the ends of the arc by stair and washroom/service cores. Along the centre of each typical tower floor, the line of 24-inch-by-78-inch columns acts as a buttress element, carrying radial reinforced concrete beams, which in turn support the cantilevered one-way reinforced concrete slabs that form the rigid horizontal diaphragms bracing the vertical shell at each floor. The 24-inch-wide concrete beams span from the back wall, over the columns, cantilevering

nearly 16 feet beyond the interior face of the columns to the glass curtain wall that forms the convex inner facade of the towers. These massive beams create concrete 'prop' elements when combined with the pier-like columns. The beams start at a 36-inch depth from back wall to column and taper to a nine-inch depth at the end of the cantilever.[1]

By virtue of the cantilevered floor slab design, the inner face of the envelope was then open and transparent, freed of obvious structural elements, with continuous glazing giving generous light and views from the adjacent open-office floor space. On the outer convex face, the structural capacity of the back wall was manifest in the carapace-like windowless cladding consisting of precast concrete ribbed panels, beautifully faced in strips of Botticino marble.

The heights of 20 and 27 floors (260.5 feet and 326.5 feet), and the unusual plan shape and different size floor plans for each office tower, made mathematical predictions of the wind loads on the structures an onerous task. Instead, scale models (1 inch = 23 feet) were constructed out of solid mahogany, and wind-tunnel tests were conducted at the University of Toronto's Institute of Aerophysics. The structural design was tested for wind speeds varying from 110 mph at the top to 60 mph at the bottom. The original competition and early design development scheme had intended for the two towers' structural systems to resolve independently to the foundation, but the wind-tunnel

Fig. 12. New City Hall office towers

testing confirmed excessive horizontal deflection at the top of the towers, which were then modified to be connected at the podium roof or third-floor slab level, thereby reducing the effective unsupported length of each vertical shell.[2]

Structural Design: Council Chamber
The Council Chamber was where the elected civic governing council would officially sit in a central circular assembly space surrounded by a semicircular public viewing gallery. According to the competition brief, it was meant to be the 'centre of interest, easy of access by the public and easily seen from the public areas.'[3] The formal image is of an inverted cone with a domed roof, a precious object atop the two-storey podium, cupped between the protective hands of the two office towers. The Council Chamber then formed a stylized bolt element, which holds everything together as the central focal point of the building composition.[4]

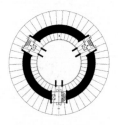

The structural design of the Council Chamber comprised three parts: the roof is a reinforced concrete dome constrained by a pre-stressed ring beam and supported by a web of inclined V-shaped precast concrete struts; the main Council Chamber form, an inverted cone with sides inclined at 30 degrees from horizontal and braced with two pre-stressed ring beams at the top and midpoint of the cone; and the cylindrical reinforced concrete shaft supporting the dome and cone (20 feet in diameter and 27 inches thick), carrying the loads down through the podium to the foundation set on local shale some 74 feet below the base of the cone.[5]

The Council Chamber's dome roof is 155-feet-3-inches in plan diameter, with a sectional radius of 150 feet, the shell of which is a concrete slab with a thickness that varies from 4.5 feet at the centre to 10 feet at the perimeter. Between the opaque concrete dome roof and cone is the visually expressive zigzag pattern of the supporting precast struts, which transfer the roof load from the ring beam down through the shell of the cone. The cone is formed by an 18-inch-thick slab supporting the amphitheatre-style gallery seating, with the top ring beam carrying the upper gallery floor and the midpoint ring beam supporting the council floor. Finally, the cylindrical shaft is comprised of structural walls with a 15.5-foot interior core diameter and that increase in thickness from 27 inches to 33 inches halfway along its 74-foot vertical length, coming to rest on a 20-foot-thick rectangular concrete footing keyed and dowelled into solid shale.[6]

Competition Winner to Built Form
Revell's competition-winning scheme in 1958 was an exciting, dynamic design, as yet untested by economic constraints and structural realities. The inevitable change wrought upon the original scheme in developing the design for construction was surprisingly minor in terms of the formal elements of the City Hall. The primary visible formal differences between competition design and built project are in the structural design for the tower, details of the tower plan outline and the structural concept for the Council Chamber volume.

The tower plans from the competition showed a dynamic parabolic arc shape, with narrow blade-like projections at the arc ends formed by the interior shell slipping past the exterior shell at the stairs. The structural concept of the massive back wall in the exterior arc was carried by a series of diminishing structural cells along the exterior, with a simple internal row of point columns. The built project's tower plans reveal how the wind-testing brought about changes to the structural design not just of each typical floor, with the back-wall/cantilever-beam/prop-column concept, but at the podium level, where the two towers were jointly stabilized. The knife-edge form of the competition scheme's towers, with its slightly disengaged exterior and interior shells, gave way to a more rounded finish to each tower arc, with an enclosing wrap of the precast exterior shell at the exit stairs.

Revell's original design for the Council Chamber did not have the concept of a main structural cylinder column. The Council Chamber was rather a true saucer shape in section that seemed to hover on more of a framework of support than the massive singular element that evolved in the built project as a result of structural design testing.[7]

Summary

While the structural design and architectural use of concrete in the City Hall's sculptural office towers is undoubtedly less expressive and visible in the resultant built forms, the project remains 40 years later perhaps the city's most notable example of concrete in architecture, from the exposed structural systems to the rich precast tower cladding. At the core of the project is the concrete design in the Council Chamber element, which can hardly be more obvious and celebratory. From outside in the civic square, within the podium entry lobby space and inside the Council Chamber interior itself, the formal volumes and heroic yet simple structural design is on display.

With a fluid formalism, Viljo Revell's competition scheme evolved with the help of John B. Parkin Associates into a built project that stands, decades later, as an expressive symbol of a city moving into the postwar modern era. A brave international design competition resulted in a timeless building, linked in spirit to works by Saarinen, Niemeyer and Le Corbusier, representing a new formal architecture that was expressed in concrete.

References

1. James A. Murray and R. J. Thom, 'Quartet: Four City Halls,' *Canadian Architect*, October 1965, 43–68.

2. Unattributed, 'Singular Symbol for Toronto,' *Architectural Forum*, 123, No. 4 (Nov. 1965): 15–23.

3. Unattributed, 'Record Special Report on Toronto City Hall,' *Architectural Record*, 124, No. 5, 10–14.

4. Unattributed, 'Toronto City Hall: Continuing Controversy,' *Architectural Record*, 138, No. 5 (Nov. 1965): 165–172.

6. Unattributed, 'Report on Toronto City Hall Competition,' *RAIC Journal*, 35, No. 10: 358–385.

7. Unattributed, 'Toronto City Hall Part 1: Civic Design,' *RAIC Journal*, 42, No. 9: 37–59.

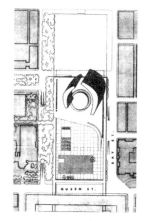

Figs. 13, 14. New City Hall original Council Chamber

Fig. 15. New City Hall original site plan

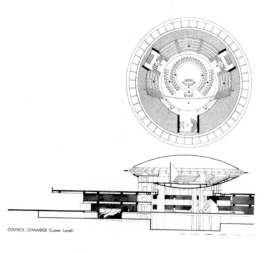

COUNCIL CHAMBER (Lower Level)

City Hall's Concrete Furniture

Marsha Kelmans

Urban designer, City of Toronto Planning, Urban Design Section

Toronto's New City Hall is fortunate to retain a small collection of its original office furniture, providing an interesting glimpse into contemporary Canadian furniture design and Toronto's exploration of modernism in the 1960s.

After citizens voted down a proposed City Hall building in classical style in the 1950s, Finnish architect Viljo Revell's design was selected following the 1958 international City Hall competition. The cultural implications of this selection were significant, resulting in Toronto's first modern concrete civic building (the seat of government, no less) prominently located in downtown's Victorian context.

Revell subsequently proposed to design office furniture for the new building and called City Council's decision to award the furniture contract by a second international competition (held in 1965) the biggest disappointment of his life. As Revell passed away before the final results of the competition, judges felt an added responsibility to award the contract to Knoll International, stating, 'More than any other competitor, this firm's designers seemed to have caught the spirit of the building and maintained it consistently in major as well as minor areas ... In addition, it was the opinion of the Committee that the Knoll International submission was one that would not have been displeasing to Viljo Revell himself.'

The late 1950s to '60s were a time of design innovation in the Canadian office-furniture sector, with the Robin Bush Prismasteel design and Jacques Guillon's Alumna office desk – with patented slotted-leg extrusion – appearing in 1958 and 1961 respectively. During this time, European furniture masters like Klaus Nienkamper and Leif Jacobsen arrived and set up shop in Toronto, later to expand or be consolidated into larger companies (Jacobsen's company was purchased by Teknion). The award of the City Hall commission to American-based Knoll, who collaborated with local Leif Jacobsen, had an effect on Toronto's furniture-design scene similar to the effect the award of Massey College to Ron Thom's office had on the history of the city's architectural production.

While the Knoll competition entry was not alone in pursuing a contemporary design, it was unique in its use of concrete and its direct response to the building. Like its host, the furniture, ranging from clerks' to Council Chamber accommodations, capitalizes on the colour, texture and sculptural possibilities of its materials. Desks and benches feature massive, precast concrete bases, oiled white oak casings with Arborite top surfaces. Furniture for the east tower, which caught the afternoon sun through its west-facing windows, was upholstered in cool shades of blue and green. The west tower's upholstery was in warm shades of yellow, gold and orange.

Scandal immediately erupted over the new furniture. For reasons that remain unexplained today, the selection committee voted on the entries without opening the envelopes containing cost information until after the winner had been announced. Knoll's bid was found to be over budget, and other competitors complained it was unfair to award the contract to a company that had not followed the requirements of the competition. Several months of wrangling between the selection committee, the Board of Control and City Council followed over what one newspaper called questions of 'ethics and aesthetics.'

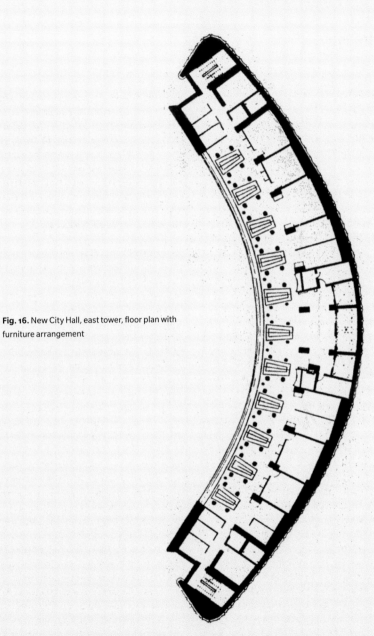

Fig. 16. New City Hall, east tower, floor plan with furniture arrangement

When the dust settled, Knoll had reduced the cost of its bid and was allowed to fulfill the contract. Mayor Philip Givens, who supported the Knoll entry, stated, 'Design is the guts of the situation. Otherwise we could have ordered from a catalogue.'

The furniture's building and completion were considered newsworthy, and once installed, the furniture's use continued to be controversial. Newspaper headlines included 'Drawerless Desk Fine with Him,' 'Furniture Row's on Again' (referring to the coincidence of desk transparency with new, shorter hemlines – 'vanity panels' were later installed), 'Wobbly Desks at City Hall Spark New Furniture Controversy' (stenographers complained that desks moved as a result of typing despite their enormously heavy concrete bases), 'Furniture Fine in Pictures But ... ' and finally, 'Bell Quits after Row over Desks.' Given Toronto's optimistic response to the design of New City Hall, it seems strange that such controversy could follow its office furniture. Perhaps the equally modern furniture design, with its mimetic use of concrete, served as an outlet for the undercurrent of anxiety about the insertion of a new form of expression into the city's fabric (construction of New City Hall was completed in 1965, the same year as the furniture competition).

Since the 1960s, a large portion of the collection was lost through renovations, as the weight and character of the furniture was not popular in later decades. Recognizing its value, Marc Barness, a former Director of Urban Design in the City Planning Division, began to collect the original furniture in the late 1980s. Today, the City Planning and Urban Design offices at City Hall continue to be a repository for the remaining original furniture, housing its largest collection, which includes chairs, desks, tables, bookshelves, credenzas and coffee tables. It remains in daily use and continues to be at risk of replacement. Original furniture (circular lounge chairs and coffee tables) can also be found in the Council Chamber members' lounge.

Still in use over forty years later, City Hall's tiny extant collection of original office furniture continues to be sturdy and beautiful, although in need of some restoration and not terribly convenient for movers. The 1960s controversy over its procurement, design and early use attests to the long-standing willingness of Torontonians to debate passionately the design of our city and to City Hall's as a banner for design innovation. It is reminiscent of recent public debate over buildings whose architectural expression is unhabitual for Toronto, offering insight for the present and future. The loss of most of the original collection is a timely reminder that the fabric of our public realm, be it furniture or architecture, cannot be evaluated merely on the criteria of 'new' or 'old,' nor can we afford to privilege the iconic over the mundane.

The original version of this text, by Manda Vranic and Marsha Kelmans, appeared as part of the 40th anniversary celebration of New City Hall.

Figs. 17, 18. 'It may be argued,' read Knoll International's Competition Entry Statement, 'that the new City Hall has been the product of European regionalism combined with North American technology and is, by reason of its successful physical fact, a "Canadian Design."'

Winning competition drawings by Clifford and Laurie Architects, Knoll International Canada

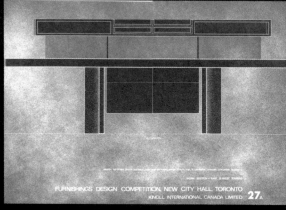

FURNISHINGS DESIGN COMPETITION, NEW CITY HALL, TORONTO
KNOLL INTERNATIONAL CANADA LIMITED. **27**A

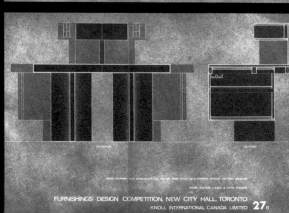

FURNISHINGS DESIGN COMPETITION, NEW CITY HALL, TORONTO
KNOLL INTERNATIONAL CANADA LIMITED **27**B

Fig. 19. Mayor's Office, 1965. The original mayor's desk weighed 800 pounds and took four people to move.

Macy DuBois:
Designing in Toronto, Designing in Concrete

Interview with Macy DuBois

Partner, Fairfield and DuBois , DuBois Plumb Partnerhsip

MACY DUBOIS is an architect who was lured to Toronto
via the New City Hall competition. His practice in Toronto
during the 1960s and '70s designed several landmark
concrete buildings. During the following round-table
discussion, held at the University of Toronto's Faculty of
Architecture, Landscape and Design in November 2006,
DuBois answered questions about his early career in
Toronto, and Canada's modern building boom.

Dr. Paolo Scrivano, modern architecture historian and
faculty at U of T, along with E.R.A. Architects, conducted
the round table. Also in attendance were Dr. Mary Lou
Lobsinger, architecture theory professor at U of T, and
Larry Richards, former dean.

Paolo Scrivano	**Macy, please tell us something about your background.**
Macy DuBois	I think my background is of interest because it affected the way I approached architecture. I always brought the engineers into the conceptual stage, often incorporating their components as design elements.

I was born in Baltimore, Maryland, and, as a teenager, I went to an
engineering high school. I continued in engineering at Tufts University,
with engineering physics. When I graduated, I went into the U.S. Navy
for three years, winding up as the commanding officer of a minesweeper
in the Korean action. Not convinced about a career in engineering, I
considered architecture as a career I might enjoy. As it so happened, when
I was considering where to go for the education, the American Institute of
Architects had its annual convention in Boston, so I thought, 'Why don't I go
to Boston, talk to the architects there and find out where I should go?' I met
some students along with some heavy hitters like Eero Saarinen, and after
talking with a few, decided I should go to Harvard.

Harvard was interesting because it has a strong reputation – perhaps, even
now, a holdover from the Gropius era. It's not necessarily the best school of
architecture, but the university itself was wonderful and it had some fine art.
The Busch-Reisinger Museum and the Fogg were two of the grandest places.

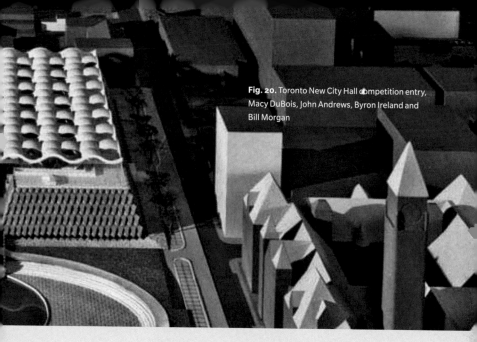

Fig. 20. Toronto New City Hall competition entry, Macy DuBois, John Andrews, Byron Ireland and Bill Morgan

I really began to understand a little bit about both art and architecture. After my first three months, I was convinced architecture was what I wanted to do.

E.R.A. Your career started early, as a student entering the Toronto City Hall competition in 1958. How did that come about?

Macy DuBois   In my last year at Harvard, a group of students in my class – John Andrews, Byron Ireland and Bill Morgan – organized a team to enter the Toronto City Hall competition. They asked me to join them and together we asked Dean Sert for a space in the school where we could develop our submission. The dean declined, saying our work on that competition would distract us from class work. So we just rented space elsewhere. But when our submission was nearing completion, we brought it into the school to finish. The whole class got into the production of documents and the model and really helped us make a wonderful presentation. We became one of the finalists. It was a real boost to us since we were only students.

Our submission had a particularly brilliant solution by Bill Morgan, of a beautiful roof over our large atrium, which was just amazing. One of the important things about a school of architecture, especially with regard to Harvard, is that you can learn an awful lot from your classmates. Working on a competition like this brought out the best in all of us.

Fig. 21. Macy DuBois discusses 45 Charles Street East

Fig. 22. Elevation, Macy DuBois competition entry

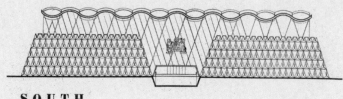

SOUTH

A few days after getting the telegram putting us in the final round, we were doing some work in the school when Ernesto Rogers, who was on the jury for the competition, came down from Toronto to visit Dean Sert. In spite of trying to discourage us from entering the competition, the dean was really proud that we had done well, so he brought Rogers in to meet us. Rogers had also brought along Gropius, so that we're standing there dazzled by all this high-powered architectural talent. They were all looking at us as if we'd won the Nobel Prize. It was really a wonderful ego-boosting experience. Of course, Revell's scheme won and when we saw it at the Eaton's on College Street we understood why.

Paolo Scrivano **Your City Hall entry is reminiscent of Boston City Hall, which was built afterward, between 1962 and 1968. What was in the air at the time? Perhaps there is no connection, but maybe there were some similar influences?**

Macy DuBois What was in the air? You mean the fact that it's a broad, low building with a hole in the centre? Well, it was the idea of the atrium coming on as a concept. One of the things that happened when we were putting our drawings together for the competition was that Siegfried Giedion, who was teaching at the school, came into our classroom as we were assembling the documents and looked at what we were doing.

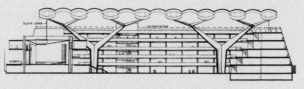

N S   SECTION

I don't know if students these days read *Space, Time and Architecture,* but 40 years ago that was our bible and Giedion had written it. And he was my most influential teacher because he opened up possibilities. The way he taught history didn't close any doors.

So he came and saw us frantically finishing the competition entry. At that time he was very interested in the idea of an indoor atrium, our indoor plaza, and he quite liked what we were up to. I can't remember what he said, but I remember being glad that he liked it. Later he wrote about our entry in *Canadian Architect,* which was incredibly flattering.

Mary Lou Lobsinger   **What is the relationship between your entry and Le Corbusier's La Tourette, which would be very similar to this and published everywhere in the early 1960s? They share many similarities such as the concrete, the cube, the low form and the interior courtyard. Siegfried Giedion, writing on the history of modernism in *Space, Time and Architecture*, puts Corbu at the top, so that's also part of the story of being educated under him. Also Paul Rudolph, in his use of concrete and forms that may have historicist resonance at the same time …**

Macy DuBois   Well, it was important because Corbu took concrete and made the crudeness of the material into a virtue. The *béton brut.* We really couldn't take that roughness in North America. You couldn't let it be crude like that.

Fig. 23

Fig. 24   Fig. 25   Fig. 26   Fig. 27

Fig. 23. Section, Macy DuBois competition entry

Fig. 24. Pinto, Parez and Marchand (Brazil) entry

Fig. 25. Andrews and DuBois (U.S.) entry

Fig. 26. Bickell and Hamilton (U.K.) entry

Fig. 27. I. M. Pei (U.S.) entry

Even Corbu, at the Carpenter Center at Harvard, was slicker than at La Tourette or the Marseille Block. But he certainly got us thinking of concrete as art. We'll get more into concrete in my later projects in these slides.

Larry Richards

While we have that image of your competition finalists' scheme, it's interesting to look at the former City Hall, which I guess was under threat, but what was in the air at the time? How did people talk about context? Nowadays people talk so much about responding to or fitting into a context. How did you think about Osgoode Hall, old City Hall and the kind of fabric around this place when you were designing this?

Macy DuBois

In fact, that was our taking-off point for the skin, which I think, in retrospect, was a mistake. We made it far too closed-in. The idea was all right – it was meant to look like huge stones on the outside – but the amount of window area it allowed was far too small.

But we felt very definitely that the building should be low. As a matter of fact, I carried that feeling through my career. I actually don't like high-rise buildings. I think they really detach people from the ground and their surroundings. So I, particularly, thought the building must be low. A government building doesn't have to be like a commercial building. It has to be something related to people, more democratic, not elitist. What we called the inside was a winter square, and the outside, of course, was a summer square. I think we could have done something a little bit more with the summer square. But it was the lowness of the building that was important for us. This really was about context.

One of the objections to Revell's solution was by the two planners on the jury who said it turned its back on the city, and there's a certain truth to it. But the somewhat arbitrary walkway around the outside of the square is successful in giving a sense of closure to the forecourt space.

E.R.A. **The City Hall competition introduced you to Toronto, and since then you've made it your home. What made you stay or even come to Toronto for an extended period of time rather than just submitting a proposal and leaving?**

Macy DuBois   Well, that's a good point. I had an acquaintance from Harvard who went to work for the Parkin office. So he knew me, and thus the Parkin office wanted me to come for an interview. John Andrews and I had worked closely together for some time and he came too. It led to the best opportunity to do important work. So John Andrews and I were courted by John C. Parkin and joined his office. In spite of my own difficulties at Parkin, I have always felt they were the leading office in Canada at the time. They really had created an aura for modern architecture in Canada. This was reinforced by the Toronto City Hall, for which Parkin was the production architect. Yet after a year I was fired. It turned out it wasn't my kind of office. It didn't really help me get where I wanted to go and, naturally, I didn't help the office.

When I was working for Parkin, I was contemplating doing one of the buildings assigned to me in concrete, and John C. said to me, 'I'm sorry, we can't do exposed concrete here in Canada. It just won't work because of our climate.' Well, I thought, there certainly are bridges made of concrete and that sort of thing that stand up all right, so I doubted that was true.

So I looked for an office I could really work in, where I could test out my ideas. One that really needed a good designer. I sort of pushed my way into the office that was Rounthwaite & Fairfield. Within a few years I became a partner of Bob Fairfield, who had, by then, split from Rounthwaite.

My work at Fairfield's office was well-received, Toronto was a busy place with a growing population, new work kept me here and Toronto itself was rapidly changing for the better.

Paolo Scrivano   **So we can move to the second project, which is the Plan for Central Toronto, 1962, that you and other colleagues published in** *Canadian Architect*. **What prompted it?**

Macy DuBois   Well, the same thing that would prompt it today, in that we don't have urban design in this city, and you see it all over Europe. I just came back from Germany and in Germany they have pedestrian walkways, and the climate isn't that much different from ours in Toronto. We were trying to get some pedestrian precincts and start a real discussion about urban design, but not necessarily to get our design implemented.

Our group included Tony Jackson, an architectural historian; Don Pinker, a planner; along with the architects Jerry Robinson, Henry Sears and me. We got together and said, 'Let's do something about urban design in this city. Let's put together a proposal that will attract some attention.'

Years later I was invited by the German government to come to Germany, with a group of architects and planners from Canada. One of the places we went to was Munich where, during the Olympics, they took the main street, which was then a vehicular street, and put a subway there, then took that main street away from the cars, making it into a wonderful pedestrian way, and never gave it back to the car. This is what was lacking in Toronto – using opportunities for significant changes in urban form.

E.R.A.   **Was there a climate of European influence in Toronto or was this unique to your group?**

Macy DuBois   There was a climate of reading *The Architectural Review*. At the time, it certainly was considered the prime English-language architectural magazine in the world. It was promoting this kind of textural pedestrian precinct, particularly with drawings and comment from the great Gordon Cullen. I think Europe has learned the lesson these essays contained, but I'm not sure we have yet. However, the Harbourfront seems to be showing progress in that respect.

Fig. 28. Central Tech, Arts Centre, interior

Fig. 29. Central Tech, ground-floor plan

Fig. 30. *New York Times* review of Central Tech,
Sunday, July 11, 1965

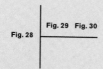

Fig. 28   Fig. 29   Fig. 30

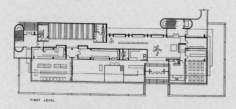

FIRST LEVEL

Paolo Scrivano	**The third project was the Arts Centre at Central Technical High School at Bathurst and Harbord streets in Toronto.**
Macy DuBois	That project was done in 1962 and it was a result of Sputnik. It was an odd thing. Sputnik scared the hell out of North Americans because the Soviets were apparently doing better technically. All over North America there was this need to improve the science teaching in some way, expand it. And what they did with Central Tech was to shove the art department out and build a separate building for them. They then expanded the science areas into the former art department.

It was like manna from heaven for the art department. They always wanted to have their own separate building. We worked very closely with the principal, Charles Goldhammer, and Dawson Kennedy, one of the teachers. It shows in the building, I think, that intimate relationship between the architect and the users.

We decided to exploit north light because of its quality of even light that artists like. So we expanded the north light by putting in sloped skylights in addition to the vertical windows and stepped the building down and out as it dropped toward the ground. We also put in a lot of artificial lighting because there was a heavy nighttime use for adult education. Between the light fixtures is expanded metal mesh so that you could see and sense the space up into the ceiling. You could hang things on this metal mesh. You could see the mechanical systems. Then we had the Venetian blinds that went in between the lights on the mullions so you could control the amount of daylight you brought in. That worked well for all kinds of uses of the studios. Every artist that I happened to run into later, whether teacher or student, told me how much they enjoyed working in those studios.

We used concrete block in the interior. We placed usually wall-lined lockers into a separate room to free the walls. We wanted to have display space for the paintings and hangings that were going on the wall. We designed a wall that would resist the graffiti that often occurs at an art school. It had to have a tough feel, a kind of primal feeling about it. All the floors were Welsh quarry tiles, which stood up very well over time to wear and materials that were dropped on them. Throughout the building we made the walls striated and changed the walls from the ordinary concrete block to one that had an insistent horizontality.

Larry Richards   **Would you say that at some point you did have some attraction to Wright and some of his organic principles? I feel about a 20 percent Wrightian factor in that corridor. Is that fair?**

Macy DuBois   When you go to a school of architecture, there's generally a line they take, and at Harvard it was Corbu. Nothing about Frank Lloyd Wright except from Giedion. So when you get out of school you have to pick up those loose ends. You can learn little tricks from Wright and other architects, but you can't mimic them. If you mimic Wright, Aalto, Corbu or Mies, it looks like mimicry. It doesn't work. I certainly became responsive to the horizontality that Wright kept emphasizing, his 'horizon line.' Wright did that with all of his brick joints, for instance. One of the other things I liked about Wright, particularly with the Usonian houses, is that he brought exterior material into the inside so you had brick and wood on the inside as well as out. It was a kind of integrity. And I said, 'That's wonderful. I want to do that.' When it comes to the linearity, I thought he did that very well.

After the Art Centre was published, I went down to Harvard for an urban design conference. One of my professors stopped me and said, 'Didn't you do – what was it? A football stadium in Toronto?' I said, 'No, no, it was an art school and I consider it a compliment that you called it a football stadium.'

Because it wasn't just a type; it was something I had designed on the basis of what needed to be done. Not a building that had to look like an art school. It was an art school.

I made the ends of the building step out slightly and the reason for that is that I didn't want it to seem like I had cut off the ends of the building. I wanted it to feel that it would not go on forever. I wanted it to look like it was a finished thing. So each floor stepped out a little bit as you went up.

One mistake I made, though, was with the glazing on the sloped windows. The water comes off the slope, down the window and over the edge, and stains the front of the building. If only I'd put a heavy gutter and flashing on and thrown the water clear of the concrete. It would have been so much better. But you make mistakes when you are young and this is one of your first buildings.

E.R.A.   **A *New York Times* article reviewing the art centre makes a small comment about the contextual use of materials, suggesting that concrete comes from your response to the heavy stone of the original building. Was this a correct observation?**

Macy DuBois   We did feel that the primitive roughness of stone and the primal quality of the concrete were related. I also felt that concrete was really appropriate for an art school. I think artists like to work from basic principles. And that's why using materials that are left untouched – like exposed concrete, concrete block, quarry tile and glass – were appreciated. It felt right for an art world.

E.R.A.   **In 1962 were there precedents for this sort of thing in the city?**

Macy DuBois   The only place I knew that had a concrete building was a synagogue on Bathurst Street. Holy Blossom was built in the '30s with poured concrete. I believe mine was the first exposed-concrete building in the city after World War II.

When I showed Central Tech to one of my colleagues when it was in the drawing stage, he said, 'You certainly were holding back at Parkin's office.'

Paolo Scrivano   **Was one of the primary concerns for the design of the New College building the proposal for building an expressway on Spadina?**

Fig. 31. New College courtyard

| Macy DuBois | Yes. There's only one side that's closed off really, and that's the Spadina facade . I talked them out of doing a high-rise, with my preference for low buildings, which also meant the building didn't require an elevator. It meant it sprawled out over the site, allowing me to create a central courtyard.

My thinking for this project goes back to my days at Parkin. I was there, alongside Revell and his team from Finland. There was a certain collegial atmosphere between the Finns and me since we were both finalists. So I was trying to find out about Finnish architecture and particularly Alvar Aalto. It was explained to me that understanding Aalto is as simple as the straight line and the curve. I thought, 'Terrific,' because I could see the potential in it. When I look at Aalto's work, I don't see these things in every building, but it did make me aware of the potential of utilizing these two geometries.

I took full advantage of all I had learned in the design of New College. It contains elements that relate to Corbu, Wright and Aalto. One has to learn from somewhere or we all would be living in caves.

The university required us to use a corridor system for the two residential colleges, and I was really worried that it was going to require a long corridor. I decided to use the space of the site to create curving corridors to break up their length and to let the outer facade maintain a rectangular idiom, reflecting the layout of the surrounding streets.

In terms of the aesthetic, I wanted it to look like a concrete building that had a skin of brick, brick being mandated by the university. Brick wasn't the supporting material; it was the veneer. And to use a lot of brick and exposed concrete on the inside, to make the interiors have some of the heft of the exterior.

E.R.A. **There are two parts to New College, Wetmore and Wilson halls, which frame the courtyard.**

Macy DuBois   That's right. They were built a few years apart. During the interval between the first and second phases, I asked Evan Walker, who was an Australian architect who became a don at Wetmore Hall of New College, to evaluate living in this building. He came up with some helpful ideas. He felt that the corridor worked well, but agreed, as I had originally proposed, that it be carpeted to keep the noise down. He asked that the don suites be put toward the centre to make them more easily accessible to the students. He had several other suggestions, some of which I used for Wilson Hall.

I'd wanted to recess the doors, which would prevent it from looking like a corridor of doors in Wetmore Hall, but the university wouldn't let me. They thought it would be a waste of space. So I showed them that it did not compromise the bedroom, and got them to do it for the second residence. Critics who have reviewed the buildings carefully mentioned that the

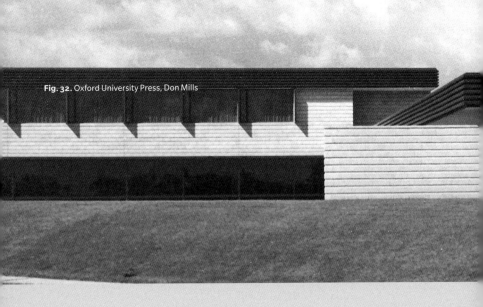

second building was improved from the first. It's not often you get to do a full-scale mock-up of a building.

One thing that was a bit of a disaster, however, was the landscaping. If you do a courtyard, landscaping is really important. I asked the university's landscape architect to present a plan of planting only and let me handle the heavy construction work, to keep the cost down, which I knew would make it easier to get approval, but he didn't. The university staff were upset when they saw the price and cancelled all the landscaping. It disturbs me every time I walk through the courtyard.

E.R.A.   **The Oxford Press building is interesting because it is situated in the suburbs, near Flemingdon Park/Don Mills. It's a relatively simple program of a light industrial building, yet this is high design. What was the climate in the mid-1960s, that a client would demand real architecture for this type of building?**

Macy DuBois   Oxford Press wanted to be distinguished, and I think that was why they were happy with it. The materials were cheap, so the design issue really wasn't about cost. We designed a concrete block with built-in horizontals for the building and used standard ribbed-steel decking for the fascias to emphasize the linearity I talked about earlier. This really engendered the feeling of 'high design' you mentioned.

E.R.A. The building is really an object in a field, different than your more urban projects. How did that influence the design?

Macy DuBois It's a kind of stand-alone element. The materials I have just mentioned, in the absence of context, freed me to create a different space-occupying complex, with a proposed wall completely around a forecourt on the street side. But the client stopped it for cost reasons. I thought a closed-off court would give more of a special impact to the building at minimal cost. We had to design much of the furniture ourselves. At that time, there weren't many desks and chairs available that were suitable.

Paolo Scrivano **And moving on to 45 Charles Street East. Can you tell us something about this project and the status of the concrete industry at that time?**

Macy DuBois This client was a contractor who had done work for us in concrete at the university and had concrete forms leftover from it that they wanted to reuse on the new building. I think they also wanted to cut down on the number of trades they had to deal with. If they did the skin and structure in concrete, they could do it themselves. If not, they would have to have a subcontractor do the exterior.

So I designed a building for them of cast-in-place concrete using the available formwork. I used the form joint texture on the concrete.

Fig. 33. 45 Charles Street East section

Fig. 34. 45 Charles Street East perspective

Fig. 35. 45 Charles Street East site plan

One thing I always enjoyed about palaces from the Italian renaissance is that they tended to have more heavily textured walls closer to people and they'd lighten the texture as they went up. I used contemporary materials to achieve that same thing here.

A large consideration for the design was that it was in mid-block of Charles Street. I figured people would be coming from the side. I shaped the building and the forecourt to respond to this. Being angled to the street is actually more attractive than being parallel.

There is also the generous use of outdoor terraces here, something unique for an office building. We made the third-level terrace parallel to the street, but we turned the building above it at an angle and we really enjoyed the angled views that came from that. It also helped us separate ourselves from our neighbours, and our neighbours certainly appreciated that we weren't so close to them. We also put plantings all through the building. We felt that bringing planting up onto the building would be a wonderful experience for an office building. We maintained the one mature tree on the site in a trapezoidal planter, which we felt was important to do.

Larry Richards   **Isn't there a little bit of Frank Lloyd Wright's remarkable Price Tower at work here?**

Fig. 36. Terrace of 45 Charles Street East, looking west

Macy DuBois	This one definitely has a touch of the Price Tower feeling. Wright changed the upstand on every second horizontal. That's what I was thinking about when I approached this, because I loved the simple way it changed the scale of the building.
Paolo Scrivano	**What about Louis Kahn? Were you paying much attention to Kahn?**
Macy DuBois	I admire Kahn. I thought Kahn was a very monumental architect. When he died I wrote a note, that they printed, to *Progressive Architecture*, that 'Kahn spoke like Moses but he built like Pharaoh.' But it was what Kahn said that really affected me. For instance, 'A client wants an entrance and I want to give a him sense of entry.' That's what architects are supposed to do. We solve problems in a poetic way.

I had lunch with Kahn once. It was in 1958, just before the City Hall competition winner was announced, when I was looking for a job in case we didn't win. I went to see Geddes, Breecher and Qualls of Philadelphia, who came second in the Sydney Opera House. And they said, 'We want to do the work you want to do, so we can't hire you, but there's one genius in town, Lou Kahn. Go see him.' So I went to see him, but he had no work. Just had a small office and no staff. We chatted for a while, I showed him some of my student work, and he said, 'Look, I'm going to lunch,' and asked me to join him.

At lunch, the conversation turned to Paul Rudolph. When Kahn said he did not like Rudolph's work, I said, 'Well ... I think Rudolph believes architecture begins where the column meets the slab.' I didn't realize it, because I'd never met Kahn before, but that's the way he talked! So I was talking his language! And he said, 'If you know that, you should go do it yourself. That's enough, that's all you need to know.' And I said, 'I think you're right, I should.' So he had that major influence on my life. When I saw him a little later at a seminar, of course he didn't remember me at all, because I was just another student who had come in to see him. But I very much admired his work. |
| **Paolo Scrivano** | **I found it very interesting that, in designing 45 Charles Street, you adopted almost the same principle one can find in the rustication of Florentine palaces of the Renaissance, such as the Palazzo Rucellai. You see there's a difference in the way the concrete is treated at this level and it changes. You used concrete out of technological,** |

functional needs, but actually you were able to use the concrete for formal expression.

Macy DuBois   It's not that you want to apply the decoration as much as you want to make it part of the elements you use on your building. I like to reduce the number of materials I use in a building as much as I can. As I said earlier, I like to use the same materials on the inside. It's completely possible to take the other approach and completely change the materials on the inside, as is done with most of the houses built in Canada. Drywall, and the outside is brick or whatever.

E.R.A.   **There is a quote in *Progressive Architecture* from August 1967, and it's very flattering. Speaking of 45 Charles East, it says: 'Canadian architecture, remarkably producing quality building after quality building at a tremendous rate, has turned out a small speculative office building that puts all the by-the-yard glass and metal stuff that is still proliferating in the U.S. to shame.' And finishes by saying: 'New York, Los Angeles, Dallas, Chicago, take heed.' Reading this, it's almost quite shocking to think of the environment you were working in: Toronto at centre stage and you and your colleagues at the forefront. So the climate was obviously very special. Charles Street and Central Tech seem to be a precedent-setting use of concrete; it seems to be a recurring theme.**

Macy DuBois   I didn't do these things because I wanted to show a common theme so much as a common approach to the problem. In order to solve it, you attack the problem based on the context, based on the client, based on the money and based on the need. As an example, the next project to talk about is the Ontario Pavilion at Expo 67, and it's a completely different building.

From the start we said it should be like a tent, it should have that feeling of a circus, it should have that temporary, exciting, dynamic feeling to it. We came up with this concept right at the beginning. The only question we got from the Ontario government Tory Caucus was, 'Has anything like this been done anywhere else in the world?' And my more experienced colleague, involved with the exhibits inside, answered for me: 'No, not to my knowledge.' And that was it. That indicated to me that when the politicians were aware of it, the whole experience of the Toronto City Hall had firmly established the idea that modern architecture was what Canada needed.

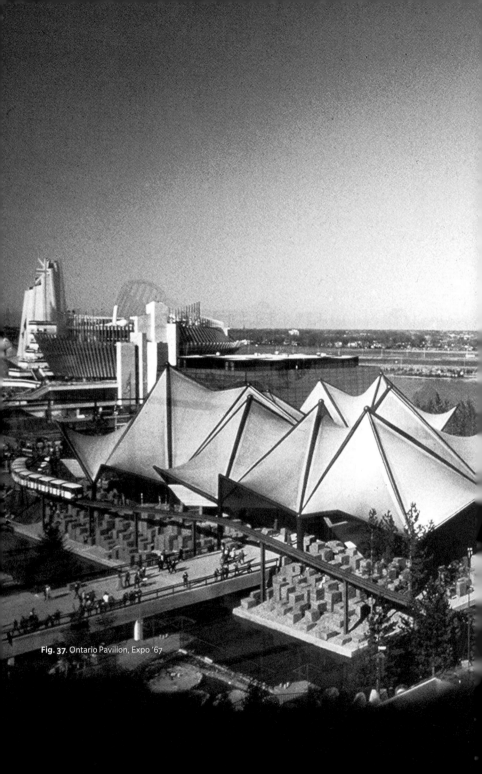

Fig. 37. Ontario Pavilion, Expo '67

This building has no reference whatsoever to any other building we've done, because it's a completely different problem. It had to be there for six months, and after that its use was over. How to construct our idea was not easy, but when we talked to the engineers they said that if we made each one of those pieces of fabric, each section as a hyperbolic paraboloid, which is a four-sided twisted figure, then they could handle the structure. We built a model to design the structure, and the drawings were made from the model. One of the amazing things about the finished building is there was not a wrinkle on the twisted forms, because not only was it designed structurally by computers, but also the fabric-cutting patterns were laid out by them.

At an early point, Expo asked me, 'Can we run the mini-rail through the pavilion?' And I said, 'Sure, that's wonderful; I'd love to see that.' That would be another experience for people, to see the pavilion without even getting off the mini-rail.

For the landscaping we wanted something that reflects an Ontario exterior, but I didn't want to have an artificially created 'natural' space. So I said to the landscape architect who had come with a natural design, 'If you abstract the landscape, then I'll take it.' What he responded with was wonderful. He took these huge blocks of granite and they had them all over the place at differing heights. They're all the same size in terms of plan form, but at different heights. They were just loaded with people at the fair, people sitting on them, kids running on them. It was wonderful to see. The landscape architect at the time was Dick Strong and he recently told me it was the best thing he ever did.

Paolo Scrivano   **How were you selected to design the pavilion?**

Macy DuBois   I think it was that the buildings we had done before that point by our firm were so different from what others were doing, and it did not hurt that Bob Fairfield, my partner, had done the Stratford Theatre. The theatre was world-famous and certainly had a lot of attention. I think all that came together.

E.R.A.   **Working on Expo must have been quite an experience. Both City Hall and Expo and the time between are considered the heyday of Canadian modernism, and you participated in both.**

Macy DuBois   It was simply exciting to be able to work at the fair. It was a national and personal high point. It was certainly the kind of challenging project that any architect would want to do.

E.R.A.   You and John Andrews came to Toronto as students and became two of the most prominent concrete designers in the city. It seems to be part of a movement. So what was going on there?

Macy DuBois   It's an interesting question. I think what was going on was, through Corbu, Kahn and others, concrete became an acceptable and noble material, the new stone. You want something that has impact. It's not really inherently beautiful, it's strong. Is that why I like using it? I'm not sure. But I certainly like the idea that I can manipulate it, I can mould it. I could include little details. All you had to do is change the formwork and get it done. I'm not sure I could have done that with a building that was considered 'normal' in this city without the climate of acceptance generated by then.

I'd like to get back to one more thing we haven't spoken about. You know the reason why the Toronto City Hall competition happened at all? It was because the students at the school of architecture began to revolt against an already accepted commissioned scheme. Peter Richardson, an architectural student I knew from Parkin's office, began to organize the students in protest against it. He got architecture professor Eric Arthur

to begin to push for an international competition as well. The success of
the competition really completely changed attitudes in the city and in the
country. Changed how it thought about architecture and about what could
be done. It's why I came, and why I stayed here.

I ran into Peter a couple of years ago and I said that the story should be
written. It's an important event in Canadian architectural history. I think
it's interesting that if you have the will, the persistence and the energy, you
can effect change – even students can.

The Sheraton Centre

Michael McClelland

Principal, E.R.A. Architects

Editor

The Sheraton Centre is a great mountain of a building. Like other big boys of the same period – the Manulife Centre or the CN Tower, for instance – it has a scale that is profoundly metropolitan. It was built on the idea that Toronto was a place for phenomenal growth and bold new urban enterprises. Completed in 1972, the Centre was planned as a companion piece for the recently completed Nathan Phillips Square. The City had expropriated the lands to ensure that the new square would be framed by a fitting urban edge, showcasing Toronto's modernity.

The architectural team selected was to be the same as for the new City Hall. John B. Parkin, from the local firm that had partnered with Viljo Revell for the City Hall, led the team. Their design consultant for the Sheraton Centre was Seppo Valjus, one of the four Finnish architects who had won the City Hall competition. It always needs to be remembered, as Revell continually pointed out, that architecture is a collaborative effort, and Heikki Castren, Bengt Lundsten and Seppo Valjus should be credited equally with him as the winners of the City Hall competition. Revell had died during the construction of the new City Hall and it was logical to encourage one of his co-workers to continue with the Sheraton Centre design.

The design of the Sheraton Centre was intended as a contextual response to the new City Hall. It was conceived as a low three-storey podium structure facing Nathan Phillips Square, with an 11-storey wing set back on Richmond Street and a large 43-storey tower placed to the south and west of the square. The massing was intended to provide a strong visual anchor to the south end of Nathan Phillips Square without blocking views from the square to the newly rising towers at King and Bay. Modern greets modern. Concrete was essential and the warm precast-concrete tones of the new City Hall were matched in the exposed concrete of the Sheraton Centre's walls, spandrels and columns. Attention was paid to the sand selection for the concrete and a light blasting was specified for the finish to ensure material compatibility.

Conceived as a microcosm of the city, the Sheraton Centre consists of almost 1.5 million square feet of space and contained shops, offices, cinemas, a spa, the hotel and a miraculous set of terraced gardens designed by Canadian landscape great Austin Floyd. The gardens start on the rooftop and descend to grade in the sky-lit hotel lobby. In a Jetsons kind of way, public space was intended to intersect with the Sheraton Centre at several vertical levels – including the very modern underground concourse of shops and a 'plus-15' walkway system with a connecting bridge to the new raised walkways around Nathan Phillips Square. A well-planned motor court allowed access to the hotel from both Richmond and Queen streets.

The reciprocity the Sheraton Centre brings to Nathan Phillips Square is almost missed today, however, and the contemporary stylistic connections go unnoticed. The cinemas are gone, the trendy bar no longer looks over the square and the plus-15 system never extended through the city. The Centre over the last few decades has started to internalize itself, like a fortress.

A modest but possibly helpful suggestion to reverse this trend and bring this mountain back to the city would be to recognize that at-grade

Fig. 39. Concrete context: the Sheraton Centre as seen from Nathan Phillips Square

public circulation needs to be continually nurtured and encouraged. I would propose one carve into the mountain a bit to open up a visible public route from Queen to Richmond, through the hotel lobby and make the wonderful interior gardens visible from Nathan Phillips Square. The sheer size of the Centre allows one to consider such modifications, and it is to the credit of these massive structures that one can continually adjust them as the circumstances of the city evolve. Metropolitan structures like the Sheraton Centre are an integral part of the downtown morphology. They are the mountains we inhabit.

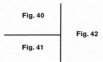

Fig. 40

Fig. 41

Fig. 42

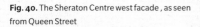

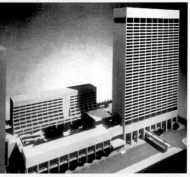

Fig. 40. The Sheraton Centre west facade , as seen from Queen Street

Fig. 41. The Sheraton Centre architectural model, showing sky garden, sky bridge, slab and tower

Fig. 42. The Sheraton Centre's public sky garden with City Hall in background

The Colonnade

Philip Evans
Associate, E.R.A. Architects

It seems almost medieval to collect $6,300 a month for a two-bedroom rental unit in Toronto, despite its mighty-kingdom-like view across Queen's Park toward the lake. Sure it's a penthouse, but the same monthly contribution could afford a mortgage payment well in excess of a million dollars. But this is the Colonnade.

Transforming Bloor Street and urban Canada with its arrival in 1964, the Colonnade by Gerald Robinson and Tampold Wells Architects at 131 Bloor Street West is an extremely well-composed mixed-use residential project that defines the character of the now urbane Bloor-Yorkville. The arrangement of 163 luxury rental apartment units, office, retail and public plaza sits as an essay on how to respond to the many challenges of integrated communities that still face architects and urban planners to this day.

The five-storey office/retail podium maintains a consistent street wall along Bloor Street and gently tempers behind the arched supports that hold 12 residential floors above to form a semi-circular forecourt. The ground plane slopes moderately toward the building's entry, levels within the shared lobby and eventually tiers down as Sultan Street comes to an end. The projecting sculpted mezzanine with its jewel-encrusted windows creates a cut through the building, allowing access to the contrasting worlds of Chanel and Prada to the north, and the cradles, cheers and applause from an animated children's play area within picturesque Victoria College to the south.

The resemblance to Le Corbusier's Unité d'Habitation in Marseilles is absolutely uncanny. Completed eights years before the Colonnade, its influence is unmistakable. Just as Le Corbusier's celebrated raw concrete mixed-use Unité d'Habitation used pilotis to free up the ground floor for pedestrians and cars, the Colonnade forms an arched succession that hovers above a raised 'artificial ground' to create interior streets lined with office and retail units. Even Corb's roof garden and exterior fire-escape stair make an appearance, the latter described as the largest free-standing exterior spiral staircase when it was built. Yet while Unité sits as an object in the field, the Colonnade seamlessly integrates into the surrounding fabric.

Across the elevations, the repetitive framework offers the illusion of a permeable skin. Despite the intrinsic opaque properties of concrete, the lattice effect formed by an intersection of solid beams and columns expresses a transparent quality comparable to many of the glass boxes.

A sales representative who'd shown me a unit proudly described an organic process by which residents had modified their units from the architect's original plans. The building's structural grid allowed floor-to-floor connections and openings through demising walls between units to suit their needs. This flexibility inherent in modern ideals may be one of the reasons the Colonnade continues to be one of the most popular rental addresses in Canada. So too might proximity to the fashionable modern neighbourhood it helped define.

Fig. 43. Drawing of concrete stair in south forecourt

Fig. 44. The Colonnade, south facade

Fig. 45. Forecourt and retail podium, the Colonnade

Toronto Hilton Hotel

Alex Bozikovic

Architecture and design writer, editor at *The Globe and Mail*

The best way to get a handle on the Hilton Hotel Toronto is to walk through its grand lobby and hop an elevator to the top floor. As the glass car whooshes up the outside of the tower, a band of precast concrete frames a view of the city's west end – a low expanse of green and asphalt stretching away to the horizon. From this point of view, the hotel feels like the very edge of downtown, a concrete cliff towering over Queen Street West.

Indeed, in terms of its raw size – 33 storeys and almost 600,000 square feet – the building is monstrous. But seen up close, from the corner of Richmond and University, the tower has a remarkably subtle impact on the cityscape. Behind the blur of the traffic, the hotel's mass rises in a grey shroud that's traced with a sober grid of lines. The corner didn't look much different in 1975, when the building opened as the Hotel Toronto. The hotel itself, though, looked fresh; Vancouver architect Reno C. Negrin was clearly inspired by the work of John Portman, the developer-architect whose concrete-atrium hotels were the height of corporate chic.

The Hotel Toronto does bear the mark of Portman's boldly drawn spaces and massive forms. From University Avenue, a staircase leads up to an elevated concrete plaza that is a time capsule of mid-'70s corporate architecture. Up here, in summer, guests sip drinks next to the hotel's outdoor swimming pool, while just metres away, workers from the office building next door take smoke breaks under a spare canopy of trees. And on the hotel, a sloping monolith of concrete window bays steps down toward the plaza. It's a bold expression of an architectural idea: anti-urban in its detachment from the streets, but powerful in its own way.

On the interior, as in so many concrete buildings of the period, there's very little concrete to be seen. The lobby, suavely redesigned in 2000 by KPMB Architects, bears a mixed palette of wood, glass, steel and onyx. There are few signs of the original interior, and at first there's little sign of the building's signature material. But KPMB made one thoughtful gesture toward it: the tower's massive structural columns, which Negrin wrapped in precast, are now brut and exposed.

The hotel's most impressive space, though, is at the back of the lobby, where it opens up into a triple-height atrium. Those stepping window bays that overlook the plaza aren't actually rooms; rather they let light into this finely proportioned atrium. Its wedge-shaped volume and the lightness of its concrete echo John Portman's crowd-pleasing massive atriums – but the atrium does so on a modest scale, without distorting the building or drawing too much attention to itself. This is concrete, Toronto-style.

Fig. 48. Hilton Hotel atrium and lobby

Fig. 49. Hilton Hotel as seen from the northwest, under construction

Sears Canada Headquarters

Jeff Hayes

E.R.A. Architects

The Toronto Sears Headquarters Building, completed in 1971, unquestionably pushes the boundaries of what qualifies as a worthy example for inclusion in this list of recently esteemed concrete buildings. Mostly because it is not a pure concrete building like the other examples found here – though it has a reinforced-concrete core. Still, it deserves an honourable mention.

Maxwell Miller, chief architect for Sears, designed the building with the greatest of Brutalist intentions, and then wrapped the entire beast in a dark brick veneer. Maybe he did this because he didn't want to appear to entirely emulate Boston City Hall. Similar to its equally monstrous cousin, opened a mere three years prior, the Sears building is a heavily cantilevered square box with elevations composed of a regular grid pattern. Unlike its predecessor, however, the exterior detailing was not left in its raw concrete form, and the dark brick used to enclose the elevations only emphasizes the oppressive nature of its top-heavy mass. Window separations on all the elevations are distinguished by outward-pointing piers, which merely adds to the overall thorniness of the structure. More like an armory (or a thick-skinned dinosaur, for that matter) than an office building, its outward treatment, along with its oppressive bulk, acts more to repulse people than draw them in. Alternatively, it's a remarkably well-executed building, and upon close examination one can appreciate the high level of craftsmanship in its construction and rigorously detailed features. It has aged very well in 35 years, perhaps to the dismay of its many detractors, who would rather see the mammoth topple or be pulled down.

Acknowledging its distinguished lineage, traced from Boston City Hall in all its Brutalist glory (and Le Corbusier's monastery of Sainte Marie de La Tourette before that), it is a further refinement of the form as a Torontofied facsimile. Recognizing the long history of brick construction in Toronto, the building's formidable mass was enclosed in a regionally acceptable material, creating perhaps the first example of Victorian Brutalism the world has seen.

But seriously, context is the issue most at odds when evaluating the Sears Headquarters, skewing the reading of what is undeniably a remarkable structure. The siting of the building, enclosed by a parking lot on the south and contradictory architectural styles in every other direction, renders its powerful architectural statement alienating. Ultimately this poor site planning makes Sears a bully of a building, a monument to overpowering bad neighbours, rather than to gravity-defying optimism, as intended.

As similar stylistically as the Sears Headquarters is to Boston City Hall, critical appreciation for each couldn't be more distanced. A recent poll of architects and historians in America, sponsored by the American Institute of Architects, voted Boston City Hall the sixth-greatest building in American history! I venture few architects in this country would currently bestow similar praise on the Sears behemoth, at least not in its present setting.

Fig. 50. Sears Canada building, as seen from southeast

Fig. 51. Sears Canada building, brick-veneer Brutalism

Fig. 52. Convent of la Tourette, Le Corbusier, 1960

Fig. 53. Boston City Hall, by Kellmann,
McKinnell and Knowles, 1968

Fig. 54. Sears Canada, by Maxwell Miller, 1971

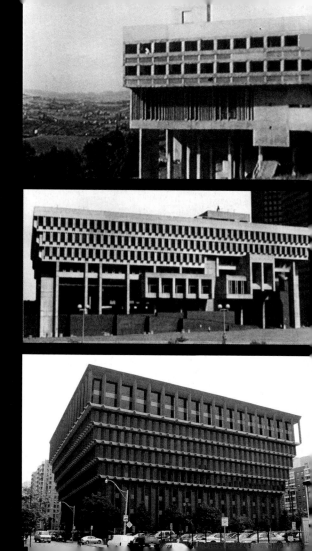

Polish Combatants Association Branch No. 20

Liam Woofter

Thesis Student, Faculty of Architecture, Landscape and Design, University of Toronto

Completed in 1973, the Polish Combatants Association Branch No. 20, located on tree-lined Beverly Street, north of Dundas, illustrates how concrete can be read as material culture. Through the skillful utilization of concrete, Wieslaw 'Winslow' Wodkiewicz's design for the Polish Combatants references the architecture of the mid-'50s movement known as New Brutalism.

Born out of the postwar English working class, and precedents set by Le Corbusier, New Brutalist architects sought to create an aesthetic that reflected the ruggedness of the new social realities of the era. Although New Brutalism had run its course through much of Britain by the late 1950s, the Brutalist aesthetic still played a role in modern architecture. The three-storey, 1,160-square-metre building consists of one floor of sub-grade parking and two floors with offices, a restaurant, banquet hall and small gallery space. The Polish Combatants Association had bought the site, which was previously home to a Jewish school, in 1947. By 1967, due to structural failures, the association had decided to commission Wodkiewicz, a member of the association himself, to design a new building to house the Polish Combatants.

The construction of the new building consists of a combination of steel, cast-in-place concrete and precast concrete panels. Columns and two-way slabs were poured on-site, while precast panels were fabricated. Steel was used on the roof of the building, reducing dead-load weight. The precast panels are assembled with inserts that are welded into connections cast into the floor slabs. The panels provide shear resistance and overall rigidity to the building. Wodkiewicz's use of the broken-rib panels was not only an aesthetic

choice – durability was also a key consideration. Two fire stairs located in opposite ends of the building, the southwest and northeast, provide resistance to wind and seismic loads. A large metal plaque mounted on the front stairway greets visitors in vintage social-realist expression.

Though materially, programmatically and architecturally the Polish Combatants is in stark contrast to its surroundings, careful sensitivity to the height and setbacks of the Victorian fabric helps make the building an icon of 'contextual' Brutalism. Its rusticated concrete panels are perhaps an homage to its Richardson Romanesque neighbour. Hidden behind a row of mature tress, the structure has remained an important piece of Toronto's Polish culture for three decades and counting.

Fig. 55. Polish Combatants: concrete piers and precast panels

Fig. 56. Polish Combatants Association Branch No. 20, Beverley Street facade

POLISH COMBATANTS ASSOC
BRANCH 20

77 Elm Street: The Nurses Residence

Now the Alan Brown Building, Hospital for Sick Childen

Ian Chodikoff

Editor, *Canadian Architect*

Completed in 1983, this 17-storey building is a beautiful, albeit strikingly idiosyncratic, Brutalist example of Toronto architecture. It is not surprising to discover that the building was designed by the legendary Uno Prii, the Estonian-born architect known for curvy, Morris Lapidus-inspired apartment buildings in Toronto's Annex neighbourhood. Prii's apartment complex at 77 Elm Street combines a series a explicit lessons regarding the possibilities of poured and precast concrete, while expressing an architecture that refuses to acknowledge the postmodern era in which it was built. Brutally honest, the building can be appreciated during daylight hours and especially at night, when its sculptural qualities allow light to permeate around the solid components of elongated concrete components at its base, creating complex spatial qualities at the street level.

Stacked atop four storeys of aboveground parking, the generous dimensions of the apartments are notable for the concrete demising walls that extend beyond the building's face – creating obvious thermal bridging challenges, not to mention chilly walls. Nonetheless, these expressive concrete fins protrude to form the basis for a modest vertical sunshade while emphasizing a clear internal organization of the building and a sculptural logic for the tower massing. With a variegated roofline, the building approaches the qualities of a semi-autonomous mega-structure, albeit one that is intimate in scale and reinforces the finesse of its overall massing, deploying many vertical elements of solids and voids to break down its largesse.

Prii's building has received unfair criticism for the brash expression of its aboveground parking configuration, but it should be acknowledged that it is sited amongst an ungainly assembly of architectural neighbours. With the building overlooking the Toronto Bus Terminal, whose buses park along nearby side streets, and situated adjacent to a variety of sterile and unforgiving hospital-related buildings which do little to enhance the quality of street life, it is understandable why Prii adopted an urban strategy replete with so many concrete elements. For better or worse, the project acknowledges a context that offers poorly defined entrances and a general lack of street life for pedestrians. If anything, the building attempts to remediate this lack of civic life at street level with a modest plaza on the northwest corner. The plaza is a hard patch of public space bounded by exuberant geometries of precast concrete enclosures that creatively screen off the numerous parking levels and provide mutable light qualities for passersby.

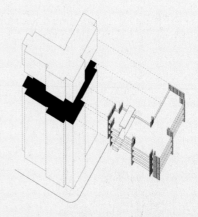

Fig. 57. Axonometric drawing, 77 Elm Street

Fig. 59. North facade , 77 Elm Street

A View of Toronto from 70 Alexander Street

Frederic Urban

Artist, writer and associate professor, Faculty of Architecture, Landscape and Design, University of Toronto

The direct axial view from my balcony at 70 Alexander Street looks west, over the tops of trees, across Yonge Street, down the centre of Grosvenor Street, across Queen's Park, to the central spire of One Spadina Crescent and beyond to the Mississauga horizon. A slightly wider view captures the concrete University of Toronto smokestack, the ornate top of the Brutalist, precast concrete Medical Sciences Building and part of the green copper dome of Convocation Hall.

The buildings to the right – Jack Daniels' 1966 Village Green Apartments with their exposed concrete frames, Jack Diamond's YMCA and a Bay Street condo – form a wall directing the axial view. The buildings to the left – Peter Caspari's 1954 City Park Apartments, which were the first modern high-rise apartments in the city (MAP P. 20), and Peter Dickinson's 1956 (remodelled) hotel – are set back and open the left foreground space.

Beyond, in the left centre, is the 80-metre-tall George Drew Building at 15–25 Grosvenor Street across from the YMCA. Its east facade of pink-sand-coloured, incised, precast concrete panels presents a blank face on which light plays subtle games. In plan, the east wall is bowed, as if it were a segment of a column. On a sunny day between 10 and 11 a.m., light does its work as the right (north) end of the curved wall falls into shade.

Rain brings out the red tones in the concrete aggregate. At night, the dark sky and the lights of the city create special effects, sometimes shifting the figure/ground and building/sky relationship. Early one stormy morning, in a strange ambience, it appeared as if the figure of the concrete wall had dissolved and become an opening in the solid ground of the sky.

Fig. 60. View from 70 Alexander Street, looking west

Sidney Smith Hall

Shawn Micallef
Writer, *Eye Weekly*; Associate Editor, *Spacing* magazine; Co-founder, [murmur]

Walking through the University of Toronto's St. George Campus is like touring an architectural zoo – you'll see just about every type of style that exists in Canada, except perhaps igloos and log houses. The visual chaos is not a bad thing, as each block is different and full of surprise for pedestrians.

This changes when you hit 100 St. George and Sidney Smith Hall. It's been an oasis of calm and serenity in the campus jumble since the cornerstone was laid in 1960, an open space ready to fit all the big brains the Arts and Science faculty can produce. Front and back, there are wide and flat patios – great cement plains, really – that help ease those students from the bustle of the street into the formality of the lecture halls inside. They were built during a time when universities could design open spaces without concern for creating riot-proof campuses, much the same way Nathan Phillips Square is Toronto's open, free and respectful civic space while Mel Lastman Square in North York is heavily programmed and all about breaking up big groups of people.

The steps up from street level to the Sidney Smith plain are thin slats of concrete that look light as a feather. Though there might be a few too many – enough that the climber will always be conscious of how many more there are to go – they're comfortable and they slow the pedestrian down, again easing mind and body into a different kind of contemplative state. This being a Canadian public institution, some of these thin steps are held up by two-by-four boards, surely not what architect John Parkin intended.

These great outdoor patios were once a bit bigger, before a 2004 infill project by Ian McDonald Architect Inc. glassed in some of the patio under Sidney Smith's front and rear overhangs, creating 8,000 square feet of additional space inside – but this interior space is almost still outside, as floor-to-ceiling glass creates study spaces and lounges made for the Toronto environment, sometimes best viewed from climate-controlled comfort. Modernism is particularly good at bringing the outside in.

Sidney Smith was the first project in the university's expansion west of St. George, vaulting the campus into a new age. The rigorously modern structure with plaza, setbacks, podium and office slab is more at home in Dessau than Oxford and must have appeared positively radical, especially to the students in the neo-Georgian Sir Daniel Wilson Residence, built for Univesrity Colege only half a decade prior.

Though the building belongs to an earlier period of modernism than famously loved and hated concrete bruts like the Robarts Library or the Med Sci building, the augmentation of its steel structure and stone cladding with large, textured and seemingly decorative concrete panels on its east and west facade place it firmly in the evolution of Toronto's concrete canon.

Much of the rest of the building, save for the abominable café on the south-facing Willcocks side, a Miami Vice–like glass-block-and-pastel explosion added at a weak and unfortunate postmodern moment, preserves Parkin's original design. Inside you'll find kids copying formulas off posters into their notebooks, their coats piled in the corner, just like they did in 1962. Like seemingly every university building, no matter what era it's from, Sidney Smith is overheated and feels a bit dirty. Perhaps deep thinking creates a fine layer of grit and dust as those rusty cogs start to turn.

The building is a maze of hallways and classrooms, with various Arts and Science offices colonizing different parts of the building. In nearly every corner of the basement there are signs directing lost faculty and students to their destinations. 600 appears to be a particularly hard-to-find destination, considering the amount of signage it requires. Even in the tight hallways, far from the outdoor expanse of patio, there is a sense of openness throughout as the walls are topped with glass, giving the feeling that though you can't see inside each office or classroom, everything is part of the same machine, working to the same end.

The entire building is anchored by the main central hall, complete with requisite warning sign prohibiting unauthorized banner-hanging, reminding that campuses are still places of radical – or frat-boy prank – ferment. The little Second Cup kiosk is an awkward add-on, but it's the centre of life at Sidney Smith and sees constant traffic, so it can be forgiven. The rest of the angular hall is given over to occasional poster sales – Jim Morrison to David Beckham to Matisse reproductions, the ubiquitous wallpaper of dorm rooms and crummy student apartments – or club days, when students can find any sub-niche to hang out in, like an old-fashioned, non-virtual Internet.

The flesh-and-blood Sidney Smith died a year before Sid Smith – as the locals call the building – was built. He was John Diefenbaker's Secretary of State for External Affairs and before that president of the University of Toronto for 12 years. A bust of this well-liked Red Tory was commissioned when the building opened, but it didn't measure up, and no other attempt was made to immortalize him. So there is just his name out front – nearly anonymous to most students, except perhaps a handful of Canadian Studies majors – marking this concrete building that looks as light and open as it did 46 years ago.

Fig. 61. Sidney Smith Hall, as seen from Sir Daniel Wilson Residence

Fig. 62. Open space, air and light: modernism comes to the St. George Campus. Sidney Smith Hall, north facade

Ontario Institute for Studies in Education

John Martins-Manteiga

Author, Founder of Dominion Modern

It was the age of concrete, and the Ontario Institute for Studies in Education (OISE) was the archetypal concrete edifice of its generation. An ad in a 1969 issue of *Canadian Architect* typifies the period, proclaiming, 'Concrete is the only material that can be moulded to conform with your ideas. It can be whatever you want. All you have to do is imagine it. That's why concrete is good for you.' (See page 295.)

OISE was first envisioned by Premier William Davis as an institution for graduate studies in education research. Davis saw OISE as 'an organization to bring about change, a driving force in Ontario's advance into education for the future.' OISE required offices, conference rooms, classrooms, libraries, underground parking and an auditorium. The architect for the project responded with an interior plan that allowed for airy spaces with lots of light. Materials such as wood, brick and concrete were interwoven inside and out and left in their natural state. Colour was used everywhere, and modern art by the likes of Jack Bush, Sorel Etrog and Kazuo Nakamura lined the building's interior walls while furnishings by Eero Saarinen, Jan Kuypers and Paul Arno graced its spaces.

Think big, be big. These were years of limitless possibilities. Canada's centennial celebrations and Expo 67 were expressions of the country's commitment to a bright and progressive future. OISE was part of the grand reinvention of Ontario brought forward by the long-governing Ontario Progressive Conservatives. The Conservative vision flourished at the time with the creation of new institutions such as TVOntario, Ontario Place, the Clarke Institute and the Ontario Science Centre, all on the vanguard of the use of new media for social policy development.

The architect K. R. Cooper, a graduate of the University of Toronto, gave OISE a monumental presence on Bloor Street. He 'imagined' an L-shaped tower atop a podium with a colonnade around the perimeter.

At that time architects were bold in their use of blank space, and Cooper's podium is a strong example of that. It doesn't apologize. It says, 'I am a blank wall: love me or leave me.' The podium is central, and Cooper works this architectural element well. It is large, but never heavy, and he softens it with incised windows that rise out of the columns that support it. The window effect is graphic on the outside while offering indirect light on the interior.

The colonnade below works in tandem with the podium. With its height and proportion, it breathes, functioning as a ceremonial and social space. It opens the building up to the street and doubles as an avenue for pedestrian traffic, leading not only to two entry doors at either end of the building, but also to the auditorium at one end of the colonnade.

The building's poured-concrete construction is dressed in precast concrete panels with a pebble surface for added texture. The tower's exterior skin is spiky, with angular precast concrete bays creating a three-dimensional effect that reflects light and shadow as the sun moves across its surface from east to west. Cooper's final dramatic feature is the double chimney stack that is utilitarian and poetic all at once.

OISE was an enormous project. And like its architectural cousins – Robarts, Tartu and Rochdale – it altered the landscape. In 1969, charming Victorians retail outlets – the likes of the first

Fig. 63. OISE, as seen from below

Swiss Chalet and Honey Dew restaurants – lined Bloor Street West. It is easy to understand why OISE was so controversial when it was built. The media at the time called it a 'monster.'

Concrete may be good for you, but concrete is a hard gig, even within the Modern Movement. The architect was sensitive to this fact. His concrete stage beckons large, but he considers the scale of the 1969 street and contains the building with setbacks and the colonnade. He frees it from becoming the beast it might have been. The OISE podium floats, aligning well with the street. Cooper pushes the podium back and then the tower back from it. He civilizes the building further by opening up the podium roof to walking areas and garden spaces.

OISE is also remarkable in that it was a complex built over subway tracks with direct entry into its concourse. Cooper was a developer-architect with experience building big projects over subways. He first did it with his Yonge-Eglinton Development, where the foundations extend down to the subway tunnels. He kept repeating this three-dimensional city integration with projects such as the Ontario Hydro headquarters that faces the Ontario Legislative Building.

The press at the time was not kind to the building, calling it a 'white elephant' and 'a soulless monster.' OISE is anything but; it has highly refined architectural scale and makes a grand statement while respecting the streetscape and pedestrian. The materials are warm and the library up front inviting. It is rare when one can walk around a building and appreciate four diverse building facades that are all sculpturally unique.

OISE has come of age and moved beyond the politics that built it and the controversies that surrounded it. It has matured to become an elegant example of classic late modern concrete architecture–an architecture that expresses one of the most progressive periods in Canada's development, when the country's architecture was as powerful and remarkable as its natural landscape.

Fig. 64. OISE, south face, as seen from Bloor Street

Tartu College

Thomas Tampold

Principal, Tampold Architects

When Graeme Stewart asked me to write about Tartu College, he referred to the 'graphic nature' of the building, and how current the design, by Elmar Tampold, looked. I was thrilled that a colleague would find my father's design from almost 40 years ago so au courant, until I discovered that he was referring only to the use of super-graphics on the facade, now so in vogue again. In the case of Tartu College, the words, cast in concrete, are set on their ends at each of the two street entrances. 'TARTU' pronounces the building's namesake – Tartu University, Estonia.

This is certainly one example of the building's interesting concrete details, as are the highly textured, cedar-board-formed exterior shear walls of each wing. However, these are not what came to mind about the significance of Stewart's observation. Perhaps the observation alluded more to the 'readability' of the design as a post-secondary student residence.

Owing, in part, to its use of concrete (which, according to the architect, was chosen for entirely rational and economic reasons), Tartu College has left us with a strong, yet surprisingly light, rendering of this student residence typology. The handsome look is achieved through three deliberate devices. First, by placing steps midway along each long street facade, the length of the precast spandrel panels is cut in half. Because of this offset, each street facade is divided like so many done-up zippers.

Second, internal shear walls that share the job (with the clothes closets) of sound attenuation between bedrooms are hidden behind the continuous windows, so that the concrete spandrels appear to float. Even at its base, the building

tends to lift off the ground, as if its only supports are those 200-millimetre end walls.

Finally, new windows were installed in 2002. The new design replaced casements with large, slimly framed, tilt-and-turn units. These units both literally and metaphorically provide more airiness and freshness to the elevations.

Next in the building's planned evolution is a library addition being contemplated for Madison Street and possible plans to add central air-conditioning ductwork on the outside of the structure – à la Piano's Lloyds of London building. It is a testament to the flexibility of the original design that each change manifests itself as a positive.

The 1971 catalogue of Canadian Housing Design Council Awards for Residential Design pointed to Tartu College as a 'good building ... clean, positive and strong.' Thus, graphically speaking, Tartu College then and Tartu College now may continue to be read in an identical manner.

Fig. 65. Typical floor plan, Tartu College

Fig. 66. Tartu College as seen from Spadina and Bloor

Rochdale College

Now Senator David A. Croll Apartments

Scott Sorli

Architectural designer, artist and sessional instructor, Faculty of Architecture, Landscape and Design, University of Toronto

Established by an act of the Ontario Legislature in 1964, Rochdale College became Canada's first free university and the largest of over 300 such free universities in North America. Based on principles of co-operative living (in the fullest sense of the term), a sociopolitical experiment played out on Bloor Street West that put into practice dreams, ambitions and ideals that were crystallized in the events of May '68.

A large concrete slab with horizontal strip windows at the edge of a typical Toronto Victorian neighbourhood, the building's scale is ameliorated by several formal tactics. A partial offset at the midpoint shortens the long elevation and seemingly narrows its width. A single line of vertical windows differentiates the 16-storey east wing from the 18-storey setback. The lobby entrance is located at this shear, benefiting from the reception area provided by the public plaza at the corner of Bloor and Huron. A corresponding second-floor terrace to the southeast provides sun and shade at appropriate times of the day and season for the 850 residents of the Rochdale community.

The west wing consisted of standard apartments, each with a kitchen, living room and one or two bedrooms (called Aphrodite and Zeus suites, respectively), while the east wing was designed to be a student residence with small single and double rooms (called Gnostics and Kafkas). In between, on each floor, was a communal unit for 12 people (called, of course, an Ashram) that included a large lounge, kitchen and washroom.

The residence opened late, a month after the start of term, and students initially shared the halls with construction workers and drywall dust, sleeping in rooms that, in some cases, didn't yet have windows installed. The entire 14th floor promptly self-organized into a commune, while each Ashram, to varying degrees, became a locus for its floor and beyond.

Two levels of underground parking, retail stores on the ground floor and offices on the second complete the program of this hybrid building. None of these details adequately describes the explosion of creativity that burned brightly and briefly for half a decade, whose cultural influence on Toronto continues to this day. These cultural forces that emerged include Coach House Press (now Coach House Books); Toronto Free Dance Theatre; House of Anansi Press; Reg Hartt's Spartan Cinema (free admission for nudists – for a screening of Hitchcock's *The Birds*, Hartt released captured pigeons and sparrows in the theatre); Toronto Filmmaker's Co-op; Nishnawbe Institute; Alternative Press Centre; Rochdale Medical Clinic; SCM Bookroom; Red White and Black (a counselling group for draft dodgers and deserters); League of Canadian Poets; Theatre Passe Muraille; resource persons Dennis Lee (Governor General Award–winning poet) and Judith Merril (who set up Rochdale's Spaced Out Library, which was later donated to the Toronto Public Library, creating North America's largest collection of sci-fi and fantasy); the first Miss General Idea pageant; civil rights lawyer Clayton Ruby (who cut his teeth defending Rochdale); a health-food restaurant, a coffee shop and a record store.

Rochdale College was a non-hierarchical, independent organization, with no entrance requirements, course structures or formal credits.

Fig. 67. Rochdale College, north facade, as seen from front plaza

Questioning institutions of authority, including academia, was encouraged, and degrees were given out casually and very inexpensively. Low-level organizational structures such as garbage cleanup and rent collection were neglected by the Toronto Student Management Corporation almost as a point of principle.

On August 5, 1971, the federal government notified Rochdale College of impending foreclosure due to default on the mortgage held through the Canadian Mortgage and Housing Corporation, and the Clarkson Company was appointed interim receiver for the building. By the end of May 1975, the last residents were evicted by force, and the doors were finally welded shut for good. Rochdale remained vacant until 1979, when it reopened as the Senator David A. Croll Apartments, the sedate seniors' residence we see today.

Any notion that formal architecture has instrumental capacity over free will and creativity was swept aside by the liberating social structures that were implemented, in what is called, in the negative sense of the term, a Brutalist building. It has also been claimed that the residents confused freedom with licence at Rochdale College, leading to its inevitable demise. But better that than, as is so commonly expected and acquiesced to today, demanding licence for freedom.

Fig. 68. Rochdale College, Canada's first 'free' university, as seen from Bloor Street

The McLaughlin Planetarium

Scott Weir

Associate, E.R.A. Architects

The McLaughlin Planetarium represents a late-20th-century response to an ongoing desire to measure or capture the cosmos within the structure of a building. As has been the tradition throughout history, a melding of innovative architectural form and the most current technology was employed to achieve this goal.

The method by which the cosmos is mapped has ranged in form through different cultures, from Stonehenge (3000 BCE), with its rings of massive stones aligned to calendar events; to the Mayan temple at Chichén Itzá (ca. 900 CE), whose stepped pyramidal form cast a shadow on the spring and fall equinoxes, illustrating the god Kukulcan slithering into the earth; to the gothic cathedrals, whose interiors attempted to embody the structure of the universe through geometry, dissolved structure and quality of light.

Rome's Pantheon (125 CE), the earliest intact example of a building enclosure constructed to accomplish that task, mapped the globe of the sun across a dome of the heavens through its central oculus. It continues to hold the record as the largest unreinforced concrete dome in existence, with an interior diameter of 142 feet and a thickness ranging from 4 feet at the oculus to 21 feet at the dome's base.

Our modern conception of a planetarium may have been formalized by Étienne-Louis Boullée when he designed the utopian project Newton's Cenotaph (1784), embodying Enlightenment ideas in architectural form. This unbuilt project imagined a structure, similar in form to the Pantheon, that could capture and invert the astronomical system – its dome would house a spherical space in which the starry sky could be referenced by holes drilled in its external masonry shell to represent constellations that would allow daylight to pierce through carefully mapped positions.

The McLaughlin Planetarium accomplished the task of capturing the cosmos by using a Zeiss planetarium projector, along with 85 other slide and video projectors, to cast an image of the stars and astronomical events onto the interior of a 75.4-foot-diameter domed projection screen. In this case, the building's structure, rather than being the vehicle through which the structure of the universe was captured, acted in a supporting role to the projector, which controlled what was to be viewed.

The space housing this program was capped by a dual-layer reinforced concrete dome that rises 83 feet from the ground, with a diameter of 91 feet, separated by an insulating layer of urethane foam. The interior cladding of this dome, which acted as the projection screen, was formed from lapped aluminum perforated sheets painted white. These perforations allowed for sound buffering on the interior and distribution of the ventilation system.

In its original conception, the building was to have included a multi-storey parking garage, a large movie theatre and a direct link to the Museum subway station, but budget cuts limited the final scope. As constructed, the building's four floors included basement storage, a ground floor with a space-themed library and shop, a second-floor exhibition space and the 340-seat theatre within the dome.

Fig. 69. Planetarium and public plaza

Fig. 70. Planetarium under construction, looking south

Attendance dropped substantially during renovations to the ROM in the mid-1970s, and part of the facilities were demolished to make way for an enlarged curatorial wing in 1978. Though attendance increased in the '80s, the building was closed on November 5, 1995, under budget cuts imposed by the Conservative provincial government of the time. The facility's exhibits, artifacts and Zeiss projector were dismantled and sent elsewhere.

Since that time, the building has been converted to offices and storage for the museum. Recently the ROM has put forward proposals for redevelopment of the site, which would include demolition of the building.

Fig. 71. McLaughlin Planetarium interior

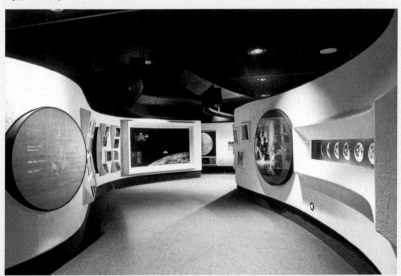

Fig. 72. The Pantheon, Rome, 126 CE

Fig. 73. Cenotaph of Newton, France, 1784

Fig. 74. McLaughlin Planetarium, Toronto, 1968

Medical Sciences Building, Toronto's Largest Modern Sculpture

Scott Sorli

Architectural designer, artist and sessional instructor, Faculty of Architecture, Landscape and Design, University of Toronto

The Medical Sciences Building at the University of Toronto, referred to as Med Sci on campus, was completed in 1969. Part of an era of ambitious academic public funding by the Province of Ontario, the very large project suited the university's growing medical research and teaching goals. Designed by an American firm that specialized in straightforward university buildings, the eight-storey, largely windowless expanse of blank facade provided perhaps less of a backdrop than hoped for to the campus's Gothic architecture that it is so neatly tucked behind.

Architect Peter Goering persuaded the university instead to incorporate the percentage for public art budget into a series of precast concrete panels that, randomly (if unintentionally so) installed by the construction crew, enlivened and softened the elevations. Not incidentally, the precast concrete panels were also part of a rain-screen system, relatively new to building science at the time, and never before used on a project of that size in Canada. (See page 292).

Robert Downing, a young multidisciplinary artist working in association with his former sculpture professor Ted Bieler, found the creative constraints of the Beer Precast company, a leading manufacturer of precast panels, frustrating. But as Elizabeth Hulse mentions in her history of the Beer family and business, the generation gap went both ways. Fred A. Beer later recalled how once, dressed in a suit and tie, he arrived at a grungy studio, was offered 'hash' and replied that he had just eaten.

As well as the twiggy rustication of the six variations on the main face (or seven, if the window-frame panels are counted) there are two half-height variants for the base, and three looser, more open patterned panel types running laterally across the penthouse as a modern frieze. Bands of blank panels aligned with horizontal balconies above and strip windows below separate the elevations into a tripartite composition. Downing also designed two precast concrete sculptured walls as part of his ongoing *Cube Series* (which was a 1969 solo exhibition at London's Whitechapel Art Gallery) and a precast concrete *Mandala* relief for the courtyard and reception to the building.

Bieler, who was awarded the 1969 RAIC Allied Arts Medal for sculpture, contributed the DNA-referencing *Helix*, placed in the forecourt, and *Muskoka Piece* (or *Wave*), located in the sheltered courtyard between the main entry to Med Sci and its auditorium just to the north. A series of cast-concrete islands embedded into the courtyard terrace, their convex forms invite being sat upon, and are much like any of a million tiny islands in northern Ontario, granite of the Canadian Shield polished smooth by lapping waves.

Peter Goering, in his retirement, is behind the world's first dark sky reserve, Torrance Barrens, a two-hour drive north of Toronto just south of Lake Muskoka, where the stars of the Milky Way remain visible on any clear, moonless night.

Fig. 75. Typical facade, Medical Sciences Building, University of Toronto

Fig. 76. Artist Robert Downing (centre) examining precast panel in Beer manufacturing plant

Figs. 77, 78. Section through sculptural wall, north elevation of Med Sci

Fig. 79. Drawings of various precast sculptural motifs, Med Sci

Figs. 80, 81, 82. Various elements of concrete sculptural program

	Fig. 80
Fig. 77 Fig. 78	Fig. 81 Fig. 82
Fig. 79	

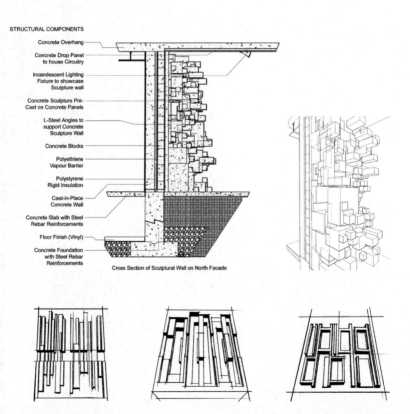

STRUCTURAL COMPONENTS

Concrete Overhang

Concrete Drop Panel to house Circuitry

Incandescent Lighting Fixture to showcase Sculpture wall

Concrete Sculpture Pre-Cast on Concrete Panels

L-Steel Angles to support Concrete Sculpture Wall

Concrete Blocks

Polyethlene Vapour Barrier

Polystyrene Rigid Insulation

Cast-in-Place Concrete Wall

Concrete Slab with Steel Rebar Reinforcements

Floor Finish (Vinyl)

Concrete Foundation with Steel Rebar Reinforcements

Cross Section of Sculptural Wall on North Facade

Building Med Sci

Anne Miller

Professional engineer, master's thesis student, Faculty of Architecture, Landscape and Design, University of Toronto

Inflexible deadlines and a limited budget presented an opportunity for the University of Toronto to take an innovative approach to the construction of the Medical Sciences Building. Knowing that the quality of the planning and administration of this project would ultimately determine its success, the university retained Canadian Bechtel Limited in the capacity of project managers very early on in the process, prior to retaining the architect.

Canadian Bechtel, a subsidiary of Bechtel Corporation, hired R. Harvey Self as the project manager. Harvey Self had worked for Ontario Hydro for 15 years and the Toronto Board of Education for 10 years before that, and brought a unique perspective to the management of an institutional building project. He wanted to build the way Hydro builds a generating station: beginning the construction process in concert with the design process. This methodology involved a short time lag – six months – between the start of design work and the start of construction, whereas conventional architectural practice would have required up to two years of planning and design prior to construction.

The construction of the building was marred by several labour strikes, including the Algoma Steel plant responsible for the production of structural steel (December 19, 1966 to January 14, 1967), the structural steel erectors and reinforcing steel rodmen (May 19, 1967 to October 16, 1967), the precast concrete manufacturers (July 31, 1968 to September 23, 1968) and a general construction strike from April 30, 1969, onward to the completion of the project. These labour-relations issues, along with design and construction status, were described in detail in Canadian Bechtel's monthly progress reports to the university. Complete with tables, charts, drawings and images, these polished reports were not only critical to the success of the project at the time of construction, but uniquely offer us the opportunity to learn a great deal more about this fascinating project.

The success of this unconventional project, fittingly declared in 1970 by the *Toronto Telegram* to be 'a real bargain,' must be attributed in part to Harvey Self and Canadian Bechtel Limited. The total project time lost due to labour-relations issues was approximately eight-and-a-half months, and yet, in spite of this, the project was completed 18 months ahead of schedule and almost $1 million below original estimates, adding another compelling dimension to this layered and significant project.

Figs. 83, 84. Application of precast panels of steel frame, Medical Sciences Building

Figs. 85, 86. Med Sci concrete sculptural installations, student lounge and east entrance

John P. Robarts Library

Mary Lou Lobsinger

Assistant Professor, Faculty of Architecture, Landscape and Design, University of Toronto

It is ugly. Or so the critics agreed upon the inauguration of the John P. Robarts Library at the University of Toronto in 1974. Labelled Fort Book, a cold-storage unit offending the senses, its building profile was likened to a peacock and the plan was said to resemble a maple leaf when viewed from above. Ron Thom, architect of the nearby Massey College, complained that the building smacked of arrogance and ego, and that it represented everything wrong with contemporary architecture. In a neighbourhood where to this day tampering with context is the gravest of sins, Robarts stands like a bull in a china shop, comparing negatively to Thom's sensitive treatment. Raising the cultural stakes, some of the more imaginative critics saw the library as a Piranesian Carceri or George Orwell's Ministry of Truth.

Since this inauspicious beginning, Robarts has continued to disturb sensibilities, again raising hackles when in 1997 it received Heritage B preservationist protection. This time the ugliness diatribe confirmed its status as a good example of Brutalism. That the robust concrete work is rather well turned out and that it signifies an unapologetic paean to the raw expression of form has passed by, barely noted in the criticism. Its provocation of affect has been considered a negative attribute, but to my mind such criticism is a sign of impoverished imaginations, the sort of stingy mentality that accompanies the unwillingness to entertain robust and uncanny aesthetic experiences.

Robarts Library is the product of planning for the forecasted boom in higher education and the expansion of graduate-level education in the early 1960s. Bowing to provincial pressure to exponentially increase graduate studies, a mantra unceasing to this day, the University of Toronto radically revised its priorities, putting aside $42 million to build a library that would give pride of place to what it hoped would become a world-class research institution. The New York–based Warner, Burns, Toan and Lunde, a practice with a track record for libraries at Cornell and Brown universities, were engaged as design consultants, with the Toronto-based Mathers and Haldenby acting as principal architects.

Sited like a giant chess piece on a razed three-acre site, the structure features a mezzanine level that connects the Faculty of Information Studies through the enclosed centre circulation atrium of the main 14-storey building to the Fisher Rare Book Library. The triangular stack organization determined much of the monolithic form, dictating the shape of the reinforced concrete structural frame and the waffle slab floors.

Even the harshest of critics had to admit that the building was well-constructed and beautifully detailed, with exquisite wood finishes of African mahogany and the dark-surfaced interiors enhanced by low light levels. Rumour has it that Umberto Eco, a frequent visitor to the university in the 1970s, found inspiration for the library in his bestselling novel *The Name of the Rose* in the four-storey hexagonal circulation core. But it is the form and rough-hewn concrete surfaces that still conjure the uneasy feelings of estrangement; that is, when it is not invoking analogy to a medieval hill town or a fortified bastion of knowledge.

Robarts is unsettling. It resists the comfortable familiarity expected of a building over time. If its ugliness provokes this effect, then I would argue that ugly is an attribute worthy of consideration. When in the mid-1950s Reyner Banham attempted to define the Brutalist aesthetic, he resorted to descriptions such as the tactile and

Continued on p. 173

Fig. 87. Robarts, north stair to raised podium and entrance to Faculty of Information Studies

Protest 1: a lesson for all

R.J. Thom

The Robarts Library, known by all on the campus of the University of Toronto as "Fort Book", represents everything in architecture that is arrogant and wrong.

It is one of those buildings that were it not for its extreme cost should be taken down and done again in a manner more befitting its important role on the Toronto campus and in the overall Ontario university library system.

The authors of the basic concept seem to have been either unaware or unimpressed by this role or by the surrounding campus and community in which the building sits. In their pursuit of some kind of monument (in itself a perverse and antiquated notion) they have created by far the most unloved building on the University of Toronto Campus.

To make any serious architectural comment is almost impossible; it is difficult to know where to start on this illustrated dictionary of architectural miseries which are so blatant and so endless they approach the absurd.

1

Begin with access to the building. One would assume that access to the most important building on any campus — its library — would be easy and welcoming, but this is certainly not so in this case with on the one side an unbelievable ramp system, and on the other side by an arrogant, monumental grand staircase.

During construction, one watched in disbelief as formwork was erected over one hundred feet in height around its periphery to form the overhanging architectural fancies now referred to by students as gun emplacements.

And the mind boggles at the architectural wit that decreed a triangular configuration on a rectangular street pattern, in a rectangular campus, containing everything from rectangular book stacks to rectangular flourescent light fixtures.

There also seems no discernable reason for the building assuming its great height, far out of scale with everything surrounding it, when it occupies only a portion of its site. It appears to retreat from the passerby while at the same time hanging over to threaten him from above.

The "empty" half of the site remains a flat and unrelieved plane of grass leading abruptly to a hard-edged collision with the mighty walls. One assumes that money for even modest landscaping was long since spent.

The only optimistic observation I can make is that perhaps the Fort will become a vivid textbook for future generations of architectural students.

It is a lesson for all to learn from.

Fig. 88. Robarts under construction, with rebar and forms for waffle slab in place

Fig. 89. Ron Thom's critique of Robarts, *Canadian Architect*, August 1974

Fig. 90. Concept rendering of John P. Robarts Library, the largest research institution in Canada

Fig. 91. Fourth- and fifth-floor reference library and reading room, under construction

Figs. 92, 93. Site inspection of concrete stair in fourth- and fifth-floor reading rooms

Fig. 94. Cantilevered stack floors emerge from base, Robarts Library, under construction

Fig. 95. Unadorned concrete waffle slab floor plates
prior to mechanical installation, John P. Robarts Library

Fig. 96. Exploded axonometric study

sensory effect produced by the immediacy of an apprehensible visual entity. Robarts is a closed form whose very materiality primes the senses through immediacy of experience, not allowing disinterested assessment. Not a thing more could be added or taken away. Sublime, the building is not. In contrast to the limitless potential of the sublime, Robarts' capacity to stir up emotion is highly determined. Rough sublime as opposed to refined beauty, perhaps. Its garrulousness speaks volumes because of its formal restraint. The bulk of concrete is a welcomed contrast to those tasteful compositions obsessed with the revealing of one material to another, a kind of Toronto style that has popped up everywhere, turning it into a graphic standard how to compose glass, Cor-Ten steel, wood and brick rather than engage with form.

In a cityscape of architectures that avoid big form and gusty materiality for the meek and tastefully composed – or worse, of banal buildings or gaudy signature baubles – Robarts still has its bite. What's more, it has global resonance. Both Kahn's British Art Museum and Rudolph's School of Architecture at Yale, any of the rough concrete buildings at Harvard, of which Le Corbusier's spectacular site-defying Carpenter Center is most famous, and the concrete wonders found anywhere from London to Chandigarh are genetically related to a specific moment in architectural theory and practice. Most reverently, the delight in visceral surface, referential formality and the raised podium speaks directly to Alison and Peter Smithson's Economist Building in London, completed in 1964; Alison coined the term Brutalism long before Banham got hold of it. This is not bad company to keep. Following these genealogical predecessors, Robarts provokes, refusing to settle comfortably or let local imaginations grow staid and self-satisfied.

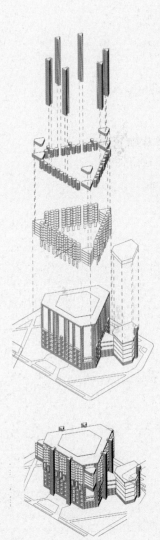

Fig. 1. Rosedale Ravine Bridge, looking west

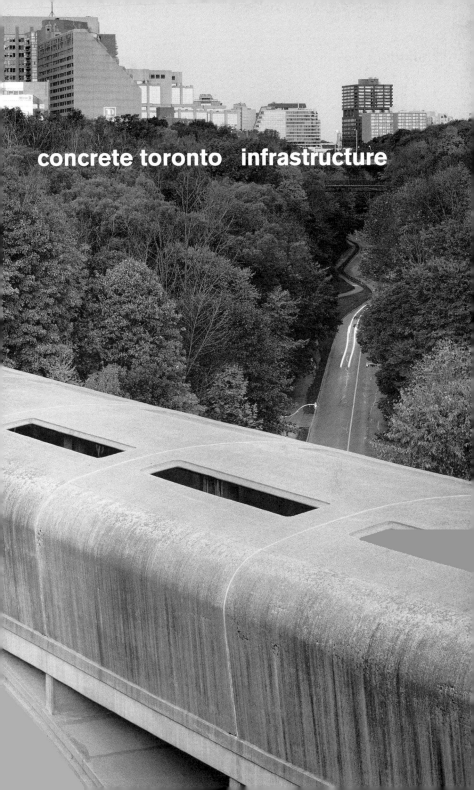

concrete toronto   infrastructure

Metro Concrete

John Van Nostrand

Partner, The Architects Alliance, The Planning Alliance

Concrete was the material of Toronto's metropolitan growth. The creation and subsequent adoption of the Plan for Metropolitan Toronto in the late 1940s launched a period of unprecedented growth and development – at the core of which was the design and construction of an extensive network of new metropolitan infrastructure to support the expanding new communities of central Etobicoke, Don Mills and north Scarborough. These included a ring of major new highways – the Gardiner Expressway, the 401, the Don Valley Parkway and the 427; unprecedented expansion of Toronto's water supply and sewage treatment systems; and the introduction of extensive controls, channelization and the outright burial of portions of troublesome water courses after Hurricane Hazel.

All of these infrastructures were rendered in an era of concrete construction that continues to define both the heroic and the ordinary characters of the metropolitan city. On the heroic side, the Gardiner Expressway and the Don Valley Parkway provided new entrances into the city and defined new relationships with nature, topography and horizon. In turn, the 401/427 interchange connected it with lands and lives beyond. On the ordinary, new concrete lighting fixtures and poles criss-crossed the city as harbingers of a new metropolitan order, and one was hard-pressed to avoid a multitude of manholes dotting our valleys and streams. In turn, metropolitan government was housed in a mysterious new series of water depots, sewerage works and modernist concrete offices and workshops that suggested to the citizenry that engineers had taken over the role of defining the city from architects, planners and even landscape architects. A new network of waterworks that pushed further north into the Don and Humber watersheds led to the creation of significant new metro parks that posited a new balance of conservation and construction – all rendered in concrete.

The concrete industry itself expanded and innovated in response to this enormous growth. Precast concrete components were scattered or laid end to end across the metropolitan landscape. At the same time, with an influx of European labour, concrete construction assumed a new quality within the public realm. Indeed, concrete was the material of the public realm and there was little room for the romantic or historic.

When the archaeologists excavate Toronto in 300 years, they will find the ruins of much of the great metropolitan period defined by concrete. It was designed to be there forever, and it will make great ruins. While some will likely still be in use, much of it will be overgrown and subsumed by the nature it set out to dominate.

Fig. 2. Channelled waterway, western Don Valley

The Donald D. Summerville Olympic Pool

Andrew Pruss

Associate, E.R.A. Architects

It can be seen from kilometres away. From the east along Lake Shore Boulevard, where the constructivist layering of the diving platforms and the embracing wings of the viewing stands inspire thoughts of competitive acrobatics, five storeys above the ground. And from the north, you can see it as you descend from the Danforth, at the termination of Woodbine Avenue. It is a turquoise water-filled tabletop at the scale of the city with sand and lake as a backdrop that brings to mind every tropical location you have ever used to escape Toronto in the winter. But this concrete monument isn't in Cuba; it is *the* architectural landmark on our Beach other than the Harris filtration plant.

The Summerville pool, consisting of two linked structures of poured-in-place concrete with impressive cantilevers, was built in the early 1960s by local architects. We imagine Olympic events scheduled at the pool, but in fact it is open a mere 10 weeks a year for recreational swimming and the occasional masters swim club. Notably, the pool's length is just short of 50 metres, a miscalculation that may have been the product of a pre-Trudeau era attempt at converting from imperial measurements.

The structure creates an elevated piazza at the pool level that has uncommon views of the lakefront. Also, cave-like loggias under the cantilevers on three sides shelter more public space, providing cover on rainy days and access to the obligatory public restrooms and a non-descript hot-dog window. Torontonians are said to have turned our back to the lake, yet this structure is an example of a public facility embracing its lakeside setting. This muscular concrete structure, from an optimistic era in the development of the city, is an example of how to build civic amenities. If it is not now used to its potential, it is still an inspiring asset waiting.

Fig. 3. Summerville grandstand and diving platform

Fig. 4. Park Pavilion, Etobicoke

The Gardiner Expressway

Calvin Brook

Partner, Brook McIlroy

In the spring of 2003 the City of Toronto completed another segment of its annual maintenance regime for the Gardiner Expressway. This portion of the eight-kilometre-long elevated structure, between Sherbourne and York streets, is an anomalous stretch of pure concrete construction, arching with angular origami-like columns up and over Lake Shore Boulevard. With relatively little effort, its simple sculptural elegance suddenly becomes apparent. Driving through the arches early in the morning, with the easterly light illuminating the rows of columns, it becomes possible to love the space created by the expressway. In contrast, the balance of the Gardiner is somewhat moribund – combining concrete columns with exposed steel rafters that are painted an unfortunate green. It is fascinating to conjure the confluence of design aspiration and bureaucratic culture in the 1950s that permitted that inspired segment to see the light of day – for it is truly artful in the manner that bridge design can occasionally be. Could it be that the expressway is beautiful – both in its form and its demonstration of a modernist ideal that is even more relevant today?

The Past: City-builders love to emulate one another. In the 1950s, when Fred Gardiner bullied the expressway into being – famously demanding that Fort York be relocated so the expressway could remain straight (he had to bend on that one) – he was merely emulating the example of American cities flush with cash from the federal highways initiative. Thankfully, Gardiner's plan for the most part largely avoided the infamy of neighbourhood destruction and social displacement that accompanied Boston's expressway program. For the elevated portion,

east of Fort York, the route of the new expressway disturbed only the marginal industrial netherland squeezed between Toronto's railway lands and its then unloved waterfront. The railway was the barrier between the city and the waterfront (and remains so to this day); the logic of placing the expressway in this lacklustre zone may have lacked foresight, but it was ... logical.

Riding the Gardiner in the 1960s was thrilling. The concrete guardrails on either side held a continuous light strip eight kilometres long weaving through the city lights. Driving into Toronto's downtown at night was the quintessential modern experience – a celebration of technology, freedom, speed and contemporary urbanism. Beneath the Gardiner was another story. Simply ignored in civic design consciousness, Lake Shore Boulevard was relegated to an ignoble status as a feeder road linking the city to the Gardiner's ramps.

The Present: The space occupied by Lake Shore Boulevard – the space beneath and beside the expressway – is a wasteland of open dirt and lacklustre lighting, without trees or vegetation. It is a cage of reflected noise and trapped exhaust fumes. The pedestrian ambience is hideous.

Herein lies the problem at the heart of the Gardiner debate – the 'barrier effect' ascribed to the Gardiner is simply misplaced. The barrier is a result of neglect of the space beneath, a blind spot in our collective understanding of civic space in the city. Yet these conditions are easily fixed, at a fraction of the cost of alternatives such as demolition and replacement with an at-grade roadway or tunnelling.

Fig. 5. Underside of western Gardiner Expressway at Strachan Avenue

Today there remains a large contingent of urbanists in Toronto who believe the Gardiner Expressway should be torn down. The biggest obstacle they face is a simple reality – it works incredibly well. For those travelling above, passing between the city's towers, it remains an efficient transportation solution and a source of unique urban vistas and exhilaration. Remember, the expressway is an eight-kilometre-long bridge – lifted above Toronto's ground level, elevating 200,000 cars and trucks each day. This allows a freedom of movement at street level that could never be achieved with an at-grade road system. Yes, the expressway could be torn down and the traffic could be inserted into a new, expanded surface-road system. But the barrier impact would be unprecedented.

The Future: Lurking in the imaginations of city dwellers is a version of an urban future free of the car. Tearing down the expressway would be a brave message – retribution for the ghastly assault on city air the car has inflicted – and a jump start on the intimate urban ambience we long for.

But the car is here to stay. It will be clean, small and very expensive to drive in the city. Another version of the future is that we embrace the Gardiner and treat it as a vast design project – a unique armature linking the city from east to west, creating landmark gateways to the waterfront and downtown. A harbinger of future urban transportation that is green and beautiful – integrating trees and planting above and below with grasses and reeds irrigated from the vast stormwater runoff of the roadways. We take the gift of an existing (already paid for) grade-separated system and introduce transit lanes above and bike lanes below. The orphan spaces beneath and beside Lake Shore Boulevard become useful, active civic places for flea markets, skateboard parks and public art demonstrations – a welcome piece of informal, happenstance place-making in the midst of the relentless, sterile and utterly predictable public realm that has emerged in the condominium canyons on either side of the expressway.

Instead of emulating once again our American counterparts – like Boston and San Francisco, who have demolished their elevated expressways – perhaps this is a chance for Toronto to embrace its own special culture and circumstances. A far more interesting future is possible. It requires serious investment, though at a fraction of the cost of alternatives. It starts with imagining the Gardiner as a thing of beauty that both heals this neglected seam in the downtown and creates a chain of surprisingly inventive civic spaces that attract people and worldwide acclaim.

Fig. 6. Underside of eastern Gardiner Expressway at Yonge Street

The Rise of Parking Garages

Marie-Josée Therrien

Assistant professor of architecture and design history, Ontario College of Art and Design

In the 1920s, the head of the McGill School of Architecture, Percy Nobbs, wrote, 'With the increasing number of motor cars, their parking and storing has become a question of utmost importance and in order to place themselves in suitable situations the garages have been forced to disassociate themselves from the class of the undesirables, and at least put on a dress better fitted to their improved status.' At the time, cities, overcrowded with Ford's Model T, began to build enclosed multi-storey parking garages. In line with the prevailing historicist trend, the more upscale garages presented facades that disguised their function. This design approach guaranteed this new 20th-century building type would be suitable for the 'aristocratic members of the building community,' as described by Nobbs.

In the booming decades after World War II, these examples of 'good neighbour' concealed parking garages were to be replaced by more utilitarian models, such as the open-deck structures. Nobbs, being of the Art and Craft tradition, might have considered those postwar examples unattractive, but functionalism, which had gained momentum by the 1950s, prompted a new aesthetic based on the intrinsic qualities (some would have said the inner beauty) of industrialized materials. Parking garages did not make the cover pages of professional magazines, but they began to occupy a prominent position in the urban fabric.

The postwar proliferation of automobiles, along with the construction of major highways, created more traffic. As a result, the parking of cars became an acute problem that required urgent action in most Canadian downtowns. While city parking authorities were established around North America, a new breed of specialists, the garage designers, devised solutions that took advantage of the most recent construction techniques: 'long-spans between columns, pre-stressed concrete, steel skeleton structures, lower ceiling heights and lower ramp grades.' Open-deck parking garages, such as the Blue Jays Parking along the Gardiner Expressway, became common features during the heyday of the functionalist era. These open decks presented real economic advantages over the early enclosed garages: they did not need venti-lating systems to expel car exhaust, fire-hazard regulations were more relaxed and the costly facades were a thing of the past. The savings allowed for the insertion of modern ornamental grills between the concrete parapets.

The garage of the Canada Life Assurance Company north of Queen and Simcoe (Webb Zerafa Menkes Housden), which holds up to 470 cars on a suspended floor area of 100,000 square feet, is articulated around a double-helix continuous ramp. Its angular shapes, firmly grounded to the streetscape, provide an elegant horizontal foreground to the office tower that seems to be rising from its upper-level deck. Perhaps this is not quite the ideal neighbour one would wish for, but considering the scale of this downtown parking garage and the nature of the back street, it is a structure well-integrated into its environment.

Circular ramps have become another common feature of parking facilities, both in underground and above-ground garages. The unusual sculp-tural shape of the circular ramp can constitute a dramatic element when properly positioned in relation to access roads. In less well-planned locations, however, their alien shapes can act as whimsical contrapuntal constituents, or simply as eyesores.

Storing automobiles became such a necessity in the second half of the 20th century that many new building owners made provisions to integrate parking space into their overall design. The Brutalist Polish Combatants Association Branch (GUIDEBOOK No. 35) on Beverley Street has resolved its problem of car storage by elevating its building on a grid of columns. The architects used the peripheral columns to create smooth transitions between the three storeys of the building. The suspended structure, with its contrasting surface textures, is a successful addition that respects the human scale of its residential neighbourhood.

The Estonian architect Uno Prii, known for his dramatic, sculptural high-rises, designed one of the most striking integrated parking garages of downtown Toronto. The Nurses Residence building on Elm Street (GUIDEBOOK No. 44) in the hospital district, is an eloquent example of

Brutalism. Rather than relegating this service to an unassuming position, Prii designed a sculptural artifact that wraps the cars within the building. The asymmetrical rhythm, with elements reminiscent of early Frank Lloyd Wright buildings, works best when looked at from a distance. From these vantage points, one realizes what Prii achieved – a high-density residential building that came to terms with the storage of automobiles. No disguise device here, just a pure expressionist concrete experience that illustrates the potential of this modernist material in the automobile age.

The parking garage that best illustrates the culture of mobility of the booming postwar decades was the rectangular structure that emerged from the doughnut shape of the late Terminal One of Pearson International Airport, by John B. Parkin Associates. From this nine-level roofed parking garage that provided storage space for more than 2,400 cars, the 'homo automobilist' was within only 300 feet from its booked airplane! Of course, security control was almost nonexistent in those days.

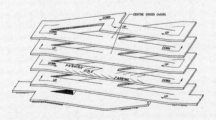

Fig. 7. Double-threaded-helix traffic flow diagram, Canada Life parking garage

Fig. 8. Central parking garage, former Terminal One, Pearson International

Eglinton West Subway Station

Ian Chodikoff

Editor, *Canadian Architect*

Perched on a modest crest of a hill overlooking a large cut into the earth constructed for Allen Road, the Eglinton West subway station is surprisingly elegant, providing an internal spatial quality that confidently cascades down onto the subway platforms and out to the bus loop. Opened in 1978, the station sits at the nexus of a significant part of Toronto's recent infrastructure history. Located at the terminus of Allen Road, the station could have been part of an ambitious plan to extend Allen Road south toward the downtown. Known as the Spadina Expressway, the controversial proposed extension of Allen Road nearly destroyed a considerable swath of Toronto's downtown neighbourhoods before it was officially cancelled in 1971, but not after considerable opposition contributed to the formation of a generation of civic advocates. Those who fought against the expressway include Jane Jacobs, former mayors David Crombie and John Sewell, and 'Stop Spadina' activist Colin Vaughan.

With the south end of the station extending beneath Eglinton Avenue and back to the Nordheimer Ravine, there once existed a plan to open a subway platform on the south side of Eglinton, across from the existing station. Slated to have been renamed Eglinton West–Allen, this proposed expansion for the subway station was part of a planned interchange for the Eglinton subway project – an initiative that was cancelled in 1994. The Eglinton subway would have travelled west to the York Centre Station at Black Creek Drive.

Today, the massive quasi-hexagonal flat concrete roof continues to hover over the station in a seemingly effortless manner. Supported by tall, round concrete columns, the roof filters in daylight through numerous skylights that are mostly clouded over, due to solar radiation. The roof construction is a deep and expressive concrete waffle slab that provides an ample and ambitious canopy for the nearly 25,000 commuters who move through the station daily.

Though the building is wrapped with large panes of glass all around its perimeter, its base is heavy, thanks to the orange-brown masonry accentuated with deftly constructed circular openings. The brick detailing, as well as the burnt-orange herringbone tile patterns, is certainly a late-'70s touch, but these elements contribute to the sensation that the station is ascending from the earth, articulating where the pedestrian emerges onto a busy stretch of Eglinton Avenue flanked by traffic streaming onto and off Allen Road.

Fig. 9. Eglinton West Station as seen from the Allen Expressway

Figs. 10, 11. Eglinton West Station, bounded by Allen Expressway

Figs. 12, 13. Eglinton West Station's suspended concrete waffle slab roof

The Manulife Centre Is a Brute

Robert Ouellette

Editor, *Reading Toronto* (www.readingcities.com)

Architecture critics in Toronto are slamming some of the city's '70s-era landmarks. Once admired as symbols of our entrance into international modernism, buildings like the Manulife and Sheraton centres are losing the battle of critical opinion.

It is easy to understand why. First, they are getting old, and we know how North American culture hates age. Second, the buildings' Brutalist lineage from practitioners like Le Corbusier through to Paul Rudolph is unselfconsciously direct in an era when everything designed stinks of precious self-consciousness. We have to ask, though, is our public pillorying of these buildings fair or are we succumbing to the vapid tides of style when we shame our Brutalist architectural heritage?

The answer to that question is personal, but I know my reply. When I first arrived in Toronto from London, Ontario, I remember standing on Bloor Street across from the Manulife Centre. I knew few people here and, with little else to do, I spent too much time searching Toronto's streets looking for 'architecture.'

Gazing up across Bloor, cloaked in the hulking winter shadow of the Manulife Centre, I remember experiencing a sense of arrival. I was sharing the street with a building whose tectonic muscle defied the winds of our Canadian landscape. Winds there were – and are today – force-fed by the undercut canyon that is Bloor and Bay. It did not matter. The building had strength.

Architects, I thought, made this raw, concrete building and the carefully hidden apartment tower behind it. They also imagined into life a labyrinth of connections under the street that would protect us from the cold, pre-global-warming Toronto climate. For a kid from small-city Ontario, the experience was cathartic.

Buckminster Fuller once wrote that modern buildings were just so many fancy nozzles on the real beauty of the city's engineering infrastructure. Given the Brutalist context of the time, he may have been right.

Nonetheless, these complex, well-engineered and forceful buildings shape a specific era of Toronto's history. They are landmarks to the public spaces beneath them they helped spawn. To say they have no place in our 21st-century city is to say that our experiment in modernity has failed. It hasn't – but our understanding of it has.

Fig. 14. The city's tallest residential block and mixed-use podium emerging at Bay and Bloor streets

Fig. 15. Manulife Centre Phase One, residential block, under construction

MANUFACTURERS LIFE CENTRE
OWNED BY ITS POLICYHOLDERS

The Manulife Centre: 1967 to Today

Michael Clifford

Michael Clifford Architect Inc. (successor to Clifford & Lawrie Architects; Clifford, Lawrie, Bolton, Ritchie Architects; Clifford & Lawrie Architects Inc.)

In 1967 the partnership of Clifford & Lawrie Architects was approached by the Real Estate Division of the Manufacturers Life Insurance Company to prepare a study for a rezoning application to the City of Toronto for the development of the entire city block above a subway station, with office, retail and residences, on a property at Bay and Bloor streets. Other Toronto architectural firms were already engaged in the same study, independent of each other. Clifford & Lawrie was selected with a solution that was apparently more relevant to Manufacturers Life in certain key areas.

There was no single 'author' responsible for the design concept of the Bloor Bay Centre (renamed the Manulife Centre in 1970). The members of the initial design team came from a mixed architectural training background – late-'40s and early-'50s RIBA qualification examinations and diplomas from art schools and schools of architecture in England, Scotland and Canada – and their influences ranged widely, including almost all the contemporary designers, from Sullivan to Mies van der Rohe, and many more. No architectural dogma or design philosophy governed the project concept, but rather the interpretation of the program created the massing and relationships of masses. The program was formulated by the client's appreciation and knowledge of the current and projected real estate market, and as architects we had no influence on these market assumptions.

Early massing studies accepted the premise that the City was looking forward to high-density, high-rise projects in the Bloor/Yonge hub, but the scale of the mixed-use components in this project was unusual for a major North American or European city at that time. To reach a 'comfort level' the client's project leaders and Clifford & Lawrie Architects principals, in pairs, visited the U.S. west coast, Chicago, New York and Boston, and France, Germany, Sweden and England, to assess built mixed-use projects.

A very significant impact on the concept was the legislation in force at that time governing the maximum cost (size) of a single real estate project by life insurance companies, expressed as a percentage of their total assets. This constraint, together with the ongoing retention of two prime retailers on Bloor Street, set up the two-phase construction framework. It also limited the gross floor area of the first phase,

Fig. 16. Precast panels affixed to concrete frame of residential block

resulting in the incorporation of the Bay Street waterfall, courtyard and reflecting pool, which did not increase the permitted zoning gross floor area.

The site-specific bylaw was approved by the City on June 18, 1969, and the design development and contract documentation started on the 51-storey tower with 797 apartments; 16-storey; 500,000-square-foot office building; 250,000 square feet of retail in three levels; and the three-level 1,200-space underground parking – ultimately some 2.1 million square feet of construction area.

The major consultants in the team included Farkas Barron (N.Y.), Jablonsky (Toronto) structural and ECE mechanical and electrical, as well as the early involvement of building science expert (the late) Kirby Garden and construction manager Goldie Burgess, with access to experienced concrete subcontractors.

Concurrent with the work on the architectural concept, the preferred structural system was evolving with poured-concrete shear walls at 24 feet on centre for the 56 floors of the apartment slab and its retail and parking substructure, with 30-foot-by-30-foot bay flat slab dropped panel in the balance of the project – the three retail/commercial podium floors, the 17-floor office building and the three levels of sub-grade parking.

Within the Phase Two office building, cranked columns and post-tensioned beams at the third through the eighth floors provide the 20-foot-wide increase at sidewalk level on Bloor and additional area for the very significant soft landscaped area between Phases One and Two, three levels above the adjacent streets. While the original-design main entrance was expressed by a second-floor exterior platform and stairs to the Bloor Street sidewalk, the current entrance experience is through the 1983 precast-concrete-clad steel-framed atrium, fully responsive to the form of the office building.

By the late 1960s, it was recognized by the National Research Council in Ottawa that all structural poured reinforced concrete (shear walls, slabs, columns, balcony slabs) needed to be thermally protected (precluding an exposed poured-concrete design that by definition is Brutalistic). Manulife was one of the first large-scale projects to follow this principle, and the visible exposed concrete is indeed a cladding system. A careful and detailed examination of the cladding alternatives covered all options – stone, brick, aluminum and glass window walls – and settled on precast concrete with a light acid-etched finish. The wall assembly is complex – a complete rain screen with deeply formed 24-foot-by-8-foot and 30-foot-by-11-foot-8-inch precast 'shingles' complete with glazed window components. These were set at the outside quarter points on the slab edge with slip joints at the top anchoring and columns, the profile maximizing shadow and light interplay on all four elevations (Toronto's grid being off true north-south) and ensuring a dominant but tolerant pattern within the discipline of the main structural grid. Large-scale details and mock-ups of the precast/glazed units were developed with industry and

Fig. 17. Public square and podium roof garden

building science participation, and construction management skills recognizing the challenge in installing the large units on the high-rise structure. The look of the building was always imagined to be textured, opaque and solid – something the precast cladding achieved to great effect.

With the original design concept for the apartment tower incorporating balconies in all the apartments, the working drawings were well underway with two central HVAC systems located at the 24-foot-high 31st floor, when a visit to Marina City in Chicago convinced the four client/architect leaders (by a vote of three to one) to make a radical change by abandoning the balconies, excepting the west and east ends of the third and fourth floors. This change allowed electrical incremental 'through-the-wall' HVAC units in each of the exterior rooms on all floors in the apartment tower. This was a relevant decision in 1970, and today is manageable because of the relatively high R-value – or heat-flow resistance – of the original wall, the

carefully designed and maintained air seals and sealed glazing units in the rain-screen wall assembly. Because of this change, significant 31-floor HVAC areas were available to accommodate even more extensive tenant amenities added to the 51st- and 52nd-floor swimming pools and fitness and recreation facilities already incorporated in the original program.

While the rental-apartment tenants include many of the original occupants, many changes to the retail areas have been made over the years and continue today. In 1986 the courtyard, waterfall and reflecting pool were replaced by a three-storey, 60,000-square-foot retail store. In time, this was replaced by the existing iconic bookstore, and in 1996 by the insertion/addition of six stadium-style cinemas and four VIP viewing lounges (MCA Inc. in joint venture with Crang & Boake), in addition to the two conventional cinemas already in use in the original Phase One construction. The Manulife Centre continues as a truly living entity!

Fig. 18. Manulife Centre Phase Two, under construction

MANULIFE CENTRE
PHASE TWO

Fig. 19. A concrete landmark, the Manulife Centre nears completion, as seen from Yonge and Bloor streets

MANULIFE CENTRE

The CN Tower: Four Small Propositions about Toronto's Tallest Concrete Building

Michael McClelland

Principal, E.R.A. Architects

Editor

First small proposition: *Recognize the CN Tower as a National Historic Site. It currently is not.*

Look at the CN Tower from a distance. Now picture that the Eiffel Tower is about three-fifths its height. Or that the Great Pyramid of Giza is only one-quarter its height. Or that Big Ben is a pocket watch in comparison. You would need six Big Bens, one on top of the other, to match the height of the CN Tower. Obviously height isn't everything, but, recognizing that Toronto has had the tallest free-standing structure in the world since 1976, one does ponder why it has so little emotional impact on our urban psyche when these other structures carry such iconic weight.

Possibly the closest comparison to the CN Tower is not the Eiffel but the Ostankino in Moscow. The Ostankino Tower was erected in 1967 and was the tallest free-standing structure in the world for the 10 years before the CN Tower was built. The Ostankino is a mere 13 metres shorter, and one can imagine the Cold War competitiveness at play. Built by the national railways as they expanded into telecommunications, the CN Tower was not so much about Toronto, but more about the play of nations and Canada within a global context. Canada's role in international affairs during the late 1960s and early '70s was felt to be one of strength, industry and optimism. Today we are as distanced from that comfortable nationalism as we are from the CN Tower.

Second small proposition: *Provide the CN Tower with a public street address and a dignified urban setting. Connect the tower to the city.*

Now try to get closer to the CN Tower. Really close. Go up and try to put your arms around it – yes, that's right, try to give the tower a big hug. It is difficult to get there because the unfortunate design that clutters the base makes close contact almost impossible. While most Torontonians have ridden to the top of the tower with visiting friends or relatives once or twice, few have experienced it as an object in the street, as it is so concealed in its context.

A basic rule of urban planning is that landmarks require carefully considered settings. They can even be used to organize the public space around them – just think again of the Eiffel Tower or even of the Ostankino, which sits in an amazingly large open space. The siting of the CN Tower is not what it could be. It is hemmed in by the operating rail tracks and blocked from the downtown by the perfectly functional, perfectly necessary, but clumsily designed Metro Convention Centre. The convention centre might be considered the clumsiest large-scale building in the city if it weren't for the CN Tower's massive friend, the Rogers Centre, which sits far too close to the tower for the creation of any generous public space.

Fig. 20. CN Tower under construction

Third small proposition: *Let the CN Tower remind us to think big; it is essential for well-planned city growth.*

The CN Tower was all that was built of the Metro Centre Plan – a gigantic proposal for the 1960s and '70s urban renewal of the CN/CP railway lands designed by WZMH and John Andrews (the eventual architects for the CN Tower). The plan was in many ways an imposition on the city. It called for the demolition of Union Station and it represented urban renewal as infrastructural change, at a time when Toronto was beginning to focus on an urbanism that valued exclusively the qualities of the smaller scale, primarily experienced in our charming older neighbourhoods.

For years afterward the railway lands lay undeveloped and only recently have they been built upon. A comparison between the Metro Centre Plan and what in fact has been built around the CN Tower would be constructive. I don't regret at all that the Metro Centre Plan did not go forward, but we may find that by ignoring and denying the infrastructural scale of city development, it has snuck in through the back door. The CN Tower reminds us that cities work at many scales, and we need to consider them all.

Fourth small proposition: *Lighten up, Toronto. Toronto needs its superheros. Toronto needs to connect with its aspirations. Sometimes it is okay to be world-class.*

I was in Japan when the CN Tower was being completed, and my then-teenaged brother Andrew reported to me frequently on how quickly the tower was rising. He was not a big architecture fan, but his enthusiasm for the building of this mammoth construction was genuine, engaged and popular. He told me he had lined up so that our names could be put in a time capsule that was placed at the top of the tower. There was a sense of positive energy about modernity in the city that worked. Torontonians were proud of the CN Tower. The CN Tower was a superhero.

While I am still impressed by the tower's elegance and phenomenal monumentality, it is true that most Torontonians are no longer buoyed by its optimism. Our current cultural mood is overcast with irony and negativity, far removed from the more innocent times of the CN Tower's construction. The tower stands as our Ozymandias, a marker of an almost distant past.

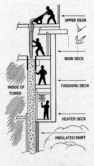

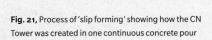

Fig. 21, Process of 'slip forming' showing how the CN Tower was created in one continuous concrete pour

Fig. 22. The CN Tower under construction

Figs. 23, 24. CN Tower slip forming in process

Fig. 25. Plan of observation deck, built out from concrete shaft 346 metres from the base

Fig. 1. Apartment at Flemingdon Park, designed by Irving Grossman

concrete toronto   the modern suburbs

Toronto's Modern Suburbs and the Concrete High-Rise

Graeme Stewart

E.R.A.Architects

Editor

*'In Toronto, an unusually large number of high-rise apart-
ments poke above the flat landscape many miles from
downtown.... [T]his is a type of high density suburban
development far more progressive and able to deal with
the future than the endless sprawl of the U.S....'*

Buckminster Fuller, 1968

Though the vastness of Toronto's suburbs is often
bemoaned as unplanned sprawl, their shape tells
a different story. Containing extensive parks and
protected natural systems, transit infrastructure,
industrial zones, cultural and community facilities, universities, modern planned communities
and, perhaps most noteworthy, hundreds upon
hundreds of high-density concrete high-rise
apartment buildings, Toronto's 'metro' suburbs
showcase a process of metropolitan growth
highly affected by regional and modern planning. Financed by the economic boom of the '60s
and '70s, these expansive areas of Toronto take
on a form unique to North America and perhaps
the world.

Created in 1954 as the only metropolitan government in North America other than New York,
Metropolitan Toronto administered a rapidly
growing region that was more rural than urban.
Aiming to fill inside its borders and leave what
lay beyond untouched, Toronto engaged in a
series of urban experiments located in what
are today known as the GTA's 'inner suburbs.'
This has left the city a remarkable modern and
concrete legacy.

In the wake of the formation of Metro, Toronto
became an attractor for internationally trained
modern planners. Some were lured by the
booming economy, rapid growth and the promise of regional planning via the metropolitan
government, while others defaulted to Toronto
due to McCarthyite politics south of the border.

Among the notables was Briton Gordon Stevenson, a leader in welfare-state planning who was
deeply involved in establishing the U.K.'s New
Towns Act, legislation encouraging the creation
of dozens of modern planned satellite communities around London and other large cities. While
in Toronto, in addition to work with the planning
department, Stevenson served a brief tenure as
the director of the nascent school of planning at
the University of Toronto. Another import was
E. G. Faludi, a Hungarian-born, Roman-trained,
modern architect and planner who was an early
advocate for Toronto's adoption of the tower-in-
the-park. His early planning work, dating back
to the 1940s, helped shape the region, particularly the boroughs of Etobicoke and North York.
Perhaps the most infamous of these characters
was German-American émigré, modern planner
and card-carrying Communist Hans Blumenfeld.
Though later villainized as the architect of the
city's highway system, he was also largely responsible for establishing regional rail transit (now
the GO system) and advocated for employment,
commerce and mixed-housing types throughout
the Metro area.

In conjunction with professional imports, a significant number of local planners and designers
received modern training internationally, while
at the University of Toronto, faculty successfully
pushed for a modern curriculum within the design
schools. The resulting combination of an eclectic
mix of eager professionals, as well as a regulatory
framework enabling the implementation of large-
scale planning, set the stage for urban growth that
was highly influenced by modern ideas.

Fig. 2. From farmer's fields to field of high-rise apartments – suburban development in Toronto, 1960s

This might explain the early success of developments such as Don Mills, Thorncliffe Park and Flemingdon Park, the plans for which were approved in 1953, '55 and '59 respectively. Beginning with E. P. Taylor's famous Don Mills, these communities were loose interpretations of the satellite town, a concept that had gained currency since the turn of the century, but had never been fully implemented on this side of the Atlantic. Macklin Hancock, who designed the Don Mills project while finishing his master's degree at Harvard, brought these European ideals to the farmers' pastures of north Toronto. These ideas were pushed further in the Thorncliffe and Flemingdon communities, which included large numbers of high-rise, tower-in-the-park apartments, a move that would have a significant impact on the future shape of the region. Providing industry, shopping, mixed-housing types, ample natural open space, and insisting that all structures be modern in character, these neighbourhoods quickly became a showpiece of high design (concrete included) and an attractive alternative to living downtown.

Fig. 4. Shops, elementary school and high-rise apartments: Flemingdon Park under construction

The introduction of high-rise towers met the growing need for rental units, and helped organize housing in high-density concentrations to better align communities with Metro's services. Influenced by similar European efforts, such as the high-rise new town of Vallanby in Sweden and London's Roehampton, and privately financed through a series of partnerships including a New York real-estate conglomerate, these communities illustrate a bold change in suburban planning internationally. They were a loosely European plans implemented by the North American free market. The result is unmistakably Torontonian, with local architects Irving Grossman and Raymond Moriyama providing the high-quality housing and cultural facilities that give these areas much of their lasting character.

Fig. 3. Model of Flemingdon Park, late 1950s

Although the master-planning approach to these early experiments didn't take hold, building suburbans tower did. Subsequently, the suburban high-rise became the most popular housing type for a period of nearly 20 years, representing some 60 percent of the development market. Thirty-thousand high-rise units were built in 1968 alone. Highways, arterials, ravine sites and the edges of bungalow communities were flagged by planners as preferred zones for apartment development, and developers were more than happy to oblige.

For the most part privately developed but publicly directed, the region was neatly organized into natural areas, and employment, institutional and residential zones, all contained within Metro's borders. Archival photographs illustrating fields of 30-storey towers at Metro's northern edge on Bathurst Street, adjacent to undeveloped pastures north of the Steeles Avenue 'greenbelt,' recently prompted *Globe and Mail* reporter John Barber to proclaim:

Not since the first bird's-eye views of the Italian Renaissance has a city looked so coherent: the densely human, heavily built-up urbe ending abruptly – and totally – at an ancient wall heavy with meaning, the Arcadian rus rolling unbroken to the horizon in striking contrast ... Although the wall surrounding 1960s Toronto was made of policy, not stone, the meaning was still there. No other city in North America built high-density suburbs like these during the long postwar boom. Few modern cities in the world, if any, were better planned than Metropolitan Toronto.[1]

Fig. 5. Bathurst and Steeles, the edge of Metropolitan Toronto, 1960s

Toronto is perhaps the only place where never-ending seas of bungalow subdivisions and concrete high-rises coexist as the typical suburban landscape. In some respects sharing closer affinity to outer Paris, Belgrade or Moscow than to the suburbs of our American cousins, Toronto's experience with modern planning has produced results unique to this continent. This perhaps calls into question the standard reading of our region and points to an enormous resource of modern dwellings worthy of further study.

In addition to housing, the suburbs of the '60s and '70s were programmed with shopping centres, religious institutions, community facilities, transportation infrastructure and universities during a period of remarkable architectural experimentation, particularly with concrete design. This provided a venue for the likes of Grossman, Dickinson, Parkin, Andrews, Moriyama, DuBois, Erickson, Prii and a long list of other giants of the era to help define the 'golden age' of modernism in Canada through their work in Toronto's periphery.

It might be argued that modernism got its start in Toronto in the suburbs. It certainly had its greatest impact there. Not all of the original ideas were realized, nor all of the results successful, yet the quality and diversity of projects speak of the climate of social investment, regional planning and great optimism, for which today there is a palpable nostalgia. Approaching half a century, this period of suburban growth deserves a second look. The articles that follow shed light on several of these remarkable projects.

Notes

1. John Barber, 'Neglected High-Rises Hold the Key to a Sustainable Future,' *The Globe and Mail*, May 27, 2007.

Fig. 6. 3380 Weston Road (MAP P. 18)

The Age of Modern High-Rise Construction

Ivan Saleff

Architect, Assistant Professor, Faculty of Architecture, Landscape and Design, University of Toronto

'We must create the mass-production spirit.The spirit of constructing mass-production houses. The spirit of living in mass-production houses. The spirit of conceiving mass-production houses.'

Le Corbusier, *Vers Une Architecture*, 1923

The esprit nouveau Le Corbusier championed so long ago, during the age of the machine, was ironically reincarnated in the space age. The purist paradox of classical formalism married with contemporary technologies and modes of production was to redefine affordable shelter in Toronto. The sublime non-stylistic aesthetic of Canadian poured-concrete grain elevators that so inspired Le Corbusier would thrive in this post-Levittown age.

The Jetsons were on TV, Yorkville was electric, Neil was young, McLuhan was in fine form, Revell's City Hall design materialized complete with Moore's *Archer*, and the Beatles, the Stones and Zeppelin were in the air. The Maple Leafs were a dynasty. While our siblings south of the border experienced the '60s as turbulent times, Toronto optimistically embraced the decade as the beginning of a new world. A variety of lifestyle choices offering new directions appeared. High-rise living was one of them.

Not since mountainside cave dwellings had such panoramic views from one's home been available. Autos were neatly stabled in the concrete belly of the tower, with speedy elevators on hand to transport occupants to their homes above. Swimming pools, landscaping, furnished lobbies, inspired entry canopies and multi-purpose rooms were among the amenities helping to convey a perception of luxury modern living.

For a 20-year period beginning in the early '60s, high-rise living embedded itself in Toronto's housing consciousness. A rare alliance occurred of unprecedented population growth and market demand, affordable urban and suburban sites, demographic characteristics, planning policies, opportunistic developers, a robust labour force and new technologies. This fertile scenario was in great part anchored by an ancient recipe of water, sand, cement, aggregate and slender steel rods. Reinforced concrete structure became the system of choice.

The technology of the reinforced eight-inch concrete one-way slab and shear wall construction provided the city's residential high-rises with highly efficient and durable armatures.

Fig. 7. Thorncliffe Park under construction

Fig. 8. Thorncliffe Park emerging from the Don Valley

The simple redundant six-metre spans complemented both unit layouts and below-grade parking. The introduction of flying-form technology, coupled with advancements in crane design, generated taller buildings. Twenty storeys high, 200 units, with two levels of below-grade parking, became a standard.

Rectangular slabs, square point towers, Y-shaped and cruciform plan typologies began to appear all over Toronto's urban and suburban horizon. The subsequent increase in living units relative to building footprint dramatically reduced construction costs on a per-unit basis. Substantial densities were achieved with relatively compact footprints. Le Corbusier's idealistic vision was to replace cramped, antiquated Parisian slums with 20th-century shelter, elevating the quality of life of its inhabitants. The agenda of our space-age megaliths was less altruistic – rather a rapid response to enormous demand.

These ordinary, underappreciated, aging megaliths may once again transform Toronto's horizon. Their sturdy poured-concrete skeletons for the most part are still in the early stages of their life cycle. Their solid-masonry exterior walls and infrastructure have, however, reached a durability threshold. Contemporary environmentally responsive over-cladding and other strategies offer viable vehicles for rehabilitation and aesthetic transformation. (See Durability, page 314.)

The present and future value of Toronto's vintage high-rise housing inventory is indisputable. How such a seemingly monolithic construct, virtually medieval in its materiality, can continue to be relevant into the next century is a testimony to both the durability of the typology and its system of choice.

The Flying Form and Development in Toronto

Lewis Poplak

Context Development

A harsh winter wind buffets the tarpaulin-walled 11th floor of a Toronto condominium building under construction. Here, gas-fired heaters work to maintain a minimum temperature required for concrete to undergo its exothermic setting process. Overhead, a tower crane boom swings as it lifts a palette of flying formwork from the 12th to 13th floors, where a contingent of workers will knit a mesh of steel rebar into the plywood and metal form, readying it for the bucket loads of wet concrete hoisted from the street below.

This scene typifies the landscape of a 21st-century Toronto residential construction boom. The industry-standard construction method is called flying-form concrete construction. It was born out of an ingenious response to increased labour costs and an ever-diminishing labour pool in Toronto's construction industry of the 1960s. Using the innovation of the climbing tower crane, first aluminum and eventually plywood forms – moulds – were hoisted from storey to storey as the building was constructed. This replaced the earlier handset-form method, and was not only less labour-intensive (a typical handset form was at largest two by four feet and had to be disassembled to move to the next floor), but also allowed much larger forms (10 or 15 feet in width), thereby greatly reducing the time it takes to construct a building.

Flying-form construction literally raised the roof in an apartment building market that had previously been comprised primarily of six- to eight-storey buildings, and introduced Toronto to the high-rise residential tower of 30 storeys and beyond. High-rise slab apartment buildings spread across the city, towering like *War of the Worlds* Martian tripods over Toronto's sleepy bungalow neighbourhoods. Working hand in hand with the creation and expansion of Toronto's highway and subway systems, starting in 1954, the flying-form-constructed apartment building helped Toronto's population double from 1 million in 1951 to 2 million by 1971. Toronto's flying-form innovators are regarded to have been the developer/builders the Greens and the DelZottos, as well as builder Nick di Lorenzo. (Engineers who worked on early flying-form buildings include Jablonsky and Yolles.)

The extremely efficient construction made possible through the local perfection of the flying form has made high-rise housing a defining feature of Toronto and its suburbs for nearly half a century. Though still popular for its simplicity and ease of construction, the double-loaded slab building of the past has been joined on the development scene by a building type – the point tower – that lends itself equally well to flying-form construction, but has a more elegant and less intrusive profile on the skyline. In the point tower – typically having a floor plate of 8,000 square feet or less, shear walls are placed in a cruciform, rather than parallel, pattern. While the '60s apartment boom has given way to today's condomania, vertical living enabled through concrete construction continues to be fundamental in shaping our city and how we live in it.

Fig. 9. High-rise apartments emerging around the 'Peanut,' Sheppard and Don Mills Road

Uno Prii: Sculptor in Concrete

Alfred Holden

Writer, and editor of the Ideas section, *The Toronto Star*

'It comes as a liquid,' an interviewer reflected, talking with Uno Prii about concrete in 1999. 'And you took that and you made it into sculptures.' Prii liked the idea of buildings that were not repeating patterns, but more flowing, sculptural wholes. Spurred on by the zoning laws of the 1960s (which in the Toronto region commonly encouraged free-standing towers on large lots), and the ease and economy with which such towers could be built using the new flying forms (reusable moulds allowing his concrete designs to be poured 'without interruption,' as *Canadian Builder* reported in 1964), the architect produced some of Canada's most distinctive urban and suburban residential architecture.

Prii's 22-storey apartment tower at 20 Prince Arthur Avenue, in Toronto's downtown Annex district, looks from the side like a soaring pair of bell-bottom pants, flaring fashionably at the base (mod meets medieval; Prii said he was inspired by the flying buttresses on European cathedrals). A few blocks west, 44 Walmer Road offered a point tower whose undulating facades of balconies were dressed (until regrettable alterations) in a fabulous railing of steel panels with circular cutouts, bisected by thin, straight lines of metal. The circle theme repeated in cutouts in the concrete entrance canopy and the building's round fountain, where water shot from a concrete trumpet beneath intersecting arches.

Prii ambitiously embellished the era's slab apartment houses. A stylized rendering of a project for Belmar Realty on Jane Street in the Toronto suburb of North York shows the proposed building in profile. The shape flares out, then tapers back as it rises to soaring points. The only straight line is an indentation that rises from base to summit in the sculpted bookend. At intervals along the front and back of the slab, matching protrusions repeat, so the building seems supported by a series of these abstract forms. The grouping of five similar buildings eventually constructed to this design on Jane Steet north of the 401, ('the Exbury buildings'), presents a startling artistic installation visible, among others, to airline passengers on approach from the east to Pearson International Airport. In Prii's own words, 'I could see apartment buildings as giant sculptures. I thought people would remember these buildings. ... I got tired, eventually, of these straight boxes,' he remembered. 'I thought, "Let's have a little fun."'

Uno Prii was born in Tallinn, Estonia, on February 28, 1924, the son of an engineer-builder. Given a pen and bottle of brown ink for his 10th birthday, he immediately showed his aptitude and got high grades for drawing in school. He left Estonia in 1943 during the German occupation and joined the Finnish navy, and after the war he earned a degree in engineering at Stockholm Technical Institute. In Sweden he married Silvia, whom he'd met in Estonia, and in 1950, after Prii enrolled by mail in the University of Toronto's School of Architecture, the couple moved to Canada.

At U of T, Prii scored top marks despite his poor English and was hired to work summers at Fleury & Arthur, the partnership of one of his professors, the famed, eccentric Eric Arthur. Opening his own practice in 1957, near the beginning of a high-rise apartment-house boom, Prii initially executed commissions he later called 'unrecognizable from other apartments.' But he began offering more expressive designs – 'a few clients were sympathetic.' His breakthrough came in meeting

Fig. 10. Jane Exbury Towers, Jane Street, north of Highway 401

Harry Hiller, an enterprising Polish-born carpenter-turned-developer whose principal instruction was 'Just don't bankrupt me.' Prii, helped by his engineering background and some hand-holding with concrete contractors ('Oh no, you can't do it,' the architect recalled one responding to an unusual specification), was able to express himself within a market-driven budget.

The architect's best-known buildings have been compared to the embellished Miami modernism of Morris Lapidus, whom Prii admired. They won no awards from a generally skeptical architectural establishment, and at one point *Toronto Life* ranked 44 Walmer with Robarts Library as among Toronto's five ugliest buildings. This outsiders' opinion notwithstanding, Prii's creations were popular with tenants, among whom they have had cult status for a generation now; in recent times there has been a reappraisal of their significance and they have enjoyed acclaim as among the most original works of the period.

'Uno Prii's buildings were a shock to the Toronto of his day,' members of the Toronto Society of Architects wrote to Toronto's preservation board in 2003, supporting the inclusion of a number of Prii's buildings on the city's list of heritage properties. 'While dealing with the difficult economies of private development, often for rental houses, his buildings showed an unbridled enthusiasm for newness and innovation.'

Responding to old controversy and new praise in 1999, Prii put it more simply: 'My designs are original. And originality is the hardest thing to come by.'

Fig. 11. 88 Spadina Road, south facade

Fig. 12. Porte cochère, 44 Walmer Road

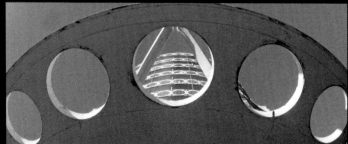

Uno Prii:
Vertical Sculpture

Interview with Uno Prii

Architect

UNO PRII was a prolific architect specializing in
concrete high-rises. The following is an Interview
conducted by Alfred Holden at the home of Uno and
Sylvia Prii in August 1999.

Alfred Holden   You're quite famous now for your work in Toronto, but have you done
any work outside of Canada?

Uno Prii   Yes, I did some apartment buildings across the lake in Ohio and I had one Toronto
client who had lots of properties in Miami, so I did some buildings over there.

Alfred Holden   You did some in Miami?

Uno Prii   I did the design, and my client took my design to Miami who hired a local
architect who did the working drawings.

Alfred Holden   Did you ever meet Morris Lapidus?

Uno Prii   I never met him, but I know him very well! I saw lots of his buildings in
Miami. I quite actually liked what he did.

Alfred Holden   What did you like about his designs?

Uno Prii   Well, I thought that some of his things, at that time – mind you, I won't
compare it to what we have now – were quite flamboyant. His buildings were
white. In Toronto, at that time, everything was dark, grey, or grey and brown.
Our climate wasn't exactly sunny, so maybe it fit into the surroundings, you
know, but this was an improvement. It made it more cheerful.

Fig. 13. Jane Exbury Tower, Jane Street north of the 401

Alfred Holden	**You chose white for a lot of your buildings.**
Uno Prii	Oh yes.
Alfred Holden	**So Lapidus's buildings were one of the influences?**
Uno Prii	I would say yes, that was one of the influences. But actually I wasn't influenced by what Lapidus did, design-wise. I just liked the whiteness of the buildings. And not only Lapidus, but a lot of other buildings in Miami were white.
Alfred Holden	**Your buildings have been compared to Miami buildings, having a sort of 'exuberant' style.**
Uno Pri	You might say so.
Alfred Holden	**I interviewed some people who lived in one of your buildings when they were new and they said it was very glamorous to move into one of your buildings.**

Figs. 14, 15. 20 Prince Arthur, perspective, elevation

Fig. 16. 35 Walmer, perspective

Fig. 17. Jane Exbury Towers, perspective

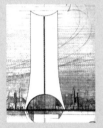  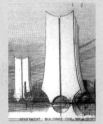

Uno Prii — I'm glad to hear it! Now at 20 Prince Arthur, they just renovated it a few years ago – new owners, and they did a fabulous job, painted the building. It looks like brand-new.

Alfred Holden — **That's your favourite one, isn't it?**

Uno Prii — My favourite. I guess so.

Alfred Holden — **Did your clients just want cheap buildings and walk away when you gave them something more exuberant?**

Uno Prii — Some of them. But others absolutely liked what I was doing. One of them was Alan Schiff. He built those buildings at Jane Street, just north of the 401.

Alfred Holden — **But you weren't involved in the development part, I gather. You were what they call a full-commission architect. That is, you didn't invest yourself.**

Uno Prii — Right. If it had to be done, I'd get involved in rezoning, especially in the City of Toronto. Around this I would design it, and they would build it.

Fig. 18. Unrealized Uno Prii design

Fig. 19. Uno Prii with model of 20 Prince Arthur

Alfred Holden   I read a few older reports prior to this interview. One of them was the Faludi report on apartment-building development in the east Annex. The report talks about zoning requirements. What they seemed to require was bonusing – I think that's the right word they used – but basically you had to put your building on a lot with more open space around it. It seems to have affected a lot of your buildings.

Uno Prii   I wasn't influenced by Faludi at all. But I had to do lots of redrawing, just to get approval to design something, build something. I did some perspectives for Faludi when I was a student, though I don't recall what for.

Alfred Holden   Another subject I wanted to ask you about was flying forms.

Uno Prii   That was actually a very good invention because it speeded up the construction considerably. I think I did the first reinforced-concrete apartment building, on St. Clair at the southeast corner of Russell Hill. And it was a great improvement. Before that, you couldn't really do much with apartments, it was simply block and brick. At that time, we had difficulty finding the workmen who knew enough about concrete formwork. But from there on it took off. Somebody invented the flying form, and there it went.

Figs. 20, 21, 22. Unrealized Uno Prii designs

Alfred Holden	**Did you go regularly to the sites and do that architect's walk-around?**
Uno Prii	I would always have to go and see what they were doing – or actually, see what they were doing wrong. [Chuckles.] Which I did very often.
Alfred Holden	**Are you doing any drawing today?**
Uno Prii	Not in summertime, but wintertime I sit where you sit over there and do little sketches of imaginary buildings, and then throw them away. It's a pleasant pastime to use your imagination as to what could be done. But on the other hand, I find that the architects today are doing very interesting buildings. Some of them, at least. They are no longer in the straitjacket of this Bauhaus thing, just square or rectangular block. That was the climate I was designing in.
Alfred Holden	**Apartment buildings are really no longer built, are they? In Canada, or in Toronto.**
Uno Prii	Condos are being built. Rental housing is pretty well out. But condos, they're going up everywhere you go.

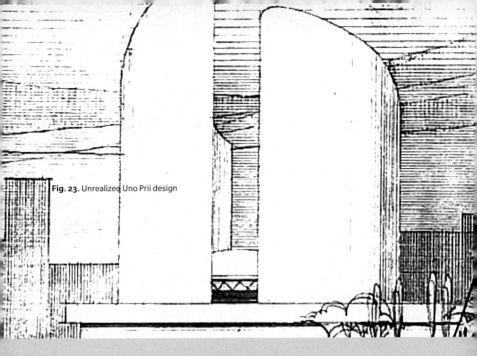

Fig. 23. Unrealized Uno Prii design

Alfred Holden	How is it the economics of the '60s allowed you to build fairly substantial concrete apartments for the middle class? These are not light, cheap buildings. And why is it they can't do that now?
Uno Prii	Well, it is rental controls. And escalating prices. Condos are a different story. You build condos, 500 square feet, just like a little hotel room, and say $100,000. Or they build half-a-million, million-dollar condos. Rich people always have the money. It doesn't make any difference what the economic situation is in the country. They have the money to buy it.
Alfred Holden	So really the middle class who used to rent apartments, now they'll buy a condo.
Uno Prii	Or they buy a condo and find it's a better deal than renting an apartment. After all, there's an investment in there and one day you sell it.
Alfred Holden	Maybe I should leave all the architecture behind for a second and ask you about your travels and your collection. One of the reasons I wanted to come here was to see what world you lived in.
Uno Prii	[Chuckles.]

Alfred Holden   Now, it looks to me like you've travelled all over the world, and collected.

Uno Prii   Not all over the world, but I have travelled a lot, especially in Europe.

Alfred Holden   Are these all mementos from your travels? Your art and your sculptures?

Uno Prii   [Gestures.] Well, this one here is a Mexican painter, Leonardo Nierman. This painting is my painting. Acrylic.

Alfred Holden   Now, you didn't mention that you painted.

Uno Prii   Oh yes yes.

Alfred Holden   Do you still paint?

Uno Prii   Yes, yes. But I haven't got enough wall space. [The apartment walls are full of paintings.]

Alfred Holden   Would you sell your paintings?

Uno Prii   No. We had a big house on Old Forest Hill Road. When I moved over here, friends took this and this and this. I figured I haven't got space for it. But maybe one painting here or so. I love to paint the flowerpots.

Fig. 24. Unrealized Uno Prii design

Fig. 25. Allen Brown Building, rendering

Fig. 26. Allen Brown Bulding, detail

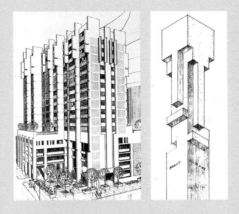

Alfred Holden	[Noticing.] Oh, yes. So you never embraced less is more, in terms of Spartan. Blank
Uno Prii	No, not quite. You know the famous saying, when some architect went to see the Seagram Building in New York, which at that time cost four times any other office building, all in bronze: 'I've never seen more of less.' [Chuckles.] I think that guy was right.
Alfred Holden	Did you ever meet Mies van der Rohe at a conference or anything?
Uno Prii	No, no no.
Alfred Holden	I wonder what a conversation between you would be like.
Uno Prii	At that time, I was a student, a young architect. If I would have met him I probably would have been influenced by him, in some ways; after all, he was such a famous architect then. It would have been a thrill to meet him. I have met Viljo Revell. That was before City Hall was completed. He died shortly after.
Alfred Holden	So did you chat with Revell about City Hall?

Fig. 27. 44 Walmer Road

Uno Prii   He was complaining that if he had known that the whole project would come in within the budget, he would have actually done some other things, which they had to cut out. His partners, who did the work, was Parkin Associates. But, anyway, as it turned out, it's a beautiful building. I like it very much.

Alfred Holden   What do you think of all the attention you're getting – people like me and also other journalists? Does it make you feel that maybe your work – ?

Sylvia Prii: I think it's wonderful, because it often happens if you are different, if you are more original – it takes time, but you get recognized.

Uno Prii   I'm gratified, personally. It's nice actually that now some people – there are a number of young architects who appreciate what I did. After all, it was my life's work. It's something I appreciate.

Uno Prii passed away in 2000. His work has had an unmistakable impact on the urban landscape in Toronto.

Ortho Pharmaceutical: Don Mills' International-Style Pinup Girl

Dave LeBlanc

Broadcaster and writer, architecture critic for the *Globe and Mail*

Like a Victorian warehouse stripped of its flesh, the bright white concrete skeleton of John C. Parkin's 1955 Ortho Pharmaceutical building shamelessly exposed itself to readers of the July 1956 issue of *Canadian Architect* like an International-style pinup girl.

But Ortho was no dumb blonde: her intelligent good looks were music to Don Mills master planner Macklin Hancock's ears, a sweet siren song to lure other white-collar industries to Canada's most important postwar planned community.

'Mack' Hancock didn't want the dirty industries associated with rough-and-tumble waterfronts sullying his new town, just as he didn't want carved stone gargoyles looking down from archways over fussy front doors on baronial mansions.

'Canada suddenly flowered – it wanted to be modern, it didn't want to be ancient,' Hancock explained to me over 50 years later in the studios of CFRB Radio.

By the 1960s, the third ring of his four-ringed community – ring one was Parkin's open-air shopping centre, ring two was housing and ring four was the protective greenbelt – was largely populated with 'clean' industry producing everything from electronics to textbooks

Fig. 28. Don Mills prior to construction

to architectural drawings. Hancock, always the persuader, convinced Parkin's firm to relocate their office to Don Mills by countering their collective raised eyebrow with, 'This is a new kind of industry, it's pharmaceuticals, it's not where you have a foundry!' Since the Don Mills rulebook specified that all buildings – whether houses, churches, banks or factories – must be modern, it proved a good move for the architects.

While sexier things like the small homes on wide 60-foot lots or the recently demolished Don Mills Shopping Centre usually get all the ink, it's worth remembering that a fully functioning town where people would live, work and play was the intention. Nothing would have made Hancock happier than seeing the town's twisty pedestrian pathways clogged with strolling commuters, but unfortunately the homes were too expensive for factory workers. In his 1993 book *The Shape of the City: Toronto Struggles with Modern Planning* (U of T Press, 1993), John Sewell estimated that 'only 5 per cent of the jobs were held by local residents,' and it's a safe bet the numbers haven't improved much.

But dismissing Mack's utopian vision of a glittering modernist new town because it didn't quite work out as planned would be like saying Plato's *Republic* has nothing to teach us. I suggest urban planners pick a street in Don Mills – perhaps forested Deepwood Crescent hard by the Don Valley Expressway – don their best stevedores and coveralls and walk Mack's intended pathway to industry ... and then figure out how to make it work the next time.

Fig. 29. Iconic image of Ortho Pharmaceutical, which graced the cover of *Canadian Architect* in 1956

The Don Valley Parkway and Suburban Growth

Graeme Stewart

E.R.A. Architects

Editor

Within the large-scale planning exercises following World War II, expressways were viewed as the key means of interconnecting the Toronto region and controlling its outward growth. Metro planners developed schemes for an extensive highway network, servicing every corner of the growing metropolis. The Don Valley Parkway was the first north-south portion to be realized.

The expressway went through several iterations before finding its final resting place along the length of the Don Valley. Originally intended to parallel the Don only downtown, north of the city it was to exist as a widened Don Mills Road. Fierce protests from developer E. P. Taylor, protective of his highly successful development of Don Mills, pushed the highway project east toward the ravine. The approval of the massive Flemingdon Park housing development on an undeveloped plateau south of Eglinton Avenue pushed the expressway off course once again, placing it in its current position. As such, it is a project shaped as much by development as by topography.

The new 'superhighway' was to enable the creation of a series of tightly designed modern communities loosely modelled after Don Mills along its length, separated by the ravine's green space. Flemingdon and neighbouring Thorncliffe Park were the first to take shape, as well as the first suburban communities in North America

Fig. 30. Don Valley Parkway, at Leaside Bridge

to consist of high-rise apartments. They were also designed to bring downtown amenities to the suburbs, including employment, retail and a new 'motor hotel.' Northern Flemingdon was originally planned to be the home of the CBC's new English-language headquarters, complete with a 'cultural village.' These developments satisfied the goal of carefully arranging highly organized suburban areas along infrastructure.

As the ideals of these satellite communities gave way to all-out suburbanization, the subsequent developments along the expressway were not as neatly conceived. However, vestiges of the planner's original intentions can still be seen in the high-density apartment clusters along the DVP's length, continuing well north of Highway 401, such as Park Forest, the Peanut and so on. The legacy of this development had made driving on the DVP one of the most modern experiences in the city and perhaps even the country. Rolling topography, a curving concrete highway and dozens of high-rise apartment buildings poking out amid the forest canopy create a linear essay in modern ideals.

Today the DVP exists as a period piece, its mere six lanes conceived long before Toronto became the congested metropolis of today. It was planned in an era when the pleasure drive was still a possibility and expressways were a novelty. For this true 'parkway,' the experience of the thoughtful curves was apparently as important to the concept as raw efficiency. Now well beyond capacity, the DVP is trapped in its bygone form by the ravine on either side, safe from development by the conservation authority. When stuck in today's endless gridlock, one can at least take in some of Toronto's most attractive vistas: big, green and thoroughly modern.

Fig. 31. Don Valley Parkway, at Eglinton Avenue, Flemingdon Park

Poured Stone Sculpture: A Tour of Toronto's Postwar Portes Cochères

Dave LeBlanc

Broadcaster and writer, architecture critic for the *Globe and Mail*

Zoomy. Zigzaggy. Womb-like. Shell-like. Sculptural.

New innovations in reinforced concrete allowed Toronto's postwar apartment builders to reinterpret the centuries-old form of the porte cochère in myriad ways. Rather than a bricks-and-mortar 'tent' surrounding the entrance, here were light, buoyant and abstracted forms, like much of the period's architecture. What had been a solid, two- or four-pillared structure designed to keep carriages and people out of the rain became yet another exercise in futuristic fancy; sometimes all that remained was a roof pitched upward at an angle so extreme it looked like it might blast off into outer space.

In 1950s Toronto, 'there was a palpable break with the past and its constricting ideas about spatial ordering and the use of decorative embellishment on buildings,' confirm Beth Kapusta and John McMinn in *Yolles: A Canadian Engineering Legacy* (Douglas & McIntyre, 2002). In other words, the porte cochère had become an excuse to create art with concrete.

One of Toronto's greatest masters of sculptural portes cochères – fronting equally sculptural apartment buildings – was Estonian-born architect Uno Prii, who passed away in November 2000 but left behind hundreds of reminders of his artistry (13 of which were designated heritage structures in early 2004). The parabolic arch hoisting the giant hula hoop that rings 44 Walmer Road is characteristic of Prii's mid-1960s work, which has often been compared to that of famed Miami Beach hotel architect Morris Lapidus.

On Eglinton Avenue west of Leslie, a Lapidus-inspired 'woggle' with a 'cheese hole' cut-out suspended by some 'bean poles' graces the front of an otherwise anonymous apartment building. Often, however, cut-outs in portes cochères were less about art and more about an effective way to transmit sunlight to plants below or liven up entryways with interesting shadow-and-light patterns.

Perhaps decorative elements like portes cochères, two-storey lobbies and jetting fountains were meant to lure a citizenry that, unlike in Manhattan, took longer to warm to the idea of apartment living (many 1950s articles questioned why people would give up single-family homes to become 'cliff dwellers').

With the high-rise taboo shattered by the 1970s, portes cochères – if incorporated into building designs at all – became utilitarian once again, taking the form of long, horizontal slabs supported by plain posts: a building sticking its tongue out. Today, like much in architecture, the trend is toward 'historical' styles, and many modern condominiums sport portes cochères that would look more at home on a 1920s hotel.

For those of us interested in real history, however, we need only cruise the wide suburban thoroughfares of yesterday to see what tomorrow was supposed to look like.

Fig. 32. Various examples of portes cochères from Toronto's stock of modern apartments

The Yonge Eglinton Centre: A Taste of Midtown Spiced with a Little Suburbia?

Robyn Huether

Associate, E.R.A. Architects

A friend and I set up on a strategically positioned bench with our Tim Hortons and Bailey's mix, preparing for a wintry afternoon of entertainment. We note the regulars – those who frequent this urban emporium – with small giggles and gestures, pondering their histories. Who is 'mystery man' with the Hawaiian shirt, who spends all day waiting. For what? The question remains. While contemplating his situation, my friend relays her joy at being the recipient of a distinguished nod from him. This officially inaugurates her as a member of this place, and I wonder when the time will come for my own inauguration.

The Yonge Eglinton Centre, the stage set chosen for our afternoon of diversion, is not a building notable for innovative design, but it's the definitive landmark of the area. Formerly the gateway to suburbia, the area was the last stop on the north-south line from Union Station when the subway originally opened in 1954. Eglinton marked the end of city concentration, yet quickly became not only the last stop but also a destination. The Yonge Eglinton Centre, designed by Toronto architect K. R. Cooper, began construction in 1968, contributing to the area's intensification and its establishment as the centre of many people's urban experience.

Breaking ground before the Manulife Centre, Toronto's other concrete mixed-used complex built atop the subway 4 kilometres to the south, the Yonge Eglinton Centre marked a bold move of suburban intensification long before the terms *smart growth* and *sprawl* were common parlance.

The development introduced a diversity that makes it part of the city's pulse: a large concrete mass that morphs into two large apartment buildings, an office tower, cinema and mini-mall for one-stop shopping. It's all within one roof or series of roofs, offering little reason to venture outside on blistering wintry days.

Built on an incline, the centre is designed to address multiple entries and street relationships that translate into an Escher-like interior, an ideal configuration for people-watching. From our perch, we note the piano player preparing for his afternoon of serenades, the elderly anxiously claiming their seats and the young professional rushing from gym to grocery store to liquor store, preparing for yet another dinner party. The tweenies race from escalator to escalator, waiting for the next matinee to begin. An urban jungle gym.

Oh, and you can't forget those residents who shop in their slippers.

Evolving along with the neighbourhood these past 40 years, the foreboding concrete mass of the Yonge Eglinton Centre, reaching low to the subway and high to the sky, claims the northwest corner at Yonge and Eglinton without any apologies.

Figs. 33, 34. Yonge Eglinton Centre under construction, amid the residential forest canopy, as well as a forest of modern high-rise apartments built in response to the subway

JCCC/Noor Cultural Centre

Raymond Moriyama, with Kathryn Seymour

RAYMOND MORIYAMA: Founding partner, Moriyama and Teshima, design architect

KATHRYN SEYMOUR : Moriyama and Teshima, Ballenford Books on Architecture, Landscape and Design

The Japanese Canadian Cultural Centre is a physical manifestation of a minority Canadian community that has struggled from social and cultural exclusion to inclusion. During World War II, discrimination, greed and political expedience bluntly forced Canadians of Japanese ancestry – 22,000 in all – into POW camps and internment camps, and to Alberta and eastern farms, in the guise of national security (security that the military denied was necessary, even at the time).

As the result of regained freedom at the end of the war in 1945, and the ability to vote for the first time in 1949, a flame was ignited in the hearts of a few community leaders. They decided to stabilize the emotionally shattered and economically impoverished community by giving it a 'home' to welcome not only its own members, but all Canadians and citizens worldwide. Its purpose was to enrich the social and cultural mosaic of Canada, moving forward through architecture that was unique, of high quality and delivered at a low cost.

Hired as the architect for the job, we saw it as our task to honour both our Japanese ancestry and Canada, embracing past and future and linking them in our design. The architecture, therefore, has a touch of Japanese, yet emerges with strength out of land that is Canada.

Contemporary Canadian technology was also employed. In addition to in situ concrete below grade, the essential structure and cladding material used was precast concrete. This enabled construction through the winter, reducing time and costs. To control quality, a key staff member, David Vickers, and I reviewed every precast and concrete block during production at the factories and during unloading at the site.

The design evokes a sense of stability and a respect for nature, while – in the '50s and early '60s – also provoking questions for the community. For example, the sidewalls in the auditorium asked, 'Are you still imprisoned by the experience of incarceration or by your memories of that time, or – instead of bars that constrain - can you also see windows to freedom and to future possibilities?'

The final cost in 1960 was $14.14 per square foot. It was low even in those days, but still over the budget by 1 percent, or 14 cents, and the architect heard about it from the client! The experience was a great lesson for a young architect just starting out: stay within the agreed budget.

In 2000, the JCCC moved to a larger facility and the building was sold to the Lakhani family. I was honoured by the Lakhanis' sensitivity, understanding and desire to have my firm convert the building into an Islamic cultural centre without destroying the original architectural integrity. The conversion was completed in 2004, and Moriyama & Teshima continue to enjoy a good relationship with the Noor Cultural Centre: a gratifying continuity from the 1950s to the present.

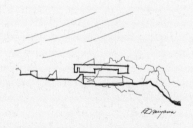

Fig. 35. Original concept sketch by Raymond Moriyama

Fig. 36. Japanese Canadian Cultural Centre, now the Noor Cultural Centre, at Eglinton Avenue and Don Mills Road

Fig. 37. Japanese Canadian Cultural Centre, south elevation

Fig. 38. Rendering of veranda

Fig. 39. Building cross-section

Fig. 40. Rendering of auditorium

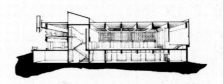

Ontario Science Centre

Raymond Moriyama, with Kathryn Seymour

RAYMOND MORIYAMA: Founding partner, Moriyama and Teshima, design architect

KATHRYN SEYMOUR : Moriyama and Teshima, Ballenford Books on Architecture, Landscape and Design

The Ontario Science Centre was a Centennial project by and for the Province of Ontario.

At the time of the commission, I was only 34 years old, making me the youngest architect to have ever been appointed by the province on any major project up to that time. In fact, at the very first meeting on the project, I was asked by the client if 'the boss' would be attending, and I had to assure those at the meeting that I was it!

Many young architects, especially those of minority backgrounds, viewed my appointment as a 'testament' and incentive that anything was possible with skill and motivation.

The project itself was late in starting, had no program and was hindered by disputes over management structure and institutional philosophy. However, the site was uniquely beautiful – its wonderfully wooded slopes and views were an architect's dream and challenge.

The initial concept was to create a new type of 'non-structure' in keeping with contemporary science and technology and to minimize impact on the site: the first iteration was an air structure like an inverted hydrofoil, without a physical covering, and the second scheme was a structure with a roof and air walls. Both schemes were rejected due to a lack of time for proper research and development. Instead, to commemorate the provincial centennial, the client requested a concrete building that would 'last a hundred years.'

The fundamental requirement was expressed in a clear, gutsy statement from then premier of the province John Robarts, who said that the Ontario Science Centre was 'to be an institution of international significance and world class.' Happily, the details were left wide open for the architect to interpret, challenge and develop.

I worked tirelessly day and night developing the program and architectural direction, and in that process a defining philosophy emerged: despite all of the emphasis on science and technology, *Homo sapiens* are intrinsically bound to earth, land and nature. Rooted in the nature of the site, the architectural concept was developed within a few short months based on this philosophy and on an old saying of Confucius made new again.

The master plan for the Ontario Science Centre was designed in the same way as for a town, in blocks of 20,000 square feet. Each block was designed as a flexible 'black box,' as the exhibit concepts were still unknown. The separate blocks were connected by linking elements that capitalized on views of nature beyond.

Ontario's provincial flower, the trillium, became a central symbol, manifested as the Great Hall that sits atop the only knoll in the valley: a symbolic unity of science, nature and people.

To control flooding in the valley around and under the lower exhibit buildings, and to preserve existing trees, the natural site contours, the watercourses and wetlands, required significant research and appropriate design measures.

The provincial cabinet of the day bravely approved an untried concept for programming the new museum that was termed 'hands-on' and based upon an old observation of Confucius: 'When you hear, you forget; when you see, you may remember some; but when you touch and

Fig. 41. Ontario Science Centre, perched atop the Don Valley

Fig. 42. Ontario Science Centre main entrance along Don Mills Road, showcasing a cast-in-place concrete surface

do, it becomes a part of you.' The team members were all convinced that 'touching and doing' were the only means by which the general public and the young could learn and truly come to appreciate the place of science and technology in their lives. The ultimate goal was to contribute to the enlightenment of future human resources in Ontario and Canada.

The needs of the physically challenged were also studied, and the design incorporated pragmatic measures to accommodate those with special needs. As a result, ramps and other features became integral to the overall design, rather than being relegated to an afterthought.

During construction, extreme care was taken to save existing trees by careful maintenance of the water table below grade and by inserting a clause in the contract specifications imposing a fine of $1,000 per tree to any contractors who carelessly allowed workers to cut unmarked trees. When the Department of Public Works first encountered this clause, their initial reaction verged on apoplectic. In the end, however, virtually no tree was lost through construction, and when the public lauded this outcome, Public Works generously accepted the accolades, even going so far as to suggest that they had instructed the architects to insert the 'tree penalty' clause in the contract.

Upon completion of the design, I recommended that the centre's programming be varied annually, with a complete overhaul and updating of exhibitions every 15 years. Unfortunately, this advice went unheeded for nearly 30 years, until attendance had fallen to far below initial levels. The internal innovation now taking place, with-

out affecting the original architectural integrity of the building, is remarkable.

However, beyond its lasting architecture, the 'hands-on' approach, shunned by most conventional institutions and curators of that era, was bravely adopted by the Ontario Science Centre. It was completely innovative at the time, and altered the subsequent approach and design of museums worldwide.

As well as an architectural legacy and museological legacy, the Ontario Science Centre also entrenched a philosophical design approach that has distinguished the work of Moriyama & Teshima since, and that defines it to this day: architecture is not simply the design of buildings, but a deeply collaborative process of 'placemaking' rooted in the connection of man, spirit and building to land, nature, site and context.

And the cost of all this groundbreaking innovation? Two million dollars under the agreed budget.

Fig. 43

Fig. 44   Fig. 45

Fig. 43. Ontario Science Centre, north facade

Fig. 44. Interior of great hall in central 'trillium' building

Fig. 45. Axonometric of OSC complex, sited within the Don Valley

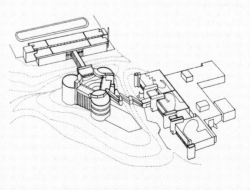

Yorkdale Shopping Centre

Veronica Madonna

E.R.A. Architects, Cindy Rendely Architexture

A curiosity that has lured shoppers from across Ontario, Yorkdale was the first suburban shopping centre in Canada that provided a real alternative to downtown retail. Opening in 1964 as the world's largest indoor shopping mall, it was based upon the most essential ingredient of suburban life – the automobile. Today one of the most popular shopping destinations outside of the Toronto urban core, Yorkdale is strategically situated with ready access to the Highway 401's daily traffic of half a million vehicles. Like the Great Pyramids perched in the desert, the Simpson's building of the Yorkdale Shopping Centre sits like a great monolithic structure in an asphalt landscape. The bold geometry of this building was designed to attract, lure and encapsulate all within its view. Even today, with over a million square feet of retail floor space, the Simpson's building stands out as the most recognizable force of the mall.

Yorkdale, like many North American shopping centres, is a product of postwar suburban development. Although some past versions of the shopping mall had surfaced as early as the 1920s, it was the postwar period of the 1940s and 1950s that saw a large increase in shopping-centre development. Yorkdale is a classic example of how, in the 1960s and '70s, the mall expanded to include not only retail stores, but also theatres and other places of activity. The shopping centre was established as a commodity for a world separate from urban life. Prior to Yorkdale, most people in the Toronto periphery did their shopping downtown. In short, the shopping centre transformed North American life in the 20th century by contributing to the rise of suburban communities. Yet, although suburban, Yorkdale was considered in no way second-rate. As in other suburban experiments in Toronto, such as Don Mills, top talent was enlisted to create on the outskirts all that was new and modern – giving the promise of a new world.

The Simpson's building is by far the most visible part of Yorkdale Mall. The project was designed by John B. Parkin Associates, with John Andrews as head designer, opening a year prior to the completion of Toronto's new City Hall. The Simpson's building established itself in the Brutalist style and demands to be seen while driving at rapid speeds. Much like the quest of suburbia, this architectural style is commonly associated with the search for a social utopian ideology. Its style is formalized in the facade of the Simpson's building through its rough, blocky appearance and the expression of its structural material and form. Its repetitious vertical piers stand like a fortress holding thousands of eager shoppers inside. Its exaggerated parapet, tilted slightly forward and reaching up to the sky, suggests endless possibilities. And as you walk inside, the concrete-vaulted ceilings make Yorkdale a shopping cathedral.

Like other suburban components established during the postwar period, the mall was developed with an individual connection to a larger external road. Built in anticipation of the Spadina Expressway, the Simpson's and Eaton's companies financed Yorkdale to take advantage of the new transportation junction at the Highway 401. While this aided in the success of the mall, some complications arose with increased traffic from shoppers leaving the complex at closing time, especially during the holiday seasons. As a result, Yorkdale has implemented seasonal all-night shopping extravaganzas to relieve traffic jams caused by hundreds of cars leaving the mall at once.

Fig. 46. North facade, Simpson's building, Yorkdale Shopping Centre

Over the decades, Yorkdale has come a long way from its isolated origins, and has in many ways become the social space for the multiple communities of North Toronto. In the 1970s, it became connected to the Spadina subway line, transforming it from peripheral to a node among nodes within Toronto's urban infrastructure. Also connected to the GO and Greyhound buses, it has become a commuter hub, and the first place of arrival for many to the city. Today, the mall continues to evolve, through multiple renovations and additions to meet changing shopping needs, and even includes several small office towers. As this trend continues, there is also the possibility of a more complex transformation, one that includes the prospect of new housing and public space networks that would change the 'Yorkdale Island' into an integrated part of adjacent communities.

Some of these opportunities may emerge in the reworking of the Lawrence Heights neighbourhood to the south. While many mid-century malls in North America lie empty or isolated as reminders of failed utopias, Yorkdale continues to thrive and grow, and may in fact become a focal point of an evolving 21st-century urbanism.

Fig. 47. Concrete vaulted sculptural ceiling, Yorkdale mall interior

Richard Serra – *Shift*

Adrian Blackwell

Artist, writer, architectural designer, urban researcher and Assistant Professor, Faculty of Architecture, Landscape and Design, University of Toronto

As his earliest site-specific work, and as a unique material experiment with concrete, *Shift* marks a double innovation during American artist Richard Serra's formative years as a sculptor.

By 1970, Serra's work had already moved through two distinct moments of development. The first was a period of experimentation with pure process, when he used lead to explore a set of material actions: tearing, rolling, cutting, melting and splashing. But Serra soon criticized this work, arguing that the function of the gallery floor as support and frame rendered the horizontal dispersion of material pictorial. In response, he initiated his prop works, using lead as a rigid material, leaning massive sheets against one another in a state of dynamic equilibrium, raising them to autonomous verticality. Here material no longer performed as an illustration of action; rather, process was perpetually re-enacted.

Shift, located in an open field by a wooded lot in King City, Ontario, allowed Serra to rethink aspects of both of these trajectories, introducing the complex relation between site specificity and sculptural autonomy that characterizes his mature work. As a series of concrete lines on the landscape, *Shift* cannot escape the pictorial, but the piece was not conceived in plan – it was sketched through the complex choreography of two bodies moving in relation to the existing topography. Just as Joan Jonas and Serra walked across the land, losing themselves behind the horizon of rolling hills, *Shift* enacts a complex oscillation between sculpture as vertical wall and horizontal line. Instead of a simple composition of figure on ground, *Shift* imbricates the experience of the viewer in a complex negotiation between these two terms. The sculpture clarifies

the contours of the site, such that one might claim the landscape as the subject of the work, but at the same time the sculpture asserts its absolute otherness in relation to its location.

Explaining why he uses steel in most of his works, Serra has argued that concrete is too architectural a material, and as a result he has used it in only two works: *Shift* and *Sea Level* (1996). In both cases, it is the architectural scale of the work and the emphasis on horizontality that pushed Serra to use a material that flows and is self-levelling, but catalyzes to solid. *Shift*'s concrete provided a bridge between the soft, sometimes liquid, characteristics of his early lead works and the machined quality of his later steel sculptures.

Figs. 48, 49. *Shift*: (1970-1972). Concrete, six sections: 5′ x 90′ x 8″; 5′ x 240′ x 8″, 5 ′x 150′ x 8″; 5′ x 120′ x 8″; 5′ x 105′ x 8″; 5′ x 110′ x 8″; overall 815′. Commissioned: Roger Davidson. Installed: King City, Ontario

Concrete Libraries in Toronto's Modern Suburbs

Chase Z. Li
Assistant Architect and Urban Designer, The Kirkland Parnership Inc.

Fairview Library and York Woods Library are two iconic North York branches of the Toronto Public Library that stand as architectural treasures in their respective areas. Both of these libraries were built during the heyday of public funding in the '70s and its consequent suburban construction boom.

These exposed-concrete libraries were a declaration of modern architecture in their neighbourhoods. They could easily be identified by their form: simple and solid concrete cube volumes designed with big frame windows and exhibiting themselves with an impassive concrete-grey colour. Their existence transformed the suburban vernacular from the traditional signature gable Carnegie building with Palladian three-part windows into the Brutal monumental style. Their design tendency, relying heavily on concrete, followed modern architecture development at that time, and the libraries were clearly inspired by Le Corbusier's milestone projects of the 1950s, such as Chandigarh (India) and Convent of La Tourette (France). By the '60s and '70s, these design ideas were widely disseminated throughout architecture and urban planning in Canada.

Fairview Library (35 Fairview Mall Dr.), designed by Brook Carruthers Shaw Architects, reveals a dramatic material confliction, with large transparent glass structures connecting solid concrete volumes. The large glass roof inclined backward to the building creates a well-lit entrance atrium

Fig. 50. Fairview Library, as seen from northwest

and reading spaces. The transparent glass wall connects and integrates indoor library activities with the outdoor civil activities. In the York Woods Library (1785 Finch Ave. W), architect Thomas Ioronyi designed the structure as a series of concrete volumes and angled walls. Taking cues from the aforementioned Chandigarh secretariat building, recessed windows with prominent angled concrete sunscreens allow controlled sun exposure and views to the street.

The designs of these buildings transmit a powerful presence on an otherwise predictable suburban landscape. Formally, they were the first considered architecture in these neighbourhoods, and they have created the context from which these neighbourhoods have evolved physically. Culturally, they represent the vital public-program key to any neighbourhood's success, and continue to thrive as much-cherished community nuclei. Within the past three decades, the demographic of each neighbourhood has changed considerably, resulting in the diverse Toronto we know today. In response, the libraries have begun providing equally diverse programming, from an expanded language collection to ESL training. The buildings themselves have also grown and evolved through subsequent renovation, yet maintain their prominent concrete character.

Rem Koolhaas has mused that shopping is the most dominant form of public activity, and it follows that the retail-dominated periphery of our large cities will grow culturally vacuous as a result. Yet the continued success of suburban public institutions such as the Fairview and York Woods libraries suggests that here, too,

Fig. 51. York Woods Library, as seen from northwest

in Toronto's modern suburbs, there is a place for thriving community and culture. Already vital anchors, these libraries and others like them can further integrate public and private services, connecting into adjacent shopping malls, high-rise apartments and bungalow neighbourhoods, creating an expanded public realm of community involvement.

Beyond their roles of housing access to free books within monumental architecture, these projects represent the postwar heritage of civic investment in a public and equitable Toronto. Expanding upon this legacy may be key to the success of 21st-century Toronto.

Ross Social Sciences and Humanities Building, York University

Philip Beesley

Architect and Associate Professor, University of Waterloo

The Ross Social Sciences and Humanities Building, opened in 1968, was designed to act as a grand front door to York University. Master-plan drawings dating from 1962 show the building as the key to the entire campus, its huge slab forming the edge of a pedestrian-oriented podium circled by a necklace of landscaped parking lots surrounded by farm fields. Gordon S. Adamson & Associates designed the project within the University Planners, Architects and Consulting Engineers (UPACE) group, a joint venture that included John B. Parkin Associates, and Shore and Moffat and Partners. The group was directed by Thomas Howarth, then director of the School of Architecture at the University of Toronto, and Hideo Sasaki, head of Landscape Architecture at Harvard.

The Ross Building was designed as an open framework with evolving functions, organized around a massive concrete frame. The building was conceived as the headquarters for a revolutionary new way of education, an integrated curriculum of two years of liberal-arts studies that encouraged general holistic thinking before moving on to advanced specialization. Exposed rows of rough-cast piers at the eastern edge, fronted by an enormous ramp stretching down from the upper podium level into parking grounds, made a great open stoa, a primordial temple front recast as an institution for the Age of Aquarius in the 1960s. Specialized areas – lecture rooms, elevators and stairs, a floating senate chamber at the top – were informally woven into this frame. In contrast to these elements, a unified swath of recessed buff precast-framed glazed openings formed a general-purpose field of six upper floors standing above the free-plan main podium. These levels were deliberately left without complete programming when the building opened, encouraging the campus to evolve.

In contrast to the east exterior front, which stood high above parking lots and farm fields, the west flank of the Ross Building shifted upward to a car-free podium. This sanctuary was intended as the main public level of the university. The Ross Building formed a porous edge to the inner campus stretching outward from the podium, cradling an open-air amphitheatre and gathering spaces that could be commanded by speeches and student demonstrations, convocation, plays and chance events. Contemporary photographs above and below the podium demonstrate the planner's vision of a labyrinthine world with chasms reaching to the underground and floating levels far overhead. This collective 'in-between' space acted like an opening within a casbah. The complex was completed by the front edges of neighbouring buildings and connected by a field of walkways, underground tunnels and interior bridges organized by slippages and offsets, making innumerable paths through the campus.

The project shares an architectural language with contemporary projects – Wallace K. Harrison's soaring acropolis of Albany, New York (begun 1965) and the lofty piers of Le Corbusier's Chandigarh (1950–65). Like those projects, the sheer primal force of the Ross Building's structural frame was conceived as a kind of counterpoint, an archaic foundation supporting the turbulent action of a free new society. Amidst the corn and potato fields of Southern Ontario, the York University designers conceived a foundation rite

Fig. 52. The Ross Building, York University

embodied in the Ross complex. The procession led from the east through a march of piers that reached down through the silt plains of agriculture into the bedrock below. Rising up the enormous ramp and through the open frame, the building gave way to the enlightened upper ground of the campus.

Windswept Canadian winters were not kind to Ross Building users, and in 1988 the building was fundamentally changed by the demolition of the entry ramp and addition of a new layer of enclosed walkways and central rotunda that emulated Thomas Jefferson's 1802 plan for the University of Virginia. The central axis of the university has since shifted eastward, moving from the pedestrian-oriented world offered by the eastern flank of the Ross Building toward a new car-oriented plaza of shopping centres served by bus drop-off lanes. Ironically, this new development renews the peripheral parking that formed the outer fringes of the original plan for the campus. The planners of the Ross complex may not have anticipated such a wholesale change, but their concrete frame still forms the robust core of this system.

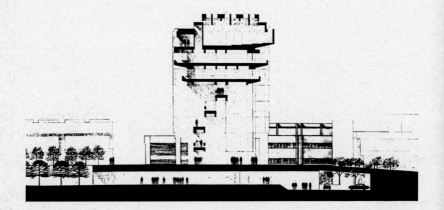

Fig. 53. Ross Building, section

Fig. 54. Students gathering in Ross forecourt

Fig. 55. Ross Building, interior courtyard

Fig. 54

Fig. 55

Fig. 53

Fig. 56. York University site under construction, Ross Building in centre of surrounding ring road

Fig. 57. Student lounge, Ross Building

Fig. 58. York University master plan, site model

Fig. 59. Ross Building, presentation model

Fig. 57

Fig. 58
Fig. 59

Fig. 1. Reginald Faryon Bridge, Trent University, Peterborough

concrete toronto   beyond toronto

Trent University

Lisa Rochon

Author, educator and architecture critic for the *Globe and Mail*

It might have been an architectural folly. The visionaries behind the Trent University commission sought a humanized university, a place of collegiate intimacy designed to reject the alienation felt by students at other post-secondary institutions in Canada. The West Coast architect Ron Thom might have overdosed on the Oxbridge collegiate tradition and built a modern-day tale of nostalgia. Instead, he worked closely with Toronto engineers Morden Yolles and Roly Bergman to deliver a masterwork remarkable not only for its innovation with rubble-aggregate concrete but for the daring way in which a river landscape is gracefully revealed through architecture.

The 1,500-acre campus spreads over both banks of the Otonabee River, about eight kilometres north of Peterborough. The university is often misunderstood as merely a series of medieval-scale pavilions, but there are also plenty of heroic gestures that match the pitch of the land: the broad sweep of the plaza and its viewing platforms drawn like prows on a boat to force views out beyond the river; and the Reginald Faryon Bridge, designed as a work of texture and plasticity – a nod to Pier Luigi Nervi's stunning concrete works – by project architect Paul Merrick with Bergman and built in concrete with a three-hinged arch and warped planes. The magic of the design lies as much in its rugged materiality as in the delicate scale of the stairs leading down to the river or the narrow vertical windows hidden behind slipped planes of concrete. I never tire of walkabouts at Trent.

Trent University (1964) represents one of Canada's most sacred modern icons of architecture. That Thom specified rubble-aggregate concrete as both architectural surface and structural material was a decision intended to offset the trend in North America during the 1960s for dull, prosaic institutional and commercial buildings made of cheap materials. And it worked. In its original form, Trent University expressed an honest, pure connection to its site and, because of its beautifully crafted concrete, appeared to have been set down hundreds of years ago. In contrast, the influential design by Eero Saarinen for the Ezra Stiles and Morse colleges, a complex of mostly four-storey buildings massed around a quadrangle and constructed of pink and grey stone cast in concrete, seems to be an exotic construct set down on the flats of Yale University at New Haven, Connecticut.

Trent, as imagined by Thom, appears to be rooted in the land. The rough texture of stone not only permeates the exterior experience of the university, but transforms interiors of, for instance, Champlain College, with rooms as grottos anchored with concrete fireplaces and benches. An elaborate process, tested with full-size models, was required to attain the correct balance between grout and split limestone faces. And masons were required to hand-finish the final exposed concrete surfaces. The result is a tribute to the individual and a celebration of concrete as sculpture.

Though there have been ill-conceived new additions to the university, the mystery of Thom's Trent continues to enchant. It is a university for all seasons, not intended to protect and shield from the bitter winter winds or the unforgiving sun of the summer, but to expose the student to the elements rudely and honestly, much like an exposure to higher learning.

Fig. 2. Trent University, situated along the Otonabee River, Peterborough

McMaster Health Sciences Centre

Tom Bessai

Assistant Professor, Faculty of Architecture, Landscape and Design, University of Toronto

The McMaster Health Sciences Centre is an impressive late-1960s mega-structure project by Craig Zeidler Strong Architects that dominates the entry to McMaster University in Hamilton. Designed and built over six years from 1967 to 1973, the enormous complex was acclaimed at the time in North America and around the world for its innovative planning and flexible infrastructure. It also demonstrated deft use of concrete both precast and poured in place.

Fig. 3. Facade detail showing composition of concrete precast panels, McMaster Health Sciences Centre, Hamilton

The ideal of absolute flexibility through modularity was central to the architectural scheme, producing compelling if not always anticipated results. Through a radical distinction between permanent and temporary infrastructure dubbed the Servo System, Eb Zeidler and his team provided a relatively inexpensive modular, long-span structural system of regular steel-frame piers and 70-foot clear span truss work. Core

mechanical and electrical infrastructure was run both horizontally and vertically into this three-dimensional matrix. These permanent installations allowed for free planning of all of the 'impermanent' fit-outs of the complex, from wards, labs and classrooms to modular facade elements.

The planning and design of the building interiors proved to be more permanent than originally theorized. Thirty-five years later, the building hasn't been significantly altered. The Servo concept delivers a truly free interior plan, but in so doing loses its ordering presence that is so clear on the building exterior. Beyond the principal 'loop' corridor and selected spaces bordering planned voids, the interiors are disorienting, particularly the massive lower floor plates. A vintage '70s graphic way-finding colour code was implemented to order the plan in primary red, yellow, blue and purple.

The exterior building skin is an excellent essay in the use of modular precast concrete facade panels. The panels are individually expressive through simple regular curves in plan and elevation. Units are set in ordered rows that accept variation in window width. The horizontal panel compositions are abstract yet dense and very

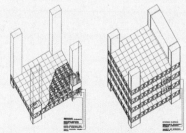

Fig. 4. Axonometric diagram of flexible Servo System, Zeidler Partners Architects

smooth. These rows are suspended between the soaring vertical steel and glass piers of the Servo towers, themselves absolutely transparent, revealing their brightly painted ducts and conduits.

The narrow outdoor 'Student Street' which bisects the bulk of the building pushes the limits of the system as the panels are made to negotiate bridges, corners and piers alike.

In Zeidler's later work, such as the Toronto Eaton Centre, this powerful, expressive functionalism gives way to more subdued modular facade treatments as he migrates away from precast concrete and clear glass to more integrated composite panel and window systems.

A final space in the project deserves mention in this context. Cast-in-place concrete was used to form the lecture theatres that animate the northern end of the building over the first two levels. Here, as with the facade panels, the sculptural effect of the cast figures is heightened via contrast with the grids and planes of the megastructure. The lecture-hall lobby successfully suspends students and faculty alike between the regular and the figural.

Fig. 5. View of 'Student Street' from the entrance to the lecture halls, McMaster Health Sciences Centre

The University of Guelph

Ian Panabaker & Wilfred Ferwerda

IAN PANABAKER: Heritage & Urban Design Planner, City of Guelph, founding member of Docomomo Ontario

WILFRED FERWERDA: Engineer at the University of Guelph and a member of ICOMOS, active internationally

The late-1960s portion of the University of Guelph represents a compelling international effort at creating a modern campus plan that highlights the sophistication and maturation of the new concrete architecture. The campus created in the late 1960s and early 1970s represents a refined Brutalism – a conscious effort toward both urbanism and monumentality.

On the campus scale, these buildings are successfully people-centred, creating identifiable, pedestrian-oriented public space. With various levels of success, the emphasis on creating an identifiable urban realm continues into the public routes in the buildings themselves.

The university was established in 1964, during that decade's major expansion of universities across the province. The university was created from three long-established colleges: the Ontario Agricultural College, the Ontario Veterinary College and the Macdonald Institute.

After a comprehensive master plan was drafted, five major concrete buildings were built within a three-year span, all using prominent architects on the Canadian and international scenes.

The Master Plan

The campus was on the edge of the growing mid-sized city of Guelph, Ontario, and was in fact outside the urban boundary until 1966. The master plan was undertaken with that edge condition very much in mind, and the fact that the projected campus population, combining students and staff, was to be roughly half of the city's population at the time (about 45,000 people), led to the proposition of the distinct campus boundary – a condition that was never realized and many years later was removed from the plan entirely.

The planning of the university is significant in that both by circumstance and by the theoretical predilection of its designers, it was to adopt an additive and conservative approach to substantially expanding an existing condition. Johnston Green, the large semicircular lawn of the Ontario Agricultural College lined with 19th-century buildings, was well-established. The expansion plan maintains this space and strategically stitches itself into the existing fabric. The new main square, Branion Plaza, is conceived as the urban centre of the campus – in contrast to, but also in balance with, the existing green.

The university's conceptual plan and initial build-out was well-published at the time and represented a successful, large-scale implementation of the period's leading urban theory and modern campus-planning ideas.

By virtue of the involvement of Josep Lluís Sert's, then head of the Harvard School of Design, and the local planning and architectural firms who undertook the work and who had trained under Sert, the early buildings of the University of Guelph are a major coherent statement of the Harvard school.

Fig. 6. The McLaughlin Library and Winegard Walk

Fig. 7. MacKinnon Building

MacKinnon Building

The MacKinnon Building, by Hancock, Little and Calvert Associates and Sert, Jackson and Associates Inc., was one of the first completed in the expansion of the university, in 1967. Its program is characteristically complex – a mix of lecture halls, faculty offices, special-purpose rooms – and its pivotal position as the first building to mediate between the old and new campuses, represents a conscious strategy of the new master plan.

It provides balance and response to Johnston Hall and is the first of the new buildings along the new north-south Winegard Walk. Where Johnston Hall is a traditional courtyard building with prominent facade and centre tower facing the lawn, MacKinnon, in a typical modernist approach, inverts the courtyard type to create a forward-facing green space around which the building's circulation is organized. The ground-floor corridor is treated as a covered open space and is described as an 'arcade' in publications at the time. Of note are the Corbusian operable ventilation panels and large sliding glazed doors along this circulation route – a gesture that does not appear to have been fully embraced in this northern climate.

The MacKinnon Building illustrates much of the formal concrete language developed by Sert in his Boston/Harvard works and sets the stage for the rest of the campus: a balanced mix of cast-in-place and precast finishes that subtly illuminate the mechanics of the construction system; the brise-soleil – more decorative than fully effective sun screens; the heavily framed skylights; a signature projecting roof element (an upper lounge area on the faculty block); colourful wood treatments; the dense yet segregated program; and the acknowledgement and studied connection to the existing and future contexts.

McLaughlin Library

A highly successful building in campus life, the McLaughlin Library, by Hancock, Little and Calvert Associates and Sert, Jackson and Associates Inc., completed in 1968, is one of the central hubs of the university. Situated on the north side of Branion Plaza, the library negotiates a complete one-storey grade change along Winegard Walk, placing its entrance not on the plaza but on the walk, directly across from the southern entrance to the MacKinnon Building.

This is the most muscular building on campus. There is an explicity strong interplay between cast-in-place and precast elements here that creates an easy legibility of vertical circulation towers set against the horizontality of the stack floors. The vertical towers are highly textured cast-in-place, done in béton brut and using vertical, diagonal and horizontal boarding patterns.

Fig. 8. University Centre

University Centre

Opposite the McLaughlin Library, across Branion Plaza, the second hub of the campus is University Centre, by Hancock, Little and Calvert Associates, completed in 1974. This building houses administrative functions as well as student services and the main campus cafeteria. As with MacKinnon and McLaughlin, the building negotiates a grade change but makes this explicit through internal level changes, taking advantage of it to animate the large interior atrium created between the banks of upper-level offices. The exterior of the building is a relatively straightforward interplay of exposed cast-in-place floor slabs and stair towers (finished béton brut), infilled with precast panels. The gymnastics are left for the interior atrium. More than any other space on

campus, the interior of University Centre is identifiably 1970s in its 'megaplex' adventurousness and programmatic energy.

MacNaughton Building

A major presence on Branion Plaza, the MacNaughton Building, completed in 1969 by Craig, Zeidler & Strong, is a tour de force of architectural concrete work. Although mainly a laboratory and lecture hall complex, the building also, purposely, houses the campus bookstore and a coffee shop, contributing to the urban character of the plaza. The ground floor is designed for a high level of flow between the exterior and interior related to the heavily used lecture halls, but also expressed in the projection of the main auditorium out into the plaza (a gesture made slightly awkward by the fact that the neighbouring Zavitz Hall was never removed as originally intended).

Fig. 9. MacNaughton Building

Fig. 10. Model of South Residence

South Residence

Perhaps the most unique architectural concept on campus is the major housing project known as South Residence. Completed in 1968, South Residence was designed by John Andrews just as he was riding the wave of success following Scarborough College. The initial plan of the university was to build a high-capacity, tall residence on the south side of a four-lane ring road that provided vehicular access from the main thoroughfare to large parking lots. Potential traffic conflicts between pedestrians and automobiles were an early concern of the architect. This dilemma generated the basic scheme of bridges over the road, connecting to an elevated internal 'street' grid at mid-level. The resultant system of wings and quads also eliminated the need for elevators, which Andrews believed were a deterrent to social interaction.

Andrews was very deliberate about creating the maximum number of choices and possibilities for socialization between students. The overall configuration was meant to optimize these factors. By locating 'houses' along the 'streets,' he attempted to create an enclosed urban atmosphere that was protected from the harsh Canadian weather.

The basic social unit is the 'alcove,' which consists of four single rooms and one double room sharing a landing and washroom. Andrews believed this to be the ideal grouping to build relationships because it resembled a typical family setting of six people. This layout has proven to be very successful as students report a high level of bonding and trust within the 'alcove.'

South Residence resembles a small city where you can run into a friend around every corner. The intersections, nooks and crannies make ideal places for impromptu gatherings or for programs and events organized by residence staff and students. This hierarchy of social spaces is the beauty of Andrews' design and the basis for the success of the building.

References

Borràs, Maria Lluïsa, ed. *Sert, Mediterranean Architecture.* Boston: New York Graphic Society, 1975.

Cheviakoff, Sofia and Alberto Duarte, *Josep Lluís Sert*, Ed. Sofia Cheviakoff, trans. William Bain, Gloucester, Ma: Rockport Publishers, 2003.

Rovira, Josep M. Ed. *Sert, 1928–1979. Complete Works: Half a Century of Architecture.* Barcelona: Fundació Joan Miró, 2006.

Sert, Josep Lluís : arquitecto en Nueva York. Ed. Xavier Costa and Guido Hartray. Barcelona: Museu d'Art Contemporani de Barcelona, ACTAR, 1997.

Taylor, Jennifer and John Andrews. *John Andrews: Architecture a Performing Art.* New York: Oxford University Press, 1982.

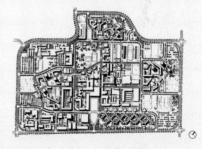

Fig. 11. University of Guelph Master Plan, 1967

Fig. 1. Application of precast panel onto steel frame, Medical Sciences Building, University of Toronto

concrete toronto   building with concrete

Concrete as a Building Material

Chris Andrews

Principal, Carruthers & Wallace Consultant Structural Engineers

Concrete is a unique, almost magical, building material. The primary constituents of concrete – including sand, stone aggregate, water and cement – appear to be benign, nearly inert, materials. However, when mixed in a carefully proportioned manner, they form a flowable slurry that can be placed into temporary forms and left to sit for as little as 24 hours; through a chemical reaction, the liquid-like material transforms into a mass with hardness, surface characteristics and colour properties similar to that of natural stone. This concrete building material has defined modern architecture.

The magic of concrete is this unique transformation from a flowable mixture to a hard, durable material that can be easily shaped into complex geometries. These shapes can be manipulated to reflect both intrinsic architectural design characteristics and efficient, load-bearing structural shapes. Building with concrete does not require artisan-level skills, as are required for stone and cut masonry work to produce fine surface finishes and intricate shapes.

The development of modern concrete as a building material goes back at least 5,000 years, to the initial emergence of lime plasters. Lime plasters were essentially high-tech building materials from at least 3,000 BCE that formed a very hard surface finish on buildings. They were likely discovered accidentally when limestone rock was heated around cooking fires. Adding water, drying and grinding the material into a powder and subsequently mixing the powder with water creates lime plaster. The Romans then improved on this material by adding what initially looked like a sand material found in the vicinity of volcanic areas. This material, rich in clay-like silica material, would chemically react with the calcium in lime to form calcium silicates and is now known as a pozzolan, named after the region of Pozzuoli in Italy where it was first mined. This early concrete material proved to be very hard and had the unique property of curing under water.

Modern concrete uses Portland cement as a binding agent to paste the mixture of stone and sand aggregates together. Portland cement was developed in the 1820s by an English mason, Joseph Aspdin. Its name reflects its similarity in appearance to limestone rock found on the island of Portland in the English Channel. Portland cement is manufactured from limestone, sand, clay and iron ore using a process of grinding, heating and further grinding.

In the Toronto area, the first Portland cement plants were located in Napanee and at Shallow Lake near Owen Sound. From 1900 to 2000, the production of Portland cement in Canada has increased 250-fold.

Concrete as a building material is extremely strong in resisting compression stresses and relatively weak in resisting tensile stresses. Reinforcing steel that is efficient in resisting tensile stresses is placed and bonded into the concrete mass in zones of tensile stress to provide tensile capacity to concrete, thereby creating a technically advanced building material. Alternatively, compressive stresses are induced into the concrete mass through prestressing steel that is pulled by jacking to induce a type of clamping force in the concrete so that critical tensile stresses are kept to safely low levels.

Other unique properties of concrete include the spontaneous heating of the material as it sets, shrinking of the material as it cures and ongoing strength gain if it is kept damp. It has a coefficient similar to that of the thermal expansion to steel. This last feature allows reinforcing steel and concrete to behave compatibly during variations in temperature and allows reinforced concrete to work in the Toronto environment.

Functionally, concrete exhibits good fire-resistance characteristics and thermal properties. Its surface patterns can be easily varied to take on the surface features of the enclosing formwork. Its structural properties can be varied to match required compressive strength design levels, density, early strength gain to allow quick removal of forms and low heat characteristics during curing to reduce shrinkage and cracking.

Sustainable considerations include the use of recycled steel, primarily from old cars, for almost all reinforcing steel used in Canada. Additionally, the pozzolan fly ash is substituted for

Portland cement. Fly ash is a by-product of industrial coal firing, and when recycled for use in concrete, significantly reduces the energy content of its production.

Concrete gained architectural and artistic expression in the projects from the 1950s, '60s and '70s outlined in this collection, and continues to shape and define much of the development in Toronto.

Fig. 2. Ontario Science Centre, exterior concrete detail

Building Parts: How Concrete Can Be Used in Construction

Anne Miller

Professional engineer, master's thesis student, Faculty of Architecture, Landscape and Design, University of Toronto

There are many ways in which concrete can be formed; however, they all fall into one of two categories: concrete that is cast where it will remain, and concrete that is cast elsewhere. Within these two categories, the most common methods are as follows.

Fig. 3. Cast-in-place pier, Robarts Library

Cast-in-Place

In this most basic method of concrete construction, formwork is erected on-site. The concrete used in this type of construction is typically ready-mixed concrete – concrete that is batched at a concrete plant and trucked to the site in a mixer truck. Typical of foundations and slabs, this method can accommodate countless types of vertical structures, the most basic of which are walls and columns.

Formwork

Concrete is inherently formless. It must be contained somehow to allow it to set into a solid. Therefore, forming techniques are not only critical to the ease with which this process takes place, they also represent the infinite formal possibilities of the material.

• *Horizontal formwork*: In a horizontal application, typical of floor slabs, concrete is deposited or placed into the form, screeded to level the surface, floated and/or trowelled and then may be finished with a broom treatment or other texture.

• *Vertical formwork*: When casting vertical elements, form ties are needed to hold the formwork together against the pressure of the concrete. The concrete is typically placed in 450–1200 mm lifts and vibrated at regular intervals to ensure proper consolidation and distribution of the mix and to minimize air pockets and bubbles.

• *Slipforming*: Typical of tall vertical or long horizontal elements with a constant cross-section, slipforming is a method by which the formwork moves incrementally along the member being constructed. The mobile forms are secured to the structure using hoisting bars that are cast into the concrete, and are lifted using hydraulic pressure. The concrete is placed in the form and, once set, the form is moved up or along the structure leaving a continuous extrusion of concrete.

Examples of Slipforming
• The CN Tower
• Service Chimney at York University

Reinforcing

Reinforcing steel, or 'rebar,' is often used in conjunction with concrete, creating a system that is strong in both compression (concrete) and tension (rebar).

Colour

As concrete is inherently a natural material, colour consistency, particularly from batch to batch, depends on many factors – from the temperature of the mix and moisture content of the aggregates to the source of the cement and other cementitious materials, to the precision with which any pigment has been added. Pigment can be added to the concrete mix – 'integral' – or can be applied after the concrete has set – 'applied.'

Texture

Formwork can also be used to affect a finish on the concrete. Whether through the use of a form liner or other patterning device, or by the placement of stone or sand in the form prior to casting, this method can drastically modify the appearance of the finished concrete.

Examples of Board Forming
• Scarborough College
• Ontario Science Centre
• House on Ardwold Gate

Curing

To develop its full potential strength, concrete needs to remain in a moist condition for at least seven days. Cast-in-place concrete is kept moist by several methods, including tarping and sprinkling. The object is not to dry it, but to 'cure' it. In our Canadian winters, concrete must be

Fig. 4. Smooth-finish cast-in-place wall, Dupont Station (MAP P. 20)

protected from freezing during the curing process

Precast

In this method of concrete construction, formwork is erected off-site, usually in a factory setting. This method is common when a consistency of colour, texture and finish is required. Though often seen as cost-effective due to its time savings on-site and the speed with which a building can be enclosed, precast concrete can also be particularly artful in its form.

Textures

The addition of texture or profile to an exposed concrete surface can be tightly monitored and controlled in a factory setting. As discussed with respect to cast-in-place concrete, an infinite number of textures can be imparted to a concrete surface: smooth surfaces can be created by smooth forming materials or form liners – such as fibreglass; aggregates can be exposed to create a rough texture by several methods, including acid etching and abrasive blasting. Notable examples of precast include:

City Hall
• Italian marble inset into the facing concrete.
• Machinery invented specifically to facilitate this.
• Panel curves vary in a fairly complex sequence
• Botticino marble strips prepared by a special diamond-sawing machine and placed into preformed grooves in the concrete form.

• Approximately 400 pieces of marble of varying lengths in each panel, with the intention that these vertical lines of marble would accentuate the height of the towers.

Medical Sciences Building
• Precast concrete as art.
• Artists retained to design the precast panels: Ted Bieler and Robert Downing.
• Between seven and 11 different panel designs were created for the hundreds of panels eventually gracing the exterior facade of the building.
• First example of rain-screen technology in Toronto.

Broken-Rib Panel

Also known as fractured rib or fractured fin, this treatment of precast panel is often used to aid in disguising wear to the exterior facade.

Examples of Broken Rib Panel
• Ontario Science Centre
• Palace Pier

Tilt-up

In this method of precasting, a cast-in-place slab floor is usually used as formwork for the walls of the building. Once the floor slab has cured, formwork is erected to form the edges of the wall slabs, which are then cast horizontally on the floor slab, sometimes in stacks on top of each other. Once cured, they are hoisted into place. This method of construction requires substantial manoeuvring space for the lifting equipment and, therefore, is not typically used in a dense urban environment.

Pre/post-tensioned

Often, it is beneficial to tension the reinforcement within the concrete, forcing the concrete into pure compression. This tensioning can be done 'pre' in the case of precast concrete elements, or 'post' in several locations from the shop floor, for a precast element, to the final resting place of cast-in-place. This technique allows for pre- or post-tensioned concrete to span farther that of an untensioned equivalent.

Fig. 5. Precast panel with inset marble, New City Hall

Fig. 6. Precast sculptural panels, Medical Sciences Building

Fig. 7. Broken-rib panels, Ontario Science Centre

Beer Precast

Elizabeth Hulse

Author of *The Beers: Canada's First Family in Precast Concrete*

By the time Beer Precast won the contract for New City Hall in 1961, the Beer family had accumulated three generations' experience making concrete in Toronto. The company, now run by brothers Fred A. Beer and Doug Beer, was widely recognized as a leader in the field of precast architectural concrete in Canada. In the 1950s and early '60s, they had worked on several projects designed by Toronto's outstanding modernist architect of the time, Peter Dickinson, including the Queen Elizabeth Building (1956) at the CNE and the Prudential Insurance Company building (1960) at King and Yonge streets in Toronto, as well as the Canadian Imperial Bank of Commerce tower (1961) in Montreal. A combination of factors ensured the Beers' success – hands-on experience, innovativeness, an ability to get on well with architects and designers, and an exceptional workforce – and they would continue to be leaders in their field in North America until the business was sold in 1976.

The Beers, who were responsible for all the precast elements in New City Hall, took on a project that was challenging in every way. Fred Beer recalled that at first architect Viljo Revell did not know what he wanted the walls to look like, and they worked together to develop his ideas. To make the more than 4,000 concave facing panels for the building, each incorporating some 400 strips of split-faced Botticino marble of random lengths and widths, the firm had to invent an automated process that could be handled by unskilled labour. The production of these panels took nearly 18 months. They were then used as the formwork for the structural walls, a relatively new technique that had never before been employed on such a large scale. By the late 1960s, marble, granite, slate and exposed aggregates, such as the river gravel used in the Lonsdale Towers apartment building (1964) and the Sutton Place Hotel (1967), were being replaced by sculptural concrete.

Although artist-designed wall panels precast in concrete had been used on a number of earlier Beer buildings, such as the Beth David Synagogue (1957) in North York, the Medical Sciences Building at the University of Toronto, completed in 1969, demonstrated a new capability. In this case, Beer Precast created a structure entirely defined by its facing panels. These were designed by sculptor Robert Downing in association with Ted Bieler. Assisted by some high-powered salesmanship from the Beers, project architect Peter Goering persuaded the university that concrete rather than stone was the appropriate modern medium. The panels, moulded in a dozen different designs, were installed at random as they came off the truck. Downing later joked that it was the construction crew who ultimately designed the building.

When the first Fred Beer had begun as a pattern maker for precast concrete in Toronto in 1904, it was for the Roman Stone Company. Ambivalence about concrete for visual building details is reflected in this and other names such as 'art stone' or 'cast stone' in the firms he worked for or founded. Not until after World War II did concrete come into its own as an architectural material, and a Beer company advertisement could boast, 'Precast concrete is like sculptor's clay in an architect's hand.'

Fig. 8. Architect Peter Goering (centre) and artist Robert Downing (left) examining a precast panel for the Medical Sciences Building, in the Beer manufacturing plant

The Broken-Rib Panel and the Virtues of Ugly

Pina Petricone

Associate Professor and Assistant Dean, Faculty of Architecture, Landscape and Design, University of Toronto

It has always seemed curious to me that elaborating the definition of concrete to include 'pertaining to or concerned with realities or actual instances rather than abstractions'[1] admits a kind of idiosyncrasy, when the realness, so to speak, of the noun form lends itself so willingly to the modernist powers of abstraction. The precast concrete broken-rib panel, developed fully in the early 1960s as an efficient rain-screen cladding system with an inherent texture, is a testament to the dynamic richness of this oxymoron. Numerous Toronto cases included in this book sport such concrete expressions, which to varying degrees provide the requisite awesomeness for concrete's sublime presence in our city.

Just as Le Corbusier passes from a strategy of béton blanché, an industrialized, machined effect of sliding formwork to achieve a consistent surface, to one of béton brut, a concrete whose surface registers with pleasure the fallible hand that formed it, for its awesome 'ugliness,' Paul Rudolph leaves smooth walls behind in favour of a highly textured ridged surface, achieved only by hand-hammering to expose the modelled aggregate after the industrialized forms are removed. While the technique changes, there is little doubt the broken-rib precast panel, diffuse in 1960s and '70s Toronto, follows this Rudolphian tradition. At the Four Seasons Hotel, the Elm Street Nurses Residence, the Sheraton Centre, OISE-UT and the Sutton Place to name a few, this, this 'corduroy concrete' works hard to render its surface massive and delightfully horrifying.

The shop-finished approach to the broken-rib panel did not preclude a machined aesthetic. To varying degrees, great lengths were taken to form and finish mass-produced panels as though each were a naturally produced one-off. From simple, gravity-ridden form surface modelling techniques to the elaborate innovations of Toronto City Hall's precast curtain wall form, the effect is uncanny – an abstraction of surface that achieves an almost sublime nature. City Hall's soaring ribbed surface of (seemingly) randomly placed three-quarter-foot and one-and-three-quarter-foot split-faced marble strips, 400 total for each concave cast panel, required the invention of an automatic two-headed diamond-cutting saw and a special form incorporating a rubber extrusion to hold the marble in place during the high-frequency vibration of the concrete pour.

These techniques are far from the implied utilitarianism of concrete and its virtue of nakedness. The virtue here seems to lie, rather, in ugliness (brut), in so far as it is ugliness that sets it apart from ideals of the artificial – the not real.

Note

1. 'Concrete,' definition #2. Dictionary.com, Random House.

Fig. 9. Precast concrete ribbed panel, Sutton Place Hotel

Selling Concrete: Advertisements from the 1960s and '70s

Anne Miller

Professional engineer, master's thesis student, Faculty of Architecture, Landscape and Design, University of Toronto

Leafing through issues of *Canadian Architect* from the 1960s makes me feel like a kid in a candy store.

I am seduced by the overall aesthetic of the publication and by the romantic notions captured in its black-and-white imagery. Nostalgia notwithstanding, the quality and quantity of the concrete projects in this era is outstanding; many of them still resonate today with their sensitivity to program and site, and with their graceful use of a material too often seen as substratum or infrastructure. Looking at particular projects in their original context and with their original design intent outlined in detail makes me grateful that I have this rearview mirror to our architectural past.

In spite of all this, the most interesting thing to me about browsing through these historic issues of *Canadian Architect* has been the notable presence of the cement and concrete industries in their pages. Not simply satisfied to let the projects speak for themselves, the industry was actively marketing its product to architects, something rarely seen today. Perhaps the nature and scale of the industry had a great deal to do with this focus. The sixties was an era of relatively small, family-owned local cement and concrete companies who were engaged in the architectural discourse of the time; they were interested in working with architects to exploit the formal strength of the material.

The marketing efforts put forth by these companies – in particular Beer Precast, Canada Cement Company, St. Marys Cement – and their industry organization, the Portland Cement Association of Canada (now the Cement Association of Canada), was instrumental in the fostering of an environment conducive to the outstanding concrete projects presented in this book. Perusing these ads will hopefully give you the same joy it has given me, along with a rejuvenated excitement about the promise of concrete.

Fig. 10. *Canadian Architect*, March 1969
(Canadian Cement Association)

Regina Caeli School, Pointe Claire, P.Q. Owner: Pointe Claire and Beaconsfield Catholic School Commission. Architect: Papineau/Gerin-Lajoie/Le Blanc, Montreal. Structural Engineer: Delorme, Carrier, Bourbonnais, Dorion, P.Q., General Contractor: Tetrault Frères Limitée, Verdun, Quebec.

1. The spectacular North York Exbury Towers, Toronto, Ont.

2. Soa

3. Bold

4. Imaginatively designed concrete panels provide unusual beauty and flawless un

Fig. 11. *Canadian Architect,* June 1968
(LaFarge Group)

Fig. 12. *Canadian Architect,* Dec. 1969
(Beer Precast Concrete Company)

Fig. 13. *Canadian Architect,* March 1968
(Beer Precast Concrete Company)

Fig. 14. *Canadian Architect,* Nov. 1968
(St. Mary's Cement Company)

Fig. 15. *Canadian Architect,* Feb. 1968
(St. Mary's Cement Company)

Fig. 16. *Canadian Architect,* March 1969
(Beer Precast Concrete Company)

BOLD, BEAUTIFUL DESIG

THE UNUSUAL IS USUALLY CONCRETE

Suddenly the most striking Canadian buildings are concrete, boldly exposed, dramatically precast, expressively sculptured. Considered from any angle, these structures express the flexibility of concrete and point out how new shapes and unusual facades can be created with concrete.

Architectural eye-catchers, they accurately reflect the mood of the sixties — dynamic, avant-garde, excitingly imaginative but eminently practical. Yes, concrete with its classic

beauty, unparal
profile and sett
Modern desi
of form and sl
make your ima
to-date informa

CANADA CEMENT COMPANY, LIMITED.

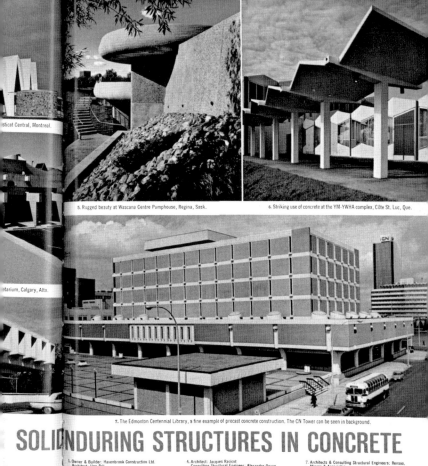

stic Central, Montreal.

5. Rugged beauty at Wascana Centre Pumphouse, Regina, Sask.

6. Striking use of concrete at the YM-YWHA complex, Côte St. Luc, Que.

etarium, Calgary, Alta.

7. The Edmonton Centennial Library, a fine example of precast concrete construction. The CN Tower can be seen in background.

SOLIDNDURING STRUCTURES IN CONCRETE

alities is carving for itself a

s, are intrigued with the free
ncrete. Let Canada Cement
est sales office for the most

1. Owner & Builder: Havenbrook Construction Ltd.
   Architect: Uno Prii
   Consulting Structural Engineers: Cooper Consultants Ltd.
   Concrete masonry units: Richvale Block Supply Co. Ltd.
   Ready-mixed concrete: Richvale Ready Mix Ltd.
2. Architect: Roland Dumais
   Consulting Structural Engineers: Jean F. Gagnon & Assoc.
   General Contractor: Albert Deschamps Ltée.
   Ready-mixed concrete: Francon (1966) Ltd.
3. Architect: McMillan, Long & Associates
   Consulting Structural Engineers: T. Lamb,
   McManus and Associates Ltd.
   General Contractor: Hashman Construction Co. Ltd.
   Ready-mixed: Consolidated Concrete Ltd.

4. Architect: Jacques Racicot
   Consulting Structural Engineer: Alexandre Opran
   General Contractor: Rapid Construction Ltée
   Precast concrete panels: Francon (1966) Ltd.
5. Owners: Saskatchewan Provincial Government
   Architects: Kerr, Cullingworth, Riches, Associates
   Consulting Structural Engineers: Reid,
   Crowther and Partners Ltd.
   General Contractor: Buildcon Ltd.
   Ready-mixed concrete: Trans-Mix Concrete
6. Architect: Harry Stilman
   Consulting Structural Engineer: Bernard Geller
   General Contractor: Leon M. Adler
   Precast concrete: Francon (1966) Ltd.

7. Architects & Consulting Structural Engineers: Rensaa,
   Minnos & Associates
   General Contractor: Alta-West Construction Ltd.
   Prestressed and precast concrete members:
   Con-Force Products Ltd.
   Ready-mixed concrete:
   Rex Underwood Concrete & Aggregates Ltd.

CANADA CEMENT

ied company plying the nation with quality cements since 1909.

Precast Sculpture Enriches Building

To achieve enrichment, free-form sculpture was added to repetitively cast, curved wall panels. Working in carefully prepared wet cement from approved drawings, the sculptors then applied individual designs on each panel at the rate of two a day. The result is an original hand finished mural that is the focal point of the building.

BEER PRECAST CONCRETE LIMITED
100 Manville Road, Scarboro 736, Ontario

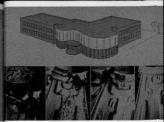

Educational Requisites—Administration Building for Windsor Separate School Board.
Architects: J. P. Thomson Associates, Scarboro, W. Leben, E. Liberis.

Working on the roughened 10 ft. x 6 ft. recessed area, sculptors apply wet cement over reinforcing mesh, adding finish with trowel.

Fig. 12

Overall Rib

Vertical Rib

Geometrical Pattern

Geometrical Pattern

Wood Pattern

Repetitive Free Form

Free Form Abstract Mural

A NEW DESIGN SERVICE FOR SCULPTURED PRECAST

The rapidly growing interest in architectural enrichment opens exciting new vistas for the creative use of precast concrete.

To assist architects in obtaining maximum freedom of design with economy, we have applied our extensive experience to the development of new production techniques. The possibilities are unlimited and range from simple textured overall patterns from a common form to repetitive abstract designs from multiforms or complete mural walls from individual forms.

In conjunction with professional designers we can now offer creative design assistance and technical advice to achieve any concept, theme or character desired.

BEER PRECAST CONCRETE LIMITED
100 MANVILLE ROAD · SCARBOROUGH · ONTARIO · PHONE 751-4121

Free Form Symbolic Mural

SCULPTURED PRECAST

For this folder please fill out and mail this coupon.

Name ....
Firm ....
Address ....
Telephone ....

BEER PRECAST CONCRETE LIMITED
TAMARVILLE ROAD · SCARBOROUGH · ONTARIO

Fig. 13

Morden Yolles:
Building in Concrete

Interview with Morden Yolles

Founder, the Yolles Partnership

MORDEN YOLLES is a pioneering Canadian engineer
who help bring postwar Toronto into the modern
era. In an interview conducted in November 2006
with E.R.A. Architects, he recalls his early experiences with concrete construction and architecture.

E.R.A.   **How did you become involved in the design of concrete structures?**

Morden Yolles   My father was in the development business. The firm, Yolles and
Rotenberg, built light industrial buildings and eventually office
buildings and hotels. He constructed the Tip Top Tailors building, the
Federal building, the Sterling Tower, the Richmond Adelaide Centre,
the Benvenuto apartments and others. He preferred and generally
built concrete structures, likely because of its economy, particularly in
achieving fire rating in light industrial projects.

My first experience with concrete was the design of a flat plate structure
for the British-American Oil Building at Bay and College Streets, a design-
build project of my father's firm. It was one of the early buildings moving
toward the modernist style. I told Father about the possibility of using
flat plate concrete slab without the standard column flares. He was very
interested in this possibility because it could achieve a shallower ceiling
sandwich, resulting in a smaller floor-to-floor height and a more effective
space for ducts and other services. The structure has drops but no flares.
It was designed utilizing a rational design process that had yet to be used
in Canada at the time, rather than the standard coefficient model the
codes required. Designing in this manner required me to gain special
permission from the City building department.

E.R.A.   Where did the idea for using this rational design method come from?

Morden Yolles   The American Concrete Institute Code was revised during the war to promote rational analysis. I had heard about it through my engineering education at the University of Toronto. So Father said, 'Well, don't go to Harvard right away – ' I had planned on doing graduate studies in architecture ' – please stay and work on this.' And he loaned me to his structural engineer, Harold Hooper. I think the British-American Oil Building was the first flat plate structure built in Canada. Subsequently my father planned the Benvenuto Apartment/Hotel on Avenue Road. With the structure here we eliminated the drops as well. It's fully a flat plate.

E.R.A.   The Benvenuto is mythologized as a major step forward in Canadian architecture.

Morden Yolles   It really was the first modernist building and we started working on that in 1950, immediately after British-American Oil. Recently I had a chance to observe the concrete in that building. A tenant, Harry Malcomson, who has a superb vintage photograph collection, remodelled his suite and took off a fair bit of the plaster on the columns, exposing the beautiful board-forming. John Hill, the site supervisor working for my father, was a highly skilled technician and the concrete was very well executed. I worked with John on many other buildings.

E.R.A.   So preference for the flat plate was related to economics?

Morden Yolles   Yes, and function. But not simply the economics of the structure itself, but rather the project as a whole. Father, with Peter Dickinson, created the floor-plan layout, which consisted of irregular bay sizes: 23 feet for kitchens and living rooms, and the adjacent bay was 16 feet for the bedroom. In response to this, I designed the larger bay as a nine-inch slab and the smaller one as a six-and-a-half-inch slab, conserving considerable material. We couldn't have done this with the coefficient design method required by the codes. I was certainly preoccupied with structural economy.

This also helped with flexibility. Father provided some of these single bedrooms with kitchenettes so they could be rented as bachelors. This meant that alternately the adjacent one- or two-bedroom units could be expanded to two- or three-bedroom units if the need arose.

E.R.A.   How did you become interested in the architectonic possibilities of structure?

Morden Yolles   I was interested in architecture because of the work of my father. At times, growing up, I would even visit the architect's office. I was particularly interested in the Tides Hotel, which he built in Miami Beach. Subsequently, in my second year of engineering at the University of Toronto, someone introduced me to Sigfried Giedion's *Space, Time and Architecture*, a book that became very important to me. I began to realize the full aesthetic and architectonic possibilities of structures, something our regular course work didn't expose us to. I then became interested in the work of the Swiss engineer Robert Maillart, as well as the Italian Pierre Luigi Nervi and the Spaniard Eduardo Torroja, among others.

To this day, I look at buildings and still feel the economy, function, working with the program, flexibility – all the primary requirements to properly satisfy, out of which you create your aesthetic.

As my practice developed, I had the great fortune to work with Roland Bergmann, with whom I became partner. He was a very skilled mathematician trained in Vienna, which enabled our office to perform design work we otherwise would've had great difficulty with. When he immigrated to Canada, he first worked on bridge design with the CNR. He was hired in 1955 and made partner by 1959. Through his exemplary design capabilities and working with the skills of various architects, we were able to realize the expression through structure, which was my initial inspiration.

E.R.A. **As you mentioned, you've worked with a highly talented group of architects over the years. Benvenuto was Peter Dickinson. What was that like?**

Morden Yolles   He was trained in England as a modernist and brought a modern vocabulary to Toronto. He brought a lot to the table in terms of design. Peter's vision required the appropriate input from his structural engineer, input I was only too eager to fulfil. I can refer to this now as a collaborative process, without my being conscious of it then. I was fortunate to be able to work with architects like Ron Thom and Peter, and Irving Grossman and so on. They were always searching with their engineers, because they could help them express what they wanted to express. This was true with Ron in particular. Things came up through conversation that wouldn't have come up otherwise.

E.R.A. **Your description of developing the flat plate is a perfect example of structural innovation. What others do you recall?**

Morden Yolles   Well, there was the Cleeve Horne Residence. Are you familiar with that? The architects were Clifford and Laurie. Cleeve Horne, the sculptor, and his wife, Jean, who was also an artist, had a piece of land that overlooks a large valley, (near Claremont, outside of Toronto) and they held a competition for the project in the late '50s. Clifford and Laurie came to us for structural engineering suggestions. I proposed a concrete hyperbolic paraboloidal shell roof. I had always been intrigued by these forms. I had read many books concerning thin concrete shelled structures which were being built in Europe, as well as in Mexico, by Felix Candela and others. This presented an opportunity to realize one here.

In the Cleeve Horne house, the roof structure consists of a concrete shell that is supported from foundation at two corners, and is prevented from rotating by ties at the other two corners. The rest is open and glass. It's two and a half inches thick, spanning 50-some-odd feet.

E.R.A.   **How was the shell formed?**

Morden Yolles   That was the interesting part. Hyperbolic paraboloids are surfaces formed by a series of straight lines called generatrices. If the surface is intersected parallel to these straight-line generatrices, the result will be a straight line. Yet if it is intersected at right angles, the edge will form a parabola or hyperbola. As a result, the shell can be formed with plywood panels. That's why I was interested in it. Because complex forms usually conflict with cost. But if you can form the shells with straight lines, you've got some bending room. That's how the surfaces of the Reginald Faryon Bridge at Trent University were formed. The surfaces on the sides are hyperbolic paraboloids.

E.R.A.   **Trent University is quite an impressive project.**

Morden Yolles   Yes. There we introduced rubble aggregate concrete to Canada. It was invented in Scandinavia and brought to America through Saarinen's Stiles and Morse College at Yale University. It's a system where four- to six-inch stones are dumped into the formwork in three-foot lifts. A retardant is put onto the face of the formwork. Mortar is then pumped in to fill the voids. As a result of the retardant on the form face, the grout can be scraped down to expose the stone.

Fig. 20. Cleeve Horne House exterior

To better understand the process, I first interviewed the contractors for the Yale buildings, who provided me with considerable information. But I concluded that we would require our own test program to establish the construction method and satisfy Ron's visual requirements. The university paid for the entire testing program, requiring experiments with a variety of aggregates and grouts, and doing test panels here in Toronto.

E.R.A.   **That kind of support for innovation really speaks of the era. The investigation of this book is the modern building boom and concrete. What are your thoughts on the preoccupation with concrete at this time?**

Morden Yolles   That is a very complex question. There isn't one simple answer. I suppose it had to do with fire codes, it had to do with developers who felt comfortable with the material. There was such a building boom, and due to economics and other reasons, concrete was often the material of choice. In the face of this, designers began to experiment with the material to develop an appropriate aesthetic. Again, going back to Benvenuto, though its aesthetics are largely of brick and glass, its structure as a concrete slab building is given expression through the exposed edge.

Later there came considerable interest in allowing the concrete itself to become the primary means of architectural expression. I'm not a historian, but there were many influences for this. Ron Thom and Arthur Erickson

Fig. 21. Detail of formwork for Reginald Faryon
Bridge, Trent University

Fig. 22. Rubble aggregate concrete, Trent
University

from the west. It also came from architectural practices in the States and of
course from Europe, going back to the Bauhaus and Perret, etc. In Toronto,
Ray Moriyama and others began to design with exposed architectural
concrete in their projects. Grossman liked working with it. Do you know
the News and Administration building?

E.R.A.   **In Montreal?**

Morden Yolles   Yes. It was built for Expo as a demonstration of the future of the office
building. Grossman was trained here at U of T and worked about three
years in England with all the contemporary architects there, as well as
some time in California. The News and Administration building is one of his
best buildings.

He asked his collaborative team's engineers, including mechanical,
electrical and myself as structural, what they thought would be the best
step forward in office design. I said that longer spans and floor flexibility
would be important. I also thought the glass box should be avoided. Glass
boxes are hothouses and they heat up and you have to cool them. Irving
took this advice and designed his building.

The result was a low structure of exposed concrete consisting of shear walls
that support 50-foot spans. To properly respond to the southern and

northern exposure, and provide shading for the continuous windows, we set back floors bottom to top, so that that the second floor protruded beyond the first and so on.

Grossman was also particularly innovative in housing designs. A concrete apartment house that comes to mind is the Somerset apartments my brother and I put up in North York. Another shear-wall structure, here he incorporated terrace units along a hillside at the base of a tower. The tower itself contained skip-stop units, allowing for northern and southern sun exposure and cross-ventilation. It was completely exposed concrete.

E.R.A.   **These projects sounds like an early implementation of ideas in environmental design.**

Morden Yolles   That's right, as well as architectural expression. In the case of the News and Administration building, each of these shear walls featured sculptures that were formed into them. Irving was one of the few architects who worked to include the artwork in the building itself, rather than applying it later.

E.R.A.   **That is some very expressive architectural concrete.**

Morden Yolles   Yes. When it came to achieving the quality for exposed concrete, we would write very exacting performance specifications, which included the requirement for sample panels, before the construction work proceeded. In the case of the News and Administration building, the contractor looked at my specs and said in his wonderful French accent, 'These are not specifications – this is poetry.'

E.R.A.   **You certainly were interested in the possibilities of exposed concrete.**

Morden Yolles   In truth, I was often disappointed with the result. We almost never achieved the quality of architectural concrete we hoped for. It didn't turn out the way it did in Europe, but I suppose that comes down to labour costs and experience.

Let me just quote myself – I wrote this in 1966 in *Canadian Architect*: 'Poured concrete is often considered as being in "the nature of the material." I am most unsympathetic with those who use this argument to rationalize such defects as honeycombs, voids, cold joint lines, severe discolourations, spalls, poor definition and the rest. This is comparable to a great *chef de cuisine* excusing his fallen soufflé as being due to a natural tendency of beaten egg whites to revert to their unbeaten state.'

E.R.A. **You've mentioned in previous conversations how the use of the flying form in Toronto made concrete construction considerably more economical.**

Morden Yolles Yes. The flying form is the ability to reuse formwork again and again and hoist it up to the next floor and so on. It speeds things up remarkably. It really changed the whole construction industry.

E.R.A. **Was it invented here?**

Morden Yolles No, it came from Europe. When I started, it was regular formwork, but there was an influx of Italian workers, and some from Finland, and things started to change. I remember by the mid-'50s seeing some apartment buildings going up on Avenue Road using the flying form. And they were Italian crews.

E.R.A. **So was it people right on the job site who said, 'Let's do this ...' ?**

Morden Yolles I'm really not sure of the history. I think the notion came from Scandinavia, but I'm not sure. We had a big influx of Italian workers from southern Italy familiar with the technique. Big influx. At first it was manually lifted, and then of course it became more mechanized when it came into standard use.

Later, other innovations occurred in forming concrete floor systems. For example, we were able to collaborate with Walter Wally, the construction supervisor for Yolles and Rotenberg, while designing the Richmond Adelaide Centre to integrate mechanical and electrical services within the concrete joist floor system, saving considerable amounts of space floor-to-floor.

E.R.A. **It seems that Toronto predominantly works in concrete, whereas, say, New York is mostly steel. You live in Toronto, you work in Toronto – it's hard to comment when it's second nature, but why concrete here?**

Morden Yolles Every city has its own construction culture; I've learned that through working in many parts of the world. Here the preference for concrete might have come from cost. The steel trades here were quite strong, actually, but we found concrete, overall, to be more economical, at least in the 1960s and

'70s. Secondly, with steel it had to be fire-protected and concrete didn't. We had the trades here, and the skilled immigrant groups, as well as a lot of good concrete suppliers. The infrastructure was here. There are many different aspects to it. It was something we often worked with. Though I have to say, by the '80s I found steel more interesting.

E.R.A. **Exposed concrete was the ethic of the '60s and '70s, but it's rarely seen today. Is the big impediment for exposed concrete environmental?**

Morden Yolles Well, it's seen today, but not as much. Many of the projects we are speaking of predate research developed by the National Research Council, which enabled a widespread understanding of building science. The big problem with a wall exposed both to the interior and exterior is that temperature differentials cause the concrete to expand and contract, causing cracks over time. There are also problems with moisture, thermal bridging and so on.

Many of these projects come out of the modernist movement. Yet the utopian notions of modernism didn't turn out as hoped. These architects were visionaries. Yet for them it was a bit of an advantage. There wasn't an understanding of the ecological, and it wasn't taken into account. The idea was you'd use the basic materials of the building to make your architecture. But there's a lot more to the building, and that's why our skins are so complicated.

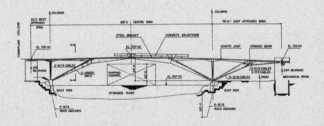

Fig. 23. Section, structural drawing, Reginald Faryon Bridge, Trent University

Fig. 24. Reginald Faryon Bridge, under construction

Durability Is Only Skin Deep

Ted Kesik

Professional Engineer, Associate Professor and Acting Assistant Dean, Faculty of Architecture, Landscape and Design, University of Toronto

An extensive stock of high-rise housing in Toronto and throughout Ontario was constructed in response to postwar immigration to large urban centres. The building technology enjoyed the benefit of well-engineered reinforced concrete structural systems; however, advanced building-science concepts were not applied to the building envelope design. For the first three decades of this building typology's service life, the envelope performed acceptably and the low cost of energy did not place economic burdens on owners and tenants. With much of this high-rise housing stock now passing some 40 years of service, deterioration of the building envelope is widely evident and the cost of energy is increasingly significant. Conventional retrofits to achieve envelope energy efficiency and durability are often producing unacceptable aesthetic outcomes.

Research in the Faculty of Architecture, Landscape and Design at the University of Toronto, through a course delivered by Toronto architect Ivan Saleff, examined relationships between the skin (building envelope) and armature (structural system) in the context of facade-retrofit technologies that extend the service life of the skin while optimizing thermal performance and maintaining, if not enhancing, the traditional aesthetic character of the building stock. A building-science component of the research assessed roof, opaque wall and glazing retrofit measures in terms of their economic viability to owners, and these indicators were compared

Fig. 25. Typical concrete slab with exposed slab edge and masonry facade

with life-cycle cost analyses. The retrofit strategy holding the most promise involved integrated overcladding, which incorporates a secondary framing system that enables the updating and integration of building services in a space between the exterior or insulation and the existing facade, and the introduction of features such as double facade systems for natural ventilation and sound control.

A building-envelope retrofit analysis was conducted on a typical 20-storey high-rise apartment building constructed in the 1970s. An integrated overcladding strategy was priced at $2.72 million and yielded an annual reduction of $241,000 in energy costs and 708 tonnes of greenhouse gases. Depending on the future escalation rate of energy prices, the payback period on the investment ranged from 8.3 to nine years, corresponding to an internal rate of return of 11.7 percent and 10 percent respectively. It is evident that a comprehensive overcladding strategy for postwar high-rise housing typology is cost-effective, delivering a reasonable rate of return. Additional benefits not accounted for in the analysis are reductions in vacancy rates, increased market value, reduced maintenance costs and possibly the economic valuation of greenhouse-gas credits.

All of these potential benefits are achievable because concrete high-rise housing possesses an extremely durable armature that can accommodate a succession of building skins, provided they are designed for obsolescence (i.e., ease of replacement). Historically, buildings were designed with excellent durability characteristics. This was largely due to the traditional nature of the structural and envelope systems employed. As a prime example, load-bearing masonry construction integrated armature and skin; hence the facade inherited the durability of the structure. Modern buildings have departed from this traditional

Fig. 26. Typical concrete slab with exposed slab edge and masonry facade

approach, but designers have not yet fully appreciated that with a separation between armature and skin, facades should be designed as sacrificial layers that will be replaced or rehabilitated several times during the useful life of a building. Magically, this DNA was incorporated into Canada's concrete high-rise housing stock.

Looking to the immediate future, there is a genuine need for considerable research and development of appropriate building-envelope retrofit strategies appropriate to high-rise housing. Enforceable municipal design standards must be developed to maintain the architectural integrity of these valuable housing resources. Sustainable retrofit solutions derived from technical research and development may further require government to formulate incentives for invest-

ments in building retrofits, possibly in the form of property-tax credits and the brokering of greenhouse-gas credits for building owners.

The commodification of housing – that is, the notion of it being a commodity to be purchased and sold for profit – obscures its importance as a social and cultural resource. Aside from its intrinsic value as shelter and home, housing is a legacy left by one generation to the next. A question to be answered is whether this legacy will be viewed as an asset or a liability. The time to responsibly address the retrofit potential of our concrete high-rise housing has arrived, and the determinant of its durability is only skin-deep.

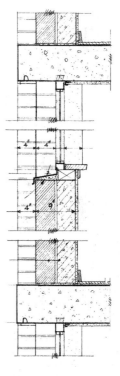

Fig. 27. Typical wall section with exposed slab edge

Concrete, Conservation and Continuity

James Ashby

Parks Canada, Docomomo Ontario

Mid-20th-century buildings that express modernity, modernism and modernization are showing the signs of middle age. For the time being, many people look at these tired buildings with indifference. Even the heritage community has been slow to embrace the legacy of the 1950s, '60s and '70s. However, today a new generation is beginning to examine this architecture with fresh eyes.

As in any period in our history, there are certain places that communicate cultural values, and these places should be identified, protected and sensitively rehabilitated. Many of these concrete buildings are undervalued and deteriorating, which makes them particularly vulnerable. Around the world, there are academics, professionals and design enthusiasts beginning to ask, 'How will we conserve this legacy?' Aging concrete has been identified as one of 'the most urgent, most prevalent, and the largest scale conservation problems' of our time.[1]

Identifying 'Heritage Character' in Concrete Buildings

The first step in preserving concrete buildings is to understand and articulate their heritage character – that is, their forms, spaces and configurations. Some of the qualities these buildings of the 1960s may share include:

• bold monumental forms;
•expressing the method of construction ;
• integrating and expressing the building systems (structural, heating, plumbing); and
• a tough, robust quality in the details.

Just as there is a vocabulary to describe the heritage character of traditional masonry buildings, there is a vocabulary to describe modern architectural concrete. These buildings were designed to honestly express the method of fabrication, so the description of the finished concrete often indicates the construction method. The specificity of concrete is demonstrated by this vocabulary:

• poured in place
• precast
• board-formed
• bush hammered
• exposed aggregate
• selectively graded aggregate
• sand-blasted
• acid-etched

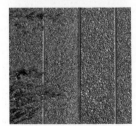

Understanding the Science of Decay

Concrete deterioration can range from superficial streaking caused by rain and pollution to complete structural failure due to rusted reinforcing bar. The forensic pathology of concrete has become an area of specialized expertise. Engineers who diagnose deteriorated concrete consider the underlying causes, which can include:
• errors made by the original designer;
• construction mistakes or shortcuts that occurred at the job site;
• lack of maintenance; and
• natural environmental processes.

Reinforced concrete is particularly prone to two types of chemical attack. A process called 'carbonation' occurs naturally when concrete is in contact with air. The chemistry of the concrete changes and makes the steel reinforcing bar susceptible to corrosion. The second threat is from de-icing salts. The salt solution can seep into the concrete and cause the steel to rust. These forms of 'concrete cancer' are manifest by cracking and then spalling.

Preserving, Restoring and Re-habilitating

Unlike other building materials from the mid-20th century, there is almost no end of products for repairing aging concrete. A multimillion-dollar industry has developed in response to the cost savings of repairing concrete rather than demolishing and replacing it. These patching compounds, coatings and other systems may be appropriate for concrete dams, bridges, tunnels or expressways. However, they may not be suitable for the very specific character of architectural concrete. Currently available repair techniques include:

Patch repairs
The 'one size fits all' approach of off-the-shelf bagged mixes is rarely successful in matching the specific visual and physical qualities of the existing concrete. Considerable skill and patience are required in the selection of aggregates, forming, finishing and curing to achieve a suitable match .

Coatings
Paints and coatings conceal patch repairs and freshen the appearance of aging concrete. However, the uniformity of the coated appearance usually lacks the subtlety of the original exposed concrete .

Cleaning

While concrete is durable, it often suffers abuse from chemicals or sand-blasting to remove graffiti and stains. In recent years, gentler techniques developed for cleaning heritage stone and brick are being adapted to clean concrete.

Electro-chemical methods: Using a low-level electrical charge attached to the reinforcing bar can change the concrete chemistry and help to resist corrosion, or even remove damaging salts.

Improving existing details: Architects make the difficult decisions of subtly altering original details to improve water-shedding and protect the original concrete.

Heritage conservation professionals need to adapt techniques from an enormous repair industry to the very specialized activities of preservation, restoration and rehabilitation of modern concrete. The challenge is how much change is acceptable while still respecting and retaining the specific character of the concrete.

Emerging Approaches to Concrete Conservation

In recent years the conservation community around the world has begun to address the challenge of aging concrete from the modern era. Following are some of the key initiatives.

• In the Netherlands, the international advocacy group Docomomo (documentation and conservation of the modern movement) held a seminar in Eindhoven called *The Fair Face of Concrete*.

• In India, a seminar was held in Chandigarh on *Conservation of Le Corbusier's work in Concrete*.
• English Heritage provided conservation guidance on historic postwar public-housing complexes such as the Alexandra Road Estate in London.
• In the United States, Wiss Janney Elstner's conservation of Mies van der Rohe's Promontory Apartments in Chicago led to a series of technical workshops sponsored by the Association for Preservation Technology International.

Technical performance, sustainability and cost-effectiveness are the current focus of concrete repair. What is emerging is an additional consideration. To preserve the legacy of our modern heritage, it will be critical to understand the cultural values and respect the character of these concrete spaces and places.

Note

1. Susan Macdonald, 'Authenticity Is More than Skin Deep: Conserving Britain's Postwar Concrete Architecture,' in *The Fair Face of Concrete: Conservation and Repair of Exposed Concrete*, Docomomo International Preservation Technology Dossier 2, April 1997, Eindhoven, The Netherlands, p. 45.

Photo credits, Figs. 28–44, page 358

Fig. 45. Architects, engineers and contractors attend a conservation training workshop in Halifax offered by the Association for Preservation Technology International.

Architectural Concrete: A Designer's Perspective

David Bowick

Partner, Blackwell Bowick Engineers

Architectural cast-in-place concrete can be tremendously rewarding and occasionally frustrating for architects, engineers and builders alike. When difficulties arise, they are often a result of unrealistic or unclear expectations, lack of objective established standards and hard-to-find information. This article is an attempt to outline the basics of good architectural concrete practice, based on my experience and research, and based on the experience and research of the tremendous architects that I have had the good fortune to work with and to learn from. It is by no means comprehensive, but with a good broad outline, the task of obtaining the specific information required to properly design and construct good architectural concrete becomes more attainable

The American Concrete Institute Committee Report 303R-2 *defines architectural concrete as 'concrete that will be permanently exposed to view and that requires special care in the selection of the concrete materials, forming, placing, and finishing to obtain the desired architectural appearance.''*

In fact much concrete that is not considered architectural concrete is permanently exposed to view and may be aesthetically pleasing. Another definition might be that architectural concrete is concrete which is subject to aesthetic requirements beyond those prescribed by the building code and referenced standards, and which can be accepted or rejected on the basis of these requirements.

The Basic Obligations of the Contractor

To understand the scope of concrete work considered architectural concrete, it might be useful to begin with an understanding of the basic requirements for concrete under the building code. The requirements most relevant to architectural concrete are contained in the Canadian Standards Association standard number A23.1, which includes sections relating to Construction Tolerances for Cast-in-Place Concrete, Formwork, Concrete Quality, Placing of Concrtete, Curing and Protection, Finishing and Treatment of Slab or Floor Surfaces, Finishing of Formed Surfaces and specifically Architectural Concrete, among others. The requirements of this standard are the obligation of the contractor to deliver, regardless of whether or not it is designated as architectural concrete. Following is a brief summary of some of these requirements

Construction Tolerances

Variation in cross section ±8 mm to ±20 mm, depending on the size of the member.

Walls and columns plumb within 1:400 and not more than 40 mm overall.

Alignment of formed surfaces 3 mm for architectural concrete, 5 mm for other concrete exposed to view, all others 20 mm.

Levelness of horizontal elements: 1:400 and not more than 40 mm overall.

Layout: ±5 mm to ±50 mm, depending on the layout dimension.

Formwork

Forms shall be constructed and maintained within the prescribed tolerances during placing.

Forms shall either be thoroughly wetted or treated with a non-staining release agent prior to placement of concrete.

Concrete Quality

Concrete shall meet the strength, slump, air content and other properties prescribed by the owner.

Concrete shall be tested by an inspection company to ensure that these properties are met.

Placing of Concrete

Equipment for placing is to be clean and in good working order.

Concrete is to be accurately placed in the forms using an elephant trunk or hopper in one continuous operation in a manner that 'prevents segratation and in a location as close as practicable to its final position.'

From A23.1, clause 19.5.2.1: 'Concrete, when being placed, shall be compacted thoroughly and uniformly by means of hand-tamping tools, vibrators, or finishing machines to obtain a dense, homogeneous structure, free of cold joints, fill planes, voids, and honeycombing. Formed surfaces shall be smooth and free from large air and water pockets. The concrete shall

Fig. 46. Board forming, Scarborough College

be well-bonded to all reinforcing steel, hardware anchors, waterstops, and other embedded parts.'

Joints
Construction joints shall be shown on formwork drawings and subject to the owner's approval.

Unless otherwise specified, slabs on grade shall be provided with control joints in square panels at a maximum spacing of 4.5 m as soon as possible after the concrete has set, to a depth between 1/4 and 1/3 of the slab thickness.

Curing and Protection
From A23.1, clause 21.1.1: 'Curing shall begin immediately following the placing and finishing operations and shall provide the temperature and moisture conditions for the period of time necessary for concrete to develop its strength, durability, and other properties.'

Concrete is to be protected from the effects of extreme temperatures during the curing period.

Finishing and Treatment of Slab or Floor Surfaces
Floors are to be finished flat within prescribed tolerances and shall be corrected by grinding if they do not meet these tolerances.

Final finishing shall consist of trowelling 'to obtain a dense, hard, smooth surface free of trowel marks.'

Finishing of Formed Surfaces
The owner shall direct the contractor to a reference sample of acceptable concrete prior to commencement.

Defects exceeding the reference sample shall be patched with mortar using the same cement and sand as the concrete. Honeycombing shall be inspected by the owner, then cut out and filled with mortar, unless the owner directs otherwise.

For concrete not exposed to view, fins exceeding 5 mm in height shall be removed. Otherwise the concrete shall be left in the condition found on removal of the forms.

For concrete exposed to view, the formwork is subjected to the additional criteria that it shall not have any defects such as chips, dents, concrete adhesions, etc., that will impart texture to the surface, and all fins shall be completely removed.

Architectural Concrete
The owner shall provide a reference sample for bidding purposes, establishing an achievable – not 'one-of-a-kind excellence' – standard.

The contractor shall prepare a preconstruction mock-up.

Form tie layout, joint and panel layout, etc., shall conform to the owners' specifications.

Forms are not to have defects that will affect the appearance of the concrete.

Methods, including construction of forms, placing techniques, etc., are to be the same as the mock-up.

Detailing and Specifying Architectural Concrete
As designers detailing and specifying architectural concrete, there are a number of basic truths we must bear in mind:

1. Concrete is an imperfect material. The greatest diligence of the architect, engineer and contractor will not result in perfection.

2. Every stage in the life of the concrete and every aspect of its construction affects its appearance, from the selection of the raw materials to the geometry of the final concrete element.

Establishing and Conveying Expectations
Because concrete is an imperfect material, its surface will inevitably be characterized by imperfections such as bug holes, cracks, stains and inconsistencies in colour and texture, among others. A common acceptance criterion is that these defects should be minimal when viewed at a distance of 6 m.

There are two ways that the expectations can be conveyed to the contractor at the bidding phase – by sample panel or by description.

A sample panel is an area of completed concrete at least 1 m² and cast in a similar orientation to the proposed concrete, with similar finishes and details. The sample panel should demonstrate a realistic, achievable standard. This should be accessible to bidders, preferably in the existing building if the project is an addition or renovation.

In the absence of a suitable sample panel, the owner may undertake to construct a sample panel in an accessible place or to describe the expectation. Following are some samples of wording that attempt to describe the visual expectation of the architectural concrete finish:

'... dense, even concrete free of major defects such as deep or extreme honeycombing, inconsistencies in plane, severe cold joint lines and major loss of fines ...'

'... concrete members of generally uniform colour ...'

'... concrete members with sharp, accurate definition at corners, rustication strips and the like, generally free of chipped or spalled areas ...'

'... members shall be visually straight ...'

'... plane surfaces without protuberances, indentations, ridges or bulges ...'

'... sandblasted surfaces with the required uniform depth of cut-back, distribution of aggregate and with colour and texture matching the sample panel ...'

The contract documents should clearly indicate the desired panel layout, form tie locations, reveal and chamfer details, etc.

Once a contract has been awarded, the contractor should construct a field mock-up to establish that he is capable of achieving the prescribed standard. The field mock-up where possible should be full-size and must be cast in a similar orientation to the proposed concrete, with similar finishes and details. Often the field mock-up is constructed as a portion of finished work. An example might be a foundation wall that is completed prior to the commencement of the architectural concrete work. Once an acceptable mock-up satisfying the standard established by the sample panel has been constructed, this becomes the standard against which the architectural concrete is evaluated.

The mock-up shall include a repaired area, since some repair is almost inevitable, even with the highest level of diligence by the contractor.

Detailing and Geometry

Establishment of the overall geometry and details is the first task of the designer, and the last to affect the appearance of the concrete finish.

One objective in establishing the geometry of the concrete is to prevent water from standing or running on surfaces and depositing airborne dirt. Some guidelines for effective detailing are:

1. Provide drips at the outside edges of soffit surfaces, as close as possible to the vertical surface but at least 25 mm away. Stop the drip slightly short of any abutting vertical surface so that water migrating laterally in the

drip will drip out rather than running down the vertical surface.

2. Where a drip is not desired or is impractical, sloping the soffit upward away from the outward vertical surface will tend to make water drip off the edge.

3. Slope horizontal surfaces. Orient the slope to drain away from a vertical surface that you wish to protect.

4. Leave the finishes on horizontal surfaces smooth where possible. Abraded surfaces will tend to impede drainage of water and accumulate dirt.

5. Make the structure robust. Larger, thicker structural elements tend to exhibit better consolidation, fewer surface defects and less cracking (both shrinkage and structural) than thinner, lighter elements.

6. Where possible, use chamfers at corners and rustication strips to protect vulnerable areas and conceal probable defects in the concrete.

Control Joints

Concrete typically dries as it cures and shrinks as it dries. The amount of shrinkage typically experienced in unreinforced concrete is somewhere around 0.04 percent to 0.08 percent, depending on the relative humidity, length of drying, reinforcement and other factors. It is roughly half of that for reinforced concrete.

Unrestrained concrete will expand and contract with no detrimental effect. Framed concrete floors and roofs are essentially unrestrained against shrinkage, and shrinkage is rarely a problem for these elements.

Concrete that is restrained against shrinkage, such as a slab on grade or foundation wall, will experience tension as the concrete tries to shrink and the ground tries to restrain it. Since concrete has very low tensile strength, the shrinkage results in cracks. The anticipated crack width then is up 0.8 mm of crack width for each metre of length. Closely spaced cracks will tend to be narrow. Widely spaced cracks will tend to be wide: up to 8 mm for an element that cracks at 10 m o/c.

The designer has two strategies for dealing with the cracking of concrete due to shrinkage depending on whether the objective is for joint-free concrete or crack-free concrete.

For crack-free concrete (understanding that crack-free means as few cracks as possible) the most effective way to deal with the cracks is by using control joints: tooled, formed or cut joints in the slab or wall approximately 1/4 to 1/3 of the thickness of the concrete. If the concrete is reinforced, 50 percent of the reinforcing should be discontinuous at the joint. These do not prevent shrinkage or cracking, but cracks will tend to form in the weak zone created by the control joints where their visual impact is minimized. The general rule for spacing of sawcuts is 30 times the thickness of the slab or wall. So a 100 mm thick slab on grade

would be sawcut at 3000 c/c. A 200 mm wall would have formed control joints at 6000 c/c.

Reinforcing steel can be an effective way to control cracking due to shrinkage. Reinforcing steel tends to reduce the amount of shrinkage and result in smaller, more closely spaced cracks. For concrete restrained against shrinkage without joints, approximately 0.7 percent reinforcing steel is recommended for control of cracking, 3.5 times the amount recommended for crack control in an unrestrained slab.

Another strategy for control of cracking is the use of concealed-crack-inducing devices. In a wall, this might be embedded Sonotube at intervals. In a slab, it might be a grid of wood, cut to a point and laid on the subgrade prior to placing the concrete. Like control joints, these do not prevent shrinkage or cracking but induce cracking at a close enough spacing so that the crack width will be acceptable at a distance of 6 m. A reasonable spacing for crack-inducing elements might be 10 to 15 times the thickness of the element.

Unfortunately, concrete, being an imperfect material, will defeat our best efforts some of the time; we have all seen examples of cracks forming right beside sawcuts.

There are various methods for repairing cracks, but a crack in dry concrete will rarely look better as a result of a repair.

Raw Materials

The basic constituents of concrete are water, cement and aggregate (coarse and fine). In addition to these are numerous admixtures to delay or accelerate curing, increase workability, reduce water content, change colour, entrain air for durability and substitute for some of the cement.

Every element in the concrete affects colour, workability or some other aspect of the appearance of the finished product. The most important objective in specifying the materials is that they come from a consistent source for the duration of the project. Even the water used in the mix contains minerals that affect the colour of the concrete.

For concrete right out of the forms, the colour is dominated by the colour of the cement, which is normally grey. White, buff, tan and light brown cements are also available. Integral pigments may also be specified to colour the concrete.

Various treatments of concrete expose some of the coarse aggregate. There are as many colours of coarse aggregate as there are colours of rock, from black to pink to grey. Specifying high contrast between aggregate and cement will tend to make variations in finishing, consolidation and mix proportions more apparent.

Because appearance is affected by the use of admixtures, it is important that the mock-up reflect the range of possible admixtures to be used. If a particular exterior concrete is intended ed to match an interior concrete, it might be prudent to specify the same air content inside as outside, even if it is not required for durability.

Formwork Construction and Detailing
There are two types of concrete formwork commonly used in construction.

Conventional formwork consists of sheathing (plywood or otherwise) supported on studs, braced by walers, tied through with form ties. Because the sheathing is typically plywood-based, a standard panel size is 1220 x 2440 mm (4 x 8 feet).

The residential foundation-forming industry makes extensive use of modular forms, which are typically 600 mm (2 feet) wide, with panel edges reinforced with steel. Forms are tied through at panel joints. The economy of these systems relies on extensive reuse of forms and are therefore not typically used for architectural concrete.

Steel, fibreglass and plastic forms are also available.

There are five main considerations in the detailing of the formwork: the fit and rigidity of the system, the selection of the sheathing or liner, the treatment of corners and joints, the selection of the ties and the stripping of the forms.

Fit and Rigidity
Fit of formwork is governed by the tolerances prescribed in the build-

ing code. The A23.1 standard has specific criteria for some aspects of architectural concrete, such as the alignment of panels. For those areas where the code is silent, it is appropriate to recommend tolerances twice as stringent as those specified in the standard for normal concrete. Anything more stringent than that may not be realistic.

The Canadian standard CAN/CSA-S269.3 recommends a deflection limit of L/270 for wood members in formwork systems. This may not be adequate to prevent visible deflection, including 'pillowing' of the sheathing. ACI 303R-12 recommends a deflection criteria of L/400 for formwork for architectural concrete applications. An appropriate standard for architectural concrete might be to limit deflections to half the deflection required by the building code.

Forms for architectural concrete should be constructed to the exact height of the element being formed, to level the top of concrete and allow a smooth, trowelled finish.

Sheathing Material and Liners
The sheathing selected determines the colour and texture of the flat uniform field of the concrete surface. In general, the more absorptive the form surface, the darker the colour of the concrete.

Regular plywood is highly absorptive and will result in a dark surface. In addition, the light summer wood is more absorptive than darker winter

wood, thus it will tend to swell more, resulting in the colour and texture of the wood grain stencilled onto the plywood.

Low-density overlay plywood and medium-density overlay plywood are each more absorptive than regular plywood and will avoid the stencilling of the wood grain. However, their absorptiveness changes with reuse, resulting in colour variation.

High-density overlay plywood is essentially impermeable and can be reused multiple times without significant colour variation, as long as it is properly cleaned and not damaged. HDO forms have a deep maroon colour that can be transferred to the concrete from new forms, leaving the concrete slightly pink. This can be avoided by coating the form with cement slurry, then washing it off prior to the first use.

Board-formed concrete (See images at the beginning of this article) is achieved by lining the form with sawn lumber boards. These can be planed smooth, rough-sawn or sand-blasted, consistent or varying widths and thicknesses, depending on the desired texture and appearance of the final product. Concrete tends to bleed between boards, creating fins, so gaps should be caulked if fins are not desired. The high absorption of the wood tends to darken the concrete and make the colour uneven. Saturating the boards will help this in a single-use application. If the forms are intended for reuse, they should be coated with cement slurry and washed prior to use to minimize the colour variation from one use to the next.

Various form liners may be used to create different effects on the concrete. Metals such as steel or aluminum, as well as fibreglass and plastic, can all be used to achieve very smooth surfaces with minimal colour variation because they are non-absorptive. Aluminum and zinc-coated forms and form liners should be used with caution because of the potential for chemical reactivity with the concrete. Steel forms and form liners should be cold-rolled to remove mill slag and treated with a corrosion inhibitor to prevent rust staining. Expanded polystyrene and vacuum-formed plastics can be used to generate complex shapes in the concrete.

Corners and Joints
Corners and panel joints each require special treatment. The leakage of water from these joints tends to result in a dark line at best, and exposed aggregate at worst, where the leakage is sufficient to include the fine cement particles, or leave inadequate water to hydrate the cement.

Joints may be caulked or taped with pressure-sensitive gaskets to seal the joints to prevent leakage. Corner chamfers and rustication assist in sealing the joints.

In addition to aiding to seal the joint, a rustication strip creates a deep reveal with a strong shadow that will tend to conceal the darkness of the panel joint or conceal a cold joint

While sharp corners are possible, corner chamfers have the advantage of softening the sharp corner, which tends to be vulnerable to breakage and difficult for consolidation of the concrete.

Chamfers and rustication strips should be back-screwed from the outside of the form to ensure a tight seal. They should non-absorptive; plastic or metal tend to perform better than wood. A draft angle or taper of at least 15 degrees will help facilitate removal.

Form Ties
Form ties are used to hold two vertical forms together, resisting the large outward pressures exerted by the wet concrete. Numerous options are available for ties.

Metal ties include snap ties, coil ties, she bolts, tapered ties and others. Each of the metal form-tie systems leave cone-shaped or cylindrical holes expressed on the surface of the concrete on a grid of roughly 600 x 600, depending on the size and spacing of the studs and walers.

Most metal tie systems leave a portion of the tie embedded in the concrete, recessed from the surface, so the tie holes must be sealed following stripping of the forms to prevent rust staining. Options for sealing tie holes include silicone caulking, manufactured plastic plugs and grout plugs, mixed on-site to a dry mix and hammered into the tie hole with a slight recess.

Fibreglass ties, being non-corrosive, can be left without further treatment. They are coloured to match the concrete, and cut and polished flush. Because of the potential for leakage around the tie hole, there is often some dark discolouration, even if the tie itself is largely invisible.

Concrete may also be constructed without ties by constructing braced forms. These are braced with rakers against the ground in a manner similar to the shoring of excavations. Low walls may also be braced at the base and tied above the top of the form, provided that the form studs are designed to span the full height of the wall.

Stripping of Forms
Stripping of forms should be done as soon as the concrete is able to support its own weight, while allowing the concrete to gain sufficient strength not to break in vulnerable areas such as corners and rustication strips – generally 24 to 48 hours.

The colour of the concrete is affected by the stripping time, so it is important that the stripping time be consistent to achieve uniformity.

Special care should be taken when stripping not to damage the 'green' concrete by aggressively attacking the forms. Prying against the new concrete is bound to damage the surface. Form-tie cones should be removed by twisting or drilling them out with a diamond bit. Rustication strips should be released from the forms prior to stripping. These can be removed later, when the concrete has gained more strength.

Form-release agents should be applied to the forms to assist in stripping. The two types of release agents are barrier types and chemically active release agents.

The barrier types include oils, paraffin wax and silicone oils. These tend to result in more stains and bugholes and are less effective than the chemically active types.

The chemically active release agents contain fatty acids, which react with the concrete, producing a thin layer of soap on the surface of the concrete. This is an excellent lubricant and tends to produce better results for architectural concrete. It is also less likely to be incompatible with any coatings that are required later.

Detailing and Placement of Reinforcing Steel
Special attention must be paid to the placement and detailing of the reinforcing steel in architectural concrete.

Extra concrete cover must be provided to accommodate rustication strips and cutback due to abrasive blasting, etc. Sufficient cover must also be provided to avoid 'ghosting' of the reinforcing steel.

Congestion of reinforcing steel can result in poor consolidation and potential honeycombing.

Walls and vertical members must be thick enough to allow 125 mm between vertical mats of reinforcement or, in walls with one layer of reinforcement, 100 mm between the reinforcement and the form, to properly vibrate the concrete. This means a minimum dimension of 230 mm for walls with a single layer of reinforcement or 250 mm for walls with two layers.

Reinforcing is held in place within the form using chairs and bolsters. These elements are necessarily in contact with the form and are visible after the forms are stripped. To prevent rust staining, these elements should be epoxy-coated, stainless steel or plastic. Concrete chairs are not recommended, because of the colour difference from the surrounding concrete.

Reinforcing tie wire is also recommended to be stainless. And care should be taken to bend it back away from the form surface and to clean up any clippings from the form.

Placing of Concrete
Proper placing of concrete is critical to its success.

The requirements for placing concrete are generally the same as for any other concrete: concrete must be appropriately placed in forms and consolidated to completely fill voids and allow trapped air to escape.

The biggest difference is control. Since patching is so undesirable, proper placement of concrete is that much more critical.

Concrete should be dispatched to prevent excessive mixing and waiting on-site prior to placement.

All conveying and placing equipment should be in good repair and thoroughly cleaned to prevent contamination from other mixes.

Concrete should be placed in shallow layers not exceeding 900 mm.

Concrete must be placed in the forms as close as possible to its final location so that it does not have to migrate laterally.

It must be placed using a chute or elephant trunk to avoid concrete spattering against the forms. Polyethylene sheets can also be dropped in to protect the form, then withdrawn as the concrete is placed.

Concrete should be consolidated with an internal vibrator dropped through the concrete at least 150 mm into the preceding layer. The vibrator should be removed vertically, moved over and replaced in the concrete close enough to ensure that the zone of influence overlaps the zone of influence of the previous drop.

A long, flat wooden stick, repeatedly inserted and withdrawn on the surface of the form, will assist air bubbles in migrating to the surface, reducing bugholes. Revibration of the top layer will also help reduce bugholes where they are most prevalent due to the lesser concrete pressure here.

Curing

Following removal of forms, the concrete should be cured in a manner that prevents drying and maintains a consistent concrete temperature regardless of ambient temperature. This will provide the most uniform colour appearance and prevent map cracking associated with thermal shock.

Moist curing is to be achieved by wetting with a constant application of water (such as a sprinkler or ponding) a continuously wetted fabric such as burlap, damp sand or other moist materials. Water must be applied at a temperature close to that of the concrete.

Waterproof paper or plastic film can be effective structurally but can result in a mottled appearance. Areas where the plastic contacts the surface will be a different colour from those areas exposed to air.

Liquid membrane curing compounds are effective in preventing drying of concrete. They should be tested for compatibility with subsequently applied coatings or repairs.

Special care is required during very hot and very cold weather.

Treatment of Formed Surfaces

Following removal of forms, several treatment options are available for the surface of the finished concrete.

Abrasive Blasting

A common treatment is an abrasive blast using sand, aluminum carbide or walnut shells. The treatment can range from a brush-off blast to a heavy blast with varying depth of cutback.

A brush-off blast will remove the surface sheen and light wood grain texture left by form ply, but may not even out the colour variations. A light blast is slightly deeper and will expose some fine aggregate and should be adequate to make the colour uniform. A medium blast will begin to expose the coarse aggregate and a heavy blast will expose much of the aggregate, leaving the surface rough and uneven.

While abrasive blasting is effective at removing or concealing some defects such as colour variation, by rounding corners it will actually accentuate others such as cracks. The more aggressive blasting is more forgiving of the operator but can reveal inconsistencies in the aggregate density.

The sample panel is important for determining the desired degree of blasting and to ensure that the operator can achieve the uniformity required. For this reason, the operator doing the final work should ideally be the same operator who constructed the sample panel.

Abrasive blasting can be done at any time after stripping the forms. Heavy blast treatments are easier if completed within the first 72 hours.

Other Treatments

Bush-hammering goes one step further than abrasive blasting by spalling the surface of the concrete with a pneumatic hammer equipped with a bush hammer or chisel to create a very rough exposed aggregate surface.

Aggregate can be exposed easily by treating the forms with a retarding agent that delays the curing of the cement at the surface. Following the removal of forms, the surface of the concrete can be washed with a high-pressure water jet to expose the aggregate. This technique doesn't abrade the aggregate, leaving its colour more pronounced.

Grinding leaves the surface smooth while exposing some or much of the coarse aggregate with an appearance similar to terrazzo. The colour of the coarse aggregate is very pronounced in ground concrete.

Hand-rubbing with an abrasive can be used to remove the surface sheen without rounding edges and cracks and without the potential non-uniformity possible with a brush blast.

Rubble concrete, a technique widely known for its application at Trent University in Peterborough, is constructed by hand-placing boulders in a form, then filling the form with grout by pumping at a high pressure from the bottom to fill the voids. Rubble is manually exposed after stripping the forms. In its original use in building and barn foundations, the construction proceeded layer by layer, laying stone in the form, then covering with a layer of ground before proceeding to the next layer.

Coatings

Coatings for architectural concrete are generally intended to prevent staining by water and airborne pollutants. They can also be used to prevent darkening of the surface when wetted, facilitate cleaning (such as graffiti) and prevent chemical attack.

Coatings vary in level of protection and visibility. Some sealers such as siloxane form an invisible hydrophobic surface layer that is water-repellant. Coatings such as urethane form a waterproof layer that can bridge small gaps and cracks. These types of coatings are visible and often darken the concrete as though wet.

Acid stains consist of metallic salts dissolved in diluted acid. When applied to concrete, the metallic salts react with the hydrated lime, changing the colour of the concrete. The colour generated is a function of the metallic salt, and ranges from earthy browns and reds to soft blues. The pigment is integral and permanent in the surface layer of the concrete. Pigmented concrete is normally sealed with a topical sealer to accentuate the colour.

Concrete Furniture

Concrete is emerging as an attractive and cost-effective alternative to stone for sinks, countertops, tubs and other furniture applications. It offers tremendous versatility in form and texture.

The design of concrete furniture is similar to the design of architectural concrete for buildings, with some additional challenges relating to scale.

Concrete is an imperfect material in furniture, as it is in building elements; however, it is intended to be experienced from a very close proximity. Acceptable from a distance of 6 m is not an adequate standard for a counter or tabletop.

Rarely is a trowelled surface an adequate surface at this scale, so the element must be cast upside down and turned over, exposing the formed face, or it must be ground and polished – a messy prospect in a residence.

Unlike some stones, concrete is porous and will tend to stain if not sealed or coated. Grinding and polishing followed by the application of a penetrating sealer yields excellent results with good longevity and little maintenance.

Thicknesses of concrete elements for furniture range from 38 mm to 50 mm. At this thickness, cover to reinforcing steel is limited to as little as 13 mm, so precise placement of reinforcing steel is critical and ghosting of reinforcing steel is more common. Dark concrete tends to be better in this regard than light concrete. Small reinforcing bars in the 6 mm range exist and are more suitable for furniture applications, but are not always available. Other types of reinforcing, such as wire and small threaded rod, can be effective.

Since vibration and consolidation of concrete in a thin vertical element is difficult or impossible, concrete for furniture is typically all cast horizontally and assembled in slabs similar to stone.

Another challenge is weight. Concrete furniture must be manufactured in segments small enough to be manhandled into place. Alternatively, it must be site-cast or precast on-site.

References

ACI 303R-04 Guide to Cast-in-Place Architectural Concrete Practice

CAN/CSA-A23.1-00 Concrete Materials and Methods of Concrete Construction

Design and Control of Concrete Mixtures, Sixth Canadian Edition, Canadian Portland Cement Association

Specification 03310 Architectural Concrete, Blackwell Bowick Partnship Limited

Wood Design Manual 2005, Canadian Wood Council

Fig. 47. Concrete bench by Toronto artist Jegan Vincent de Paul

Scarborough College Is Concrete

Interview with John Andrews in the mid-1960s on the topic of Scarborough College's concrete. First appeared on Vincent Tovell's CBC television program *Explorations* in 1966.

Vincent Tovell
: You've stated the form of your buildings are derived from their programs, their interior spaces. If that true of Scarborough College?

John Andrews
: I think so. I like to believe that to the best of my ability it's the result of the way it wants to be, not what I wanted it to be.

  There are 40,000 cubic yards of concrete in this building, and somebody did a calculation that if you lined up all the concrete trucks that brought it, they'd stretch from here to Buffalo end to end. That can give you some idea of what 40,000 cubic yards means.

  The use of a natural material, or the use of natural light – to me, these are things that are available for free. They're not necessarily something that has to be paid for. The light's always there. It's a case of making use of it rather than ignoring it. The materials were always there, so why hide the type of material?

Vincent Tovell
: What made you decide to use concrete?

John Andrews
: The nature of the program for getting this building built in two years. The normal time of getting a building built this size would probably be twice that. We had to develop a system of integrating the architectural process with the building process, which meant that these two things worked somewhat in parallel, rather than doing the architecture first and following this with the building process. Now, in order to do this we had to make certain guesses. Concrete as a material allowed us to make much broader guesses than if it had been a steel frame with a very specific structure.

Vincent Tovell
: Is it cheaper?

John Andrews
: It's difficult to say – it's certainly no more expensive ... Whereas let's say a steel structure, you'd have to put in a steel column system and beams. You would then have to encase the columns in concrete to fireproof them. You would then put a brick wall between the columns in order to provide the space. You would then plaster the wall and paint it in order to provide the finish. With concrete however, one operation, the pouring of the wall, provides the space, provides the structure, and provides the finish.

Vincent Tovell
: What about concrete? No two architects use it the same way. Has it got a lot of possibilities, decoratively speaking?

Fig. 48. Scarborough College under construction

John Andrews   Well, it's a very flexible material. Poured as a liquid, you can make it do
almost anything you can provide a form for. Certainly the decoration on
this building, if you can call it that, has come solely from organizing the
formwork pattern, the wall type pattern in which you hold up the formwork
in concrete. You have to be very careful about where you stop pouring for
a day and where you begin the next day. And just taking care of these very
practical, maybe even minor things, but placing quite some emphasis
on them and solving them, has led to the pattern of holes you see in the
concrete or raised V-joints or continuous slots that occur vertically up
a massed wall. These things are a result of solving practical concrete-
pouring problems.

Vincent Tovell   **What about cold weather and pouring concrete?**

John Andrews   Well, the concrete has to be protected. They built a plastic skin around
it. Sometimes the construction looks more like the bridge on the River
Kwai than it did the University of Toronto. They built a wooden enclosure
and encased it in plastic and heated this so that the temperature was
maintained sufficient to pour the material of the concrete.

Vincent Tovell   **Does temperature affect the colour?**

John Andrews   Yes, it does. Anything can affect the colour. A change of two or three
degrees can affect the colour of the concrete. A change in the temperature
of the water. A different water. A slight change in the mix. Many, many
things can affect the colour, so the obvious thing to do is not to try to
achieve the same colour, but set up a means of accepting variation. The
areas that receive large amounts of sunlight will bleach. The areas that
receive little sunlight, or none at, will gradually darken. As time goes by,
the building will change and will respond even more to the climate in
which it is situated.

Vincent Tovell   **Will it become a mellower, warmer kind of environment?**

John Andrews   I think it will mellow. I wonder if it isn't warm already as an environment.

Vincent Tovell   **Is it easy to maintain?**

John Andrews	It certainly will be easy to maintain because of the way the materials have been used. The materials are really rather basic – there are basically only four major ones: concrete, glass, wood and quarry tile. None of which need any maintenance other than the cleaning of the floor.
Vincent Tovell	**Do people want to paint it?**
John Andrews	Oh yeah. Of course they want to paint it, you know. But then they get an estimate of how much it would cost to paint and they get another idea.
Vincent Tovell	**... Do you have a definiton of architecture?**
John Andrews	Not really, but it should be fun! ... As I said, it's an attempt to find out what the building wants to be, not what you want it to be.

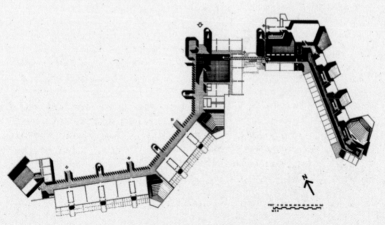

Fig. 49. Scarborough College ground-floor plan

Fig. 1. Scarborough College, terraced along the topography of Toronto's ravine system

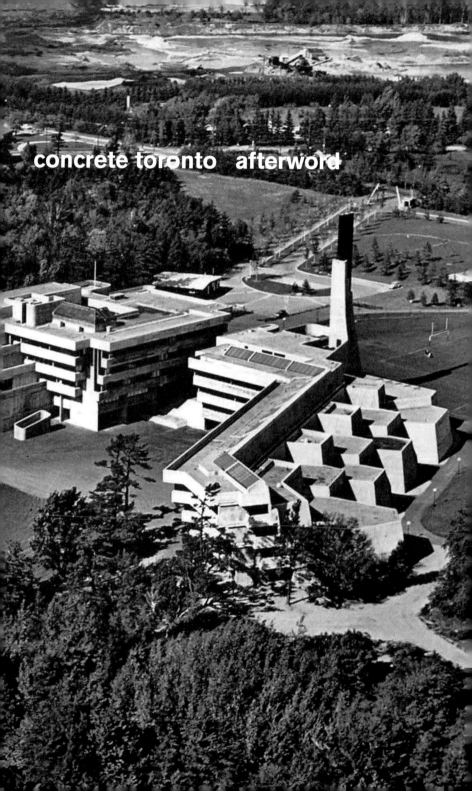

concrete toronto   afterword

Scarborough College's Brutalist Dreams

Paolo Scrivano

Assistant Professor of Modern Architectural History at Boston University; Former professor, University of Toronto's Faculty of

Architecture, Landscape and Design (2002 to 2007), lectured extensively on Toronto's modern architecture

In 1969, four years after its official opening, University of Toronto's college at Scarborough became the setting for a 63-minute movie by director David Cronenberg. In *Stereo*, the first film produced by the Toronto artist, the college was portrayed as a place evoking alienation and estrangement. A fictitious 'Canadian Academy for Erotic Enquiry,' the building provided the stage for a story in which seven young adults are first given drugs and aphrodisiacs in order to eliminate their repressions and then isolated from each other for long periods. At the end of the film, two of them commit suicide.

Built in little more than 24 months, between the summer of 1963 and the summer of 1965, Scarborough College embodied the hopes and expectations of the moment, both socially and architecturally. Conceived of from the onset as a 'TV college,' the complex tried with its design to address the question of how pedagogy could be adapted to the needs of the age of mass education; and, built as a long, rectilinear reinforced concrete structure, it openly referred to models and paradigms – specifically Brutalism and mega-structural urbanism – that were widely debated by the international architectural discourse of the 1960s. Even if in tune with the climate of its age, however, by the time of Stereo's release, Scarborough College had already lost its cutting-edge appeal. Now considered an out-of-scale and hard-to-reach university facility, in the following years it would have come to be seen only as the epitome of all the aversions surrounding Toronto's concrete architecture.

Behind the initial conception of Scarborough College was a young member of the Department of Zoology, William Beckel. Educated as a biologist, Beckel began experimentation in the use of closed circuit TV (CCTV) in his classes on the St. George campus in response to the challenges presented by the mounting number of university students. With the release of the Sheffield Report in 1955, in fact, the Province of Ontario had adopted public policies of mass higher education, a move that would induce the University of Toronto to plan its expansion in the expectation of the increase of the student population. In the early 1960s, Beckel had been involved in the development of the new zoology building, where he had fine-tuned his concept of a 20-people classroom equipped with CCTV.

It was probably this previous experience that, in the fall of 1962, prompted Carl Williams, the university's Director of Extension, to invite Beckel to become a member of the planning group for the construction of two new colleges, one in Mississauga and one in Scarborough. When a design team for Scarborough was formed, Williams and Beckel were joined by architect John Andrews, landscape architect Michael Hough and planner Michael Hugo-Brunt to work on a master plan for a teaching facility with an initial enrollment of 1,500 students (expected later to increase to 5,000). The allocated budget for the project was $6.3 million. Jim Sykes (a draftsman from Andrews' office) and Ed Galanyk completed the staff. The group took over a floor of the university's old chemistry building: they had two years to plan, design and realize the complex.

Scarborough College was to be sited on 202 acres of land furrowed by a ravine, already purchased by the university in 1962. When climatologist F. B. Watts discovered that the ravine floor was unsuitable for construction, the

Fig. 2. Scarborough College as seen from ravine bed

project team decided to focus on the northern edge of the rift, a choice that reduced the available area to 39 acres. The college would be organized into two wings, one for the humanities and one for the scientific disciplines, connected by a hinge containing the administration and the library. The university selected Page & Steele Architects for the technical design, with Robert Anderson – a junior partner in the firm – as partner-in-charge for the project. A design committee was formed by Andrews (in charge of the architectural design), Anderson (in charge of the building process), Williams and Beckel (representing the college), and Frank Hastie (in his capacity of director of the university's Physical Plant department). After the completion of the master plan, the following months were devoted to the detailed definition of the humanities building and, later, of the wing for the sciences.

To accelerate construction, Anderson decided to combine design with building management: as a consequence, a 'Critical Path schedule' (a chronological diagram of activities) and a management contract approach with sequential tendering were prepared. The selection of reinforced concrete as the main building material was determined by the urgency to complete Scarborough College on time for the 1965-66 academic year. As Andrews recalls in the book *John Andrews: Architecture a Performing Art*, 'with concrete, by pouring excessive footings and leaving other margins,' it would be possible to 'move in stages, dealing with each problem as it arose.' Sometimes construction began even before design was concluded: for example, footings were poured 10 percent oversize because the designers had yet to calculate the exact loadings. For the same reason, the flying buttresses marking the south façade of the science building were added during the building process: at the time of the elevation of the third floor, in fact, the engineers discovered that the beams were not wide enough at the top to allow buckling.

Since the college was intended to be based on CCTV, upon Beckel's suggestion small classrooms for 20 students replaced the traditional laboratories for 100 people. The adoption of TV technology as a main pedagogical device was unquestionably the peculiar trait of Scarborough College. In the expectations of the design committee, CCTV would cover every space in the complex and every course offered: more than one-half of all the teaching would be done by presentation of TV material. The project provided for 200-seat, 100-seat and 50-seat lecture theaters, and 20-people labs. The large theatres had rear projection on wide screens, plus TV monitors at the front and on the sides. The smaller theaters and labs had TV monitors at the front.

Each classroom was connected to TV production facilities: one large studio of professional size and quality and four smaller ones equipped for informal lecture presentations, seminars or panel discussions, and lab talks and demonstrations. It was expected that all professors at Scarborough College would be trained to use CCTV. The university also enlisted the help of commercial TV networks – such as the local station CFTO – to collaborate in the production of programs to be used for pedagogical scopes. Between 1969 and 1970, for example, Scarborough College's studios realized shows on a variety of subjects, including an interview with critic and historian Reyner Banham on the Bauhaus.

Fig. 3. Scarborough College, section through central atrium

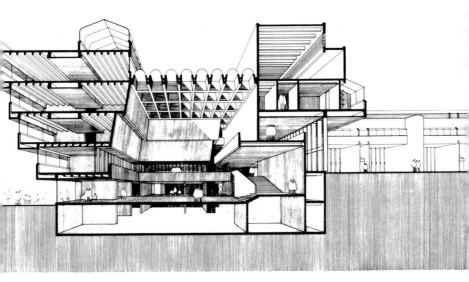

Fig. 4. Scarborough College, south facade, Science wing

The construction of Scarborough College took place during a period of unprecedented enthusiasm for and activism toward university expansion. Simon Fraser University, in Burnaby, B.C., was developed during the same years. In the United Kingdom, the 1963 Robbins Report, which recommended the broadening in numbers and social profile of the country's student base, led to the foundation of the New Seven (the universities of Warwick, Lancaster, Kent, Sussex, Essex, York and East Anglia), establishing the principle that higher education could be supported entirely by the state.

But despite this fervour, Scarborough College fell victim to its own distinguishing features. The new facility, in fact, faced problems such as changes in the university's curricula that made the use of CCTV less convenient economically: among them was, for instance, the abolition of the distinction between honour courses, intended for small classes of highly qualified students, and general courses, geared to large undergraduate audiences.

The use of TV technology also met the opposition of students – who feared the increasing distance between teaching and learning – and instructors – who found the preparation of recorded lessons more burdensome than traditional teaching. Unions also raised questions about recompense for the creation of teaching material that could potentially be used by the university almost endlessly, anticipating modern issues of intellectual copyright. Finally, Scarborough College became an involuntary paradigm of Brutalist architecture, even though the adoption of reinforced-concrete technology had been dictated by incidental factors: for sure, the supposed alien-ating environment depicted by Cronenberg's Stereo reflected the negative reactions this kind of architecture was beginning to elicit at the threshold of the 1970s.

It is rather ironic that Scarborough College's fate suffered from such a rapid change of perception, if we think that immediately after its completion the new complex was enthusiastically endorsed by architectural magazines such as *Canadian Architect* and *Architectural Forum* or main-stream periodicals such as *Time* and *Harper's Magazine*.

In spite of this quick shift from consent to condemnation (or perhaps because of it), Scarborough College appears today as a case study worthy of further examination. It offers in fact an accurate testimony of a precise moment in time when issues of architectural language and technique, pedagogy and mass culture, politics and societal change, came together in a way that can rarely be found elsewhere. It is not a matter of 'good' or 'bad' architecture: it is exactly through examples like Scarborough College that Torontonians can learn to look at the architectural history of their city with a broader and more critical perspective.

References

Lee, John A. *Test Pattern: Instructional Television at Scarborough College, University of Toronto*. Toronto-Buffalo: University of Toronto Press, 1971.

Taylor, Jennifer and John Andrews. *John Andrews: Architecture a Performing Art*. Oxford-New York: Oxford University Press, 1982.

Unattributed. 'Scarborough College, Ontario,' *Canadian Architect* 11/5, May 1966, 41–62.

Toronto's Experience in Preservation Has Not Always Been Concrete

Kathryn Anderson

Heritage Preservation Services, City of Toronto

The City of Toronto's role in preserving heritage properties began formally in 1958 when City Council established the Toronto Historical Board. Threats to beloved landmarks like Old City Hall and Union Station spurred the Board to begin the identification of Toronto's heritage sites, and in 1973 City Council declared nearly 500 buildings heritage structures. While the Queen's Quay Terminal was one of a handful of concrete structures on the initial list, it was recognized as an example of commercial architecture rather than as one of Toronto's earliest documented examples of poured-concrete construction, dating to 1926. In 1974, the THB adopted criteria that recognized materials as a contributor to a building or structure's heritage import, but no special effort was made to identify those built from concrete.

With the passage of time, a deeper appreciation of other aspects of heritage buildings evolved, including construction methods and materials, and since the original heritage list, a number of visible concrete edifices have been added to the heritage inventory, ranging from the new City Hall (1965) to the Benvenuto Place Apartments (1955) and the lesser-known Mauren House (1968) in Forest Hill. Recognition of the CN Tower, constructed as the tallest slipform concrete structure in the world, triggered little reaction. However, in 1997, the identification of the University of Toronto's Robarts Library inspired a more complex response. A column in the *Globe and Mail* questioned the listing of a building that exhibited the raw concrete Brutalist style and opined that 'in the big ugly department, it is legendary.'

Inclusion on Toronto's heritage inventory does not mean that these concrete edifices will be preserved. Recently, the 1928 Dominion Coal Silos on Mount Pleasant Road – listed on the inventory since 1978 and recipients of an award from the City for their distinctive painted signage – were demolished with barely a whimper. While the recent changes to the Ontario Heritage Act strengthen Toronto's ability to identify and protect all manner of buildings and structures for their cultural heritage value, much work remains to be done. The ongoing recognition of Toronto's concrete heritage may yet prove Ruskin's words that 'endurance is nobler than strength, and patience than beauty.'

Fig. 5. Regent Park North, demolition

Concrete Ideas

Pina Petricone

Associate Professor and Assistant Dean, Faculty of Architecture, Landscape and Design, University of Toronto

On December 13, 2006, a group of thirteen graduate students presented a series of speculative proposals in concrete for six strategic Toronto sites identified in the Petricone Option Studio: Concrete Ideas at the University of Toronto's Faculty of Architecture, Landscape and Design. The studio was designed to test the capacity for a building material such as concrete to be an urban catalyst with a reconsidered poetic expression, in light of its shifting cultural status in our -30° C to $+30^\circ$ C Toronto.

It is now common knowledge that depolluting nanocoatings can be applied to concrete surfaces, making them smog-eating machines. As was used in the Jubilee Church in Rome, designed by Richard Meier & Partners, photocatalytic titanium dioxide nanoparticles in the precast panels (by Italcementi) trap then decompose airborne pollutants – all in a few thousandths of an inch. This kind of invisible treatment of concrete entirely inverts some of its fundamental and recognizable qualities, as does the super-thin, almost ductile, high-performing and deconstructable prefabricated concrete members used in Jacques Ferrier's Hypergreen tower. We must ask, then, to what extent these nanotechnologies impact the slow shift in the cultural status of concrete, which until very recently carried inherent implications of a non-sustainable heaviness.

Concrete Ideas posed these questions along with those inherent to the City of Toronto – arguably the Canadian city with the highest concentration of concrete buildings, and one of North America's richest resources of 1960s and '70s concrete stock. These richly Canadian shining moments in concrete do not necessarily fit the decidedly beautiful sculptural moulds of Nervi, Calatrava, Candela or Niemeyer, or even the inventive genres of Le Corbusier, Ando, Kahn and Scarpa. The studio examined this collection of mostly '60s and '70s building stock with fresh eyes and some distance in order to push the boundaries of contemporary design in concrete and ideas of its representation. Through six strategic sites, which punctuate a city swath along the spine of Toronto's University Avenue, where we find opportunities to create new urban links in and around some of our often forgotten Toronto concrete treasures, the studio asked whether a more self-conscious aestheticization of the material as infrastructure/building/surface might heighten the presence of these existing architectures that have slipped into our urban subconscious.

The studio was broken down into three overlapping projects of research: experiments in representation, speculations into design and tectonic innovation, and finally creative sustainable practices. The focus of this research was the creation of new urban links that collectively forge a (fugitive) city museum of Toronto's concrete heritage. The resulting proposals developed innovative tectonic strategies, at various scales, to positively inform the current cultural, aesthetic and sustainable status of this age-old material. Through buildable solutions, these student projects reconsider concrete as lush and poetic, affording it a new voice that is not merely utilitarian or 'cold.'

Fig. 6. Med Sci surface abstraction, *Delamination* by Vanessa Graham

Fig. 7

Fig. 8

Fig. 9

Fig. 10

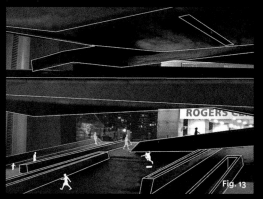

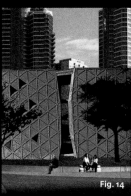

Fig. 7. Anne Miller's infrastructural public plaza

Fig. 8. Vanessa Graham's network pavillion

Figs. 9, 10. Kenzie Thompson's culvert 'link'

Fig. 11. Jessie Grebenc's Wayfinding Station

Fig. 12. Shirley Lee's parking 'gallery'

Fig. 13. Tangie Genshorek's Sky beach

Fig. 14. Eric Van Ziffle's transport hub and arts centre

Fig. 15. Liam Woofter's roofscape pedestrian corridor

The Canadian War Museum: A Case Study

Brian Rudy

Moriyama and Teshima Architects

Many aspects of concrete construction can be controlled – it can be told where to go, how to get there and how quickly to cure. There is one aspect to concrete, however, that often seems elusive in the hands of designers and builders: what it will look like once the formwork is stripped away. Anyone who has tried to achieve an architectural finish on a concrete wall can attest to a moment of bewilderment when the walls in the parking garage look more interesting than the walls for which an architectural finish was specified.

Perhaps because of this unpredictable nature, many architects in the recent expressivist resurgence are turning back to concrete as a material not to be tamed, but to be given a voice. In recent projects such as Zaha Hadid's Phaeno Science Centre in Wolfsburg, Germany, Moshe Safdie's Holocaust History Museum in Jerusalem and UN Studio's New Mercedes-Benz Museum in Stuttgart, concrete lends a highly expressive heft to the curved and challenging forms of the structures.

Justo García Rubio Arquitecto's Cáceres Bus Station in Spain is hard to imagine in any material other than concrete. The folded pastry-dough forms – at times thick and furrowed, at times stretched and impossibly thin – are further animated by a deliberately rough and unrefined board-formed finish. In Artengo Menis and Pastrana's Magma Arte y Congresos in Tenerife, Spain, a highly expressive form is realized with a masterful play between bush-hammered and board-formed finishes.

As a common thread to these recent projects, the expressiveness of the form is complemented by the expressiveness of the material finish – the two go hand in hand. Concrete is used structurally to achieve the complex shapes demanded by the design and is also left exposed as the final finish for the building – celebrated instead of being buried beneath stone or drywall. Concrete works for these buildings because of their very bulk: the vast, raw and unfinished expanses on which the material is expressed. The inconsistencies and blemishes on the small scale become part of the overall patina on the large scale.

A similar usage and treatment of concrete was applied to the Canadian War Museum in Ottawa, completed in 2005. Concrete was selected as the primary structural material and, simultaneously, as the predominant finish for the building. This choice made itself clear early in the design process for several complementary reasons: design concept, environmental benefits and economy.

Raymond Moriyama writes eloquently about the concept of regeneration for the museum in his recently published book, *In Search of a Soul*: 'Ours was to be an architecture of remembrance and regeneration. Our building would house the memories of devastation and sacrifice while expressing the power of survival and rebirth, acting as a visceral link between the "truths" of yesterday and the possibilities of tomorrow.' Anyone wanting a beautiful and detailed account of this building should turn to Raymond's book.

Throughout the design and construction process, the project team had to frequently remind itself of several seemingly obvious mandates: this was a *Canadian* war museum; this was a Canadian *war* museum. The spirit of the place had to express what was unique about Canada

Fig. 16. Canadian War Museum, interior

and its position as a nation relative to war. *Glory* or *grandeur* were not words that were used – *honesty, humility* and *honour* were. Through the architecture, we also wished to rouse discomfort in the visitors as a reminder of the horrors of war.

For these reasons, the rawness and honesty of concrete made perfect sense. Walls were left unfinished, folded and leaning at varying angles to express distress. Floors were sloped to cause unease in visitors – enough, hopefully, for an emotive and contemplative effect.

It felt wrong conceptually to clad the structure with secondary and potentially expensive materials such as stone. Luckily, this also dovetailed well into the economic benefits of choosing concrete. The cost in time and money of detailing finishes and claddings over the concrete structure would have been prohibitive, as the budget and construction schedule for the project were extremely tight.

Also in support of the regeneration concept, the objective was to produce as environmentally sustainable a building as possible, and in this regard concrete was again the perfect choice. The museum is almost entirely concrete construction, with a poured-in-place concrete rain screen on the extrior, all of which provides an energy-conserving mass. Concrete accumulates heat slowly from the daytime sun, then radiates this heat off slowly during the cooler nighttime hours, thus reducing the loads on the building's heating and cooling systems. Concrete also provides a natural barrier to the movement of heat energy and humidity from the climate-controlled spaces that hold the museum's sensitive collections.

Another sustainable measure that concrete afforded us was the use of recycled fly ash in the concrete mix. A by-product of burning coal for power generation, fly ash is an excellent green alternative to Portland cement, whose production contributes to global warming by releasing large amounts of CO_2 into the atmosphere. Fly ash also has the tendency to increase the dark-to-light gradations in concrete. In our case, this helped to give the exposed concrete wall surfaces the desired war-torn appearance. As an added bonus, the use of fly ash over cement resulted in an overall capital cost savings to the project.

Fig. 17. Canadian War Museum, detail

To maximize the unique expressive qualities of the concrete finishes, the contractors were requested to execute 'controlled imperfection' in the assembly of the formwork and the pouring of the concrete. Three prevailing patterns were developed to help express how the concrete itself was formed: the vertical board pattern, the random plywood pattern and the memorial pattern.

With the vertical board pattern, rough-sawn boards of random widths, lengths and thicknesses spaced apart with varying gaps insured that the concrete would ooze out between boards, creating sharp and irregular shadow patterns across the wall surfaces.

With the random plywood pattern, the contractors were instructed to find old and discarded plywood from previously used formwork, cut it up and arrange it into random sizes and shapes for the new formwork. Missing knotholes and rough edges were encouraged. The final effect is perhaps evocative of some of the wartime aerial photography found in the museum's collection.

The memorial pattern, used in the Hall of Remembrance, was designed as a deliberate contrast to the other two patterns. The finish here was to be smooth, clean and organized, to promote a sense of calm and meditation inside the space. An offset pattern was applied to the concrete to evoke a field of gravestones. The proportions of this pattern are based on the only artifact displayed in the space: the headstone of the Unknown Soldier. Controlled imperfection again plays a role here: irregular striations visible in the walls are the result of different concrete truck deliveries to the site during the continuous pour. In this way, the walls map a progression of time, while – for the individual contemplating within the hall itself – the experience is one of time standing still.

For the design and construction teams on the Canadian War Museum, there existed periodic moments of fear and anxiety as the formwork was stripped away from key walls. On some of the very first walls, excessive honeycombing and irregularities in the concrete almost made us second-guess ourselves. A particularly poignant moment was when the memorial walls were stripped. They were poured entirely in one single lift – this was a one-shot deal. The results were not exactly what we were expecting; the concrete, it seemed, had a slightly different idea of what a memorial space should look like. However, after we shed our preconceived notions for the space, we came to see the concrete in a different light and now consider these walls as among the most beautiful and expressive in the museum.

Over time, we learned to embrace that aspect of concrete which is the hardest to control: the quality of the finish. We were even disappointed sometimes with walls that were too 'perfect' or didn't show enough surface blemishes or discolourations. When viewed up close, some of the most beautiful walls in the museum appear to have almost excessive irregularities. But seen from a distance, in the context of the much larger whole, the glitches add up to a wonderful patina, giving the building a texture that would have been impossible to achieve with any other material.

Fig. 18. Canadian War Museum, roofscape

Acknowledgements

Graeme Stewart and Michael McClelland
Editors

We would like to thank all those who contributed to this publication. We were flooded with responses and pleased that the project evoked such strong interest. We are indebted to all of those across the country whose insights and efforts have helped expand the current understanding of Canadian cities and their architecture. Their dedication is a testament to the health of architectural culture in Canada and to the spirit of collaboration, without which this publication would have been impossible.

First, we would like to thank our sponsors, who have been gracious and helpful. Special thanks are due to the Canada Council for the Arts. Their help speaks of the public support for culture that resonates through the projects in this book.

We are grateful for the work of the professional staff and the architecture students, from both the University of Toronto and Ryerson University, who greatly furthered our effort and brought the topic of the recent past directly into the classroom. We would especially like to thank Dr. Paolo Scrivano, whose enthusiasm for Toronto's modern history had a great influence in shaping this collection.

Thanks are also due to the many far and wide who provided access to archival material. We are grateful to *Canadian Architect* magazine, the Canadian Architectural Archives at the University of Calgary, the archives of the Cement Association of Canada, the archives of the University of Toronto, the archives of the City of Toronto, and to so many private professionals and firms who have allowed us to use their archival materials. Special thanks are due to David Clusiau (NORR Limited Architects & Engineers, formerly John B. Parkin and Associates), Marnee Gamble (Special Media Archivist, University of Toronto), Anne Miller (Cement Association of Canada), Ian Chodikoff (*Canadian Architect*), Brian Rudy (Moriyama and Teshima Archiects) and Katharine Harvey (Halcrow Yolles) for their incredible dedication to this project.

We would like to thank the array of talented local photographers who added new perspectives of these aging buildings. And we are incredibly grateful to the photographers of the era, whose talent and eloquent documentation of the period are an invaluable cultural resource and themselves works of art.

Worth special mention is the work of Panda Associates, a Toronto-based commercial-architecture photography firm founded by Hugh Robertson, Paul Rockett and Lockwood Haight in 1946, whose work makes up the majority of photographs in this volume. A retrospective recently held at the Eric Arthur

Gallery at the University of Toronto, curated by Larry Richards, described Panda Associates as 'documenting the built environment [during] the birth of the modern Canadian city and reflect[ing] how Canadians lived, dreamed, and defined themselves ...while the country and its architecture developed its own voice.' We are incredibly grateful for the ability to display this wonderful work here.

We would like to thank Stan Bevington, Alana Wilcox, Christina Palassio, Evan Munday, Rick/Simon and the entire talented team at our co-publisher Coach House Books, as well as the heroic efforts of our copyeditor, Stuart Ross. As always, Coach House has been a wonderful collaborator and we thank them for their support of a complicated project of this kind.

Many thanks are due to Steven Chong, our extremely talented designer.

The full staff of E.R.A. Architects must be thanked for their assistance, contributions and patience as the book has developed. Special thanks go out to Edwin Rowse, who has nurtured and supported the production of this book over its gestation of several years, and to Doug Gibbons, whose variety of efforts, big and small, helped bring this book from idea to reality.

We would especially like to thank the architects, engineers, planners and designers whose work is the subject of this book. We thank those who participated directly for their time, and to all others for their wonderful contributions to the Canadian architectural landscape.

And finally, we would like to thank you, the reader, for braving this subject and entering into the discourse of modern heritage.

Fig. 19. Hugh Robertson:

'I learn first what the architect likes, I shoot to please him and then I shoot photographs to please myself.'

Contributors

Contributors

Kathryn Anderson	Christopher Hume	Andrew Pruss
Chris Andrews	George Thomas Kapelos	David Rich
James Ashby	Marsha Kelmans	Larry Richards
George Baird	Ted Kesik	Lisa Rochon
Philip Beesley	Dave LeBlanc	Brian Rudy
Tom Bessai	Chase Z. Li	Ivan Saleff
Adrian Blackwell	David Lieberman	Kathryn Seymour
David Bowick	Mary Lou Lobsinger	Paolo Scrivano
Alex Bozikovic	Ronald Mar	Scott Sorli
Calvin Brook	John Martins-Manteiga	Graeme Stewart
Ian Chodikoff	Michael McClelland	Thomas Tampold
Michael Clifford	Shawn Micallef	Marie-Josée Therrien
Macy DuBois	Anne Miller	Vincent Tovell
Philip Evans	Veronica Madonna	Frederic Urban
Wilfred Ferwerda	Raymond Moriyama	John Van Nostrand
Jeff Hayes	Robert Ouellette	Scott Weir
Robert G. Hill	Ian Panabaker	Liam Woofter
Alfred Holden	Pina Petricone	Morden Yolles
Robyn Huether	Lewis Poplak	
Elizabeth Hulse	Uno Prii	

Photographers

James Acland	Jeff Hayes	Payam Rajabi
Tom Arban	Alfred Holden	Lindsay Reid
James Ashby	Jesse Jackson	Hugh Robertson
Tom Bessai	J. R. Jowett	Gordon Stewart
Ian Clifford	Rohit Jigyasu	Joan Stewart
Wiss Janney Elstner	Robert Lansdale	Frederic Urban
Steven Evans	Dave LeBlanc	Peter Varley
Douglas Gibbons	Chase Z. Li	Jegan Vincent de Paul
Miloš Glišic	Andrew Louis	L. F. Webster
Jennifer Haliburton	Nick Nelson	Derek Wuenschirs
David G. Harris	Gilberto Prioste	

Students from the University of Toronto
(ARC 3015, Concrete Ideas, Fall 2006)

Gary Chien	Leigh Jeneroux	Kenzie Thompson
Tangie Genshorek	Shirley Lee	Eric Van Ziffle
Vanessa Graham	Anne Miller	Liam Woofter
Jessie Grebenc	Shi Ning	
Jennifer Haliburton	Alessia Soppelsa	

Students from Ryerson University

(ARC 512, Theory III, Fall 2006)

Purul Bahguna
Jake Black
(Jenny) Ching Chan
Samuel Chan
Hsaio Chung Cheih
David Correa
Sheila Crowe
Gavin Daly
Lisiane D'amico
Phu Dinh
Nasim Erfanirad
Brett Fine
Jason Fong
David Goymour
Elise Hing
Kevin Hutchinson
Yin Jai
Jana Jirasek
Paul Kim

Shognik Koujekian
Brandon Kupers
Emma Lee
Richard Li
Desmond Lo
Michael Lock
Kevin Lower
Michelle Luk
Stanley Lung
Jordon Machett
Sean MacLean
Azeem Magood
Amanda Massender
Jordon Matchett
Raschelle McGill
Ava Moshaver
Gillian Nasser
Cameron OíNeil
Kevin Quan

Sana Samanian
Juan Saona
Shirin Shirvanifar
Melody Taghipoor
Edwina Tam
Keleng Tran
Nicki Tran
Micah Vernon
Tara Whelan
Zella Sze Wong
Michael Yau
Brian Yip

E.R.A. Architects

Rachel Delph
Ameera Dennis
Yusef Dennis
Philip Evans
Joey Giaimo
Doug Gibbons
Maggie Goodfellow
Martin Guthier
Jeff Hayes

Richard Holland
Robyn Huether
Ben Huntley
Jan Kubanek
Kenneth Luk
Veronica Madonna
George Martin
Michael McClelland
Andrew Pruss

Lindsay Reid
Edwin Rowse
Matthew Somerville
Kirsten Stein
Graeme Stewart
Shawn Tubbs
Sonya Tytor
Scott Weir

Coach House Books

Stan Bevington
Evan Munday

John De Jesus
Christina Palassio

Rick/Simon
Alana Wilcox

Credits

FOREWORD

Pp. 6–7, Beth David Synagogue: Panda Fonds, Canadian Architectural
Archives, University of Calgary, PAN62102-5
Quote: Irving Grossman: 'Building a Stage Set for Life' Edie Yolles. 2005
Pp. 8–9, Ontario Science Centre: Courtesy of the archives of Moriyama
and Teshima Architects
Quote: Unattributed. 'Tower on Bias,' *Progressive Architecture*. August
1967: 166–168.
Pp. 10–11, New City Hall: Courtesy of the archives of *Canadian Architect*
Quote: Giedion, Siegfried. 'City Hall and Centre,' *Canadian Architect*.
April 1959: 49–55
Pp. 15. Fig. 4. John P. Robarts Library: Nick Nelsons

GUIDEBOOK

Text: Graeme Stewart, Michael McClelland, Philip Evans, Douglas
Gibbons, Robyn Huether, George Martin, Andrew Pruss, Scott Weir
Maps:
Steve Chong/Graeme Stewart
Photos:
01. New City Hall:
Hugh Robertson, Panda Associates
Courtesy of NORR Limited (previously John B. Parkin Associates)
02. CN Tower:
Gilberto Prioste
03. Yonge Eglinton Centre:
Graeme Stewart
04. Yorkdale Shopping Centre:
Courtesy of the archives of *Canadian Architect*
05. Gardiner Expressway:
Miloš Glišic
06. Rosedale Valley Bridge:
Hugh Robertson, Panda Associates
Courtesy of NORR Limited (previously John B. Parkin Associates)
07. Eglinton West Station:
Nick Nelson
08. Don Valley Parkway:
Gordon Stewart
09. Bata Headquarters:
Hugh Robertson, Panda Associates
Courtesy of NORR Limited (previously John B. Parkin Associates)
10. Imperial Oil:
Hugh Robertson, Panda Associates.
Courtesy of NORR Limited (previously John B. Parkin Associates)
11. Ortho Pharmaceutical Plant:
Hugh Robertson, Panda Associates
Courtesy of NORR Limited (previously John B. Parkin Associates)
12. Oxford University Press:
J. R. Jowett, Courtesy of the Archives of Macy DuBois
13. 45 Charles Street East:
Graeme Stewart

14. Sears Canada:
Jeff Hayes
15. National Life:
Hugh Robertson, Panda Associates
Courtesy of NORR Limited (previously John B. Parkin Associates)
16. The Manulife Centre:
Hugh Robertson, Panda Associates
Courtesy of Michael Clifford and Manulife Financial
17. The Sheraton Centre:
Hugh Robertson, Panda Associates
Courtesy of NORR Limited (previously John B. Parkin Associates)
18. Toronto Hilton:
Andrew Louis
19. Four Seasons Hotel:
Nick Nelson
20. Sutton Place Hotel:
Graeme Stewart
21. Rochdale College:
Courtesy of City of Toronto Archives: Fo068_floo19_idil44c
22. Tartu College:
Courtesy of Thomas Tampold and the Archives of Tampold and Wells
23. OISE:
Courtesy of John Martins-Manteiga and the OISE Collection
24. The Clarke Institute:
Hugh Robertson, Panda Associates
Courtesy of NORR Limited (previously John B. Parkin Associates)
25. Sidney Smith Hall:
Hugh Robertson, Panda Associates
Courtesy of NORR Limited (previously John B. Parkin Associates)
26. New College:
Courtesy of the archives of Macy DuBois
27. Robarts Library:
Andrew Louis
28. Medical Sciences:
Andrew Louis
29. Central Technical Art Centre:
Hugh Robertson, Panda Associates
Courtesy of the archives of Macy DuBois
30. The McLaughlin Planetarium:
Courtesy of City of Toronto Archives: Fo068_floo21_idj9a
31. Ontario Science Centre:
Courtesy of the archives of Moriyama and Teshima Architects
32. Ross Building:
Hugh Robertson, Panda Associates
Courtesy of the archives of *Canadian Architect*
33. Holy Blossom Temple:
Douglas Gibbons
34. Beth David Synagogue:
Panda Fonds, Canadian Architectural Archives, University of Calgary
PAN62102-5 Beth David Synagogue